Adoption and After

Adoption and After

LOUISE RAYMOND

Revised by

COLETTE TAUBE DYWASUK

HARPER & ROW, PUBLISHERS
New York, Hagerstown, San Francisco, London

Designed by C. Linda Dingler

Library of Congress Cataloging in Publication Data

Raymond, Louise, 1907–1973
  Adoption and after.
  Bibliography: p.
  1. Adoption. I. Dywasuk, Colette Taube.
II. Title.
HV875.R3 1974   362.7'34   73–14285
ISBN 0–06–013531–X

Contents

Contents

Foreword

Since this book was first published, adoption has undergone vast changes. The eligibility requirements, the application procedures, the adoption study, the process of selecting a specific child for a specific couple, even the atmosphere of most adoption agencies has changed dramatically. In 1955 it was difficult for a childless, infertile couple to adopt a child. Today, not only is it easier for these couples to adopt, but it is now possible for fertile couples with other children and even single persons to adopt if their interest is not limited to an infant. Yet throughout the years this book has remained relevant. This is because even though the process of adopting children has changed, adoption itself essentially remains the same. The day-to-day adjustments, the problems, the real-life situations that adoptive families have to deal with are as they have always been.

Over the years, *Adoption and After* has become well known in the adoption field. It is referred to by social workers and recommended by them to adopting parents. It has helped countless adoptive families adjust to adoption—exactly how many it is, of course, impossible to estimate although it is interesting to note that within the nearly twenty years since this book first appeared over two million children have been adopted.

In revising *Adoption and After* I've changed only what is essential to bring the book up to date. I've tried to retain as much as possible Miss Raymond's original flavor that made the book what it is. I'm proud to have had the opportunity to be even a small part of this marvelous, helpful book.

COLETTE DYWASUK

I Screening Yourselves— and the Child

1 What You Should Know About Yourselves

In spite of much that has recently been written, many people "thinking about adoption" to whom I have talked and who have talked to me seem to be floundering in a sea of anxieties and misconceptions. There are a few who seem to know that adoption is for them; who are relaxed about it, and intellectually and emotionally are on the way, at least, to being prepared for its special aspects. There are others who never seem to get beyond a sort of wistful interest in the stories of couples they know who have adopted. And there are some even today who think that all they have to do is call at an agency and pick up the blue-eyed little girl they have set their hearts on. There are still others—and these are the most numerous, I think—who genuinely want to adopt a child, and believe they would make good parents, but who are confused and discouraged by some of the things they have heard about adoption.

They don't understand why there are so few babies to fill the demand, when "everybody knows" that institutions and foster homes are full of infants who need homes. Most of these people, rightly, steer away from the black market because they have been informed of its dangers, but when they consider adopting through an agency, they are put off by the prospect of "waiting two or three years" and perhaps in the end not getting a child because they don't measure up to some agency's standards. Just what these are they don't know, but they have heard that long forms must be filled out, that the many interviews strip the applicants of all privacy, that the home is inspected quite critically, and that to be considered acceptable, one has to be rather well off, especially now that living costs have gone up.

Some of these notions are quite false. Others are basically true but have so often been misinterpreted that it is no wonder people quail at the grilling they think they may have to undergo. Adopting a child today is not a difficult procedure. At one time it undoubtedly was. Fifteen, even ten years ago, most would-be adoptive parents were childless couples who wanted to adopt a "perfect" baby to satisfy their own natural yearning for a child. There weren't enough such babies to go around (about one baby to every ten or twenty couples), so adoption agencies set up forbidding guidelines and standards in order to choose the most "worthy" parents out of the many who applied to adopt. Only those who were considered young enough, in perfect health and free from any chronic illness, financially above average, married for the first time and to a man or woman of the same race and religious faith, and who didn't have and were able to prove they couldn't have children were considered eligible to adopt a child. But this has all changed.

Because of the phenomenal rise in illegitimate births and the increasing efforts of agencies to find a home and family for every parentless child who can benefit by adoption, more and more children (many previously considered "unadoptable" because of physical, mental, or emotional handicaps) became available for adoption. The need for more adoptive homes became apparent. Adoption agencies began reviewing and revising their standards, rules, and procedures. They became more flexible in their requirements in order to allow more people to adopt. Many prospective adopters who were previously refused are now welcomed by adoption agencies. They include: the older couple, the less affluent, the previously divorced, the couple with different racial or religious backgrounds, the couple with biological or adopted children, the fertile, even the unmarried. So today, it isn't only the childless couples who have the best chance of adopting a child. Agencies are seeking and accepting a wide variety of adoptive parents. The only applicants invariably ruled out by every single adoption agency are those not considered potentially capable of providing good care and a warm, loving home to a child not born of them.

Some adoption agencies are much more flexible in their requirements for adoption than others. Some states have more or less stringent adoption laws than others. Policies differ from adoption agency to adoption agency, and from state to state, so that the experience of an adopting couple in the Middle West may differ considerably from that of a couple in a large city elsewhere. Whatever your experience may be, you may be sure that you and the agency workers will be quite well acquainted before you are through. They need to know whether you and your husband are actually or potentially good parent material. And when you stop to think of it, that's something you need to know, too!

Let us look at the reasons for the very thoughtful consideration that agencies are obliged to give the couples who come to them.

In the first place, it is not at all true that whole hordes of foster mothers are taking care of whole hordes of babies on whom you or I would love to confer a permanent home. Nor is it true that grim welfare workers insist on caging other adoptable darlings in institutions of various kinds. It is the simple fact that although there may be an occasional exception, these babies and small children are not available for adoption. Sometimes a mother has left her child, promising to return, but disappears. (Even if she never returns the authorities are powerless to place such a child for adoption until long and complicated abandonment proceedings have been carried out.) Sometimes a father has had to call on the state for help in looking after his motherless children. Sometimes grandparents, physically or financially unable to take over the whole care of lively young ones whose parents have died, arrange for them to be boarded, and visit them at intervals. Many of these situations are far from ideal, but neither you nor I nor the state has the right, legal or moral, to decide that in any one of them adoption would be a better solution. (There have been increasing efforts recently to obtain the release for adoption of children who have been left *indefinitely* in foster care or institutions.)

In the second place, of the children in foster homes or institutions, most are not babies at all. They are the children who are older, those with physical, mental, or emotional handicaps, and those who have sisters or brothers to be placed in the same adoptive home. Although these children desperately need homes, few people seem to want to adopt them. Most people, when they think of adoption, picture a perfect infant, less than a year old, the younger the better.

Right now there are few infants available for adoption—especially healthy white infants. This is due to the increasing tendency of white unwed mothers to keep their babies, the prevalence of birth control, the availability of abortion, and the widespread popularity of adoption. Some adoption agencies have for a time stopped accepting applications for infants unless they have or expect to have one available. Some agencies have waiting lists. Others leave it up to the would-be adopters to keep calling periodically to see if the agency is accepting applications. It is possible, even if a prospective adopter calls often, to never hit the right time. Those who want a white healthy infant *may* have to wait for years before a child can be placed in their home. If, however, the prospective adopters are flexible in the kind of child they are willing to accept—if they are willing to take a child who desperately needs and is waiting for a home—it is often possible for a child to be placed in his new adoptive home within a very few weeks.

However long the adoption takes—weeks or months—a child will never be placed in an adoptive home until the agency is insured that the would-be adopters have the capacity to meet the child's needs. The agency exists in the child's interest to see that this absolutely helpless child gets the home and parents best suited to him. Not the most famous, the richest, the most brilliant, or the most insistent, but the ones the agency feels will make the best parents for that particular child.

Naturally, agencies want some assurance of security for the children in their care, but they are not interested in the fact that you can boast about owning your own home, that you have money in the bank, or have an excellent credit rating. They are looking for much more than that. They are looking for real homes for the children to grow up in. Warm understanding and affection are far more important than swimming pools or the best of schools.

And so far as the roof over his head is concerned, the agency expects that the child will have heat, light, and air; a bed of his own; space for his toys and clothes. A separate room may be preferable, but far from essential. As far as money is concerned, the agency expects reasonable security—a regular income, sensibly managed, sufficient for the needs of three.

In some cases families who want to adopt have plenty of love and emotional security to offer but just can't afford to assume full financial responsibility for a child. Why, say the agencies, should a family who has so much to offer be refused? In cases like these many states now provide for a prearranged financial reimbursement (called a subsidy) so that lower-income families can adopt. Usually subsidies are paid in cases involving a child who may otherwise have a difficult time or be unable to find an adoptive home.

Adoption agencies are much more flexible than they used to be about the age of adopters. It used to be that the majority of agencies didn't consider a couple over forty for an infant or a young child. Most agencies no longer set an exact age limit for prospective adopters (although applicants should generally be within the age range usual for biological parents). The physical condition and life expectancy of the individual applicants are taken into consideration.

Anyone nearing middle age who is considering the adoption of a very young child should remember: It is an inescapable fact that emotional and physical resiliency *does* start to decline in the middle years. Wrestling off four muddy snow suits from your squirming child and three of his playmates is just another chore when you're twenty or twenty-five; if you're pushing forty-five this and the hundred other daily chores that a toddler creates may so deplete your energy and frazzle your nerves that you just can't be the warm, sunny, unruffled mother he is entitled to have.

Furthermore, some middle-aged couples adopting a child find that it is surprisingly difficult for them to provide for their child friends and playmates of a suitable age. The children of their own friends and their relatives may all be much older, so that if the neighborhood is a settled one, and if the adopted child is probably going to be an only child, it may become a real problem to give him companionship and the education he needs most: the give-and-take of play with other children.

Then, as your toddler grows older, while the physical strain is lessened, the stress on emotions and nerves is likely to increase from pre-adolescence on, along with an infinite capacity to worry on your part. When your child is adolescent, you will undoubtedly be considered even further behind the times than the parents of his contemporaries, unless you make a constant effort to be abreast of, and sympathetic with, the ever-changing customs of the teen-ager.

All of these difficulties can be overcome by gifted parents, and in many cases they have been. Everyone knows at least one older couple who added an infant to their family and managed just beautifully. But be sure that *you* have the physical, emotional, and mental resiliency necessary to bring up a young child before you take on the job.

In the past, the majority of people seeking adoption were couples who were childless. They turned to adoption only after they found out it was impossible for them to have biological children. Today many couples turn to adoption for different reasons. Some couples who *could* bear children see adoption as an answer to frequent miscarriages, difficult pregnancies, or the possibility of bringing an imperfect child into the world; others who could have additional biological children wish to adopt rather than add to the population explosion; still others believe they have a responsibility to provide a home to a child who needs one. Many single persons, too, who want to be parents but not a husband or a wife, believe they can offer love and security to a child. In the past, adoption agencies would not even have considered fertile married couples or single men and women as potential adopters. Many agencies are now welcoming such persons (although some, because of the current shortage of high-demand babies, give priority to couples who don't have—and can't have—any children, and only accept applications from others for older children, handicapped children, or children of certain minority groups).

There has been some tendency, too, toward the relaxation of religion requirements by adoption agencies. In certain states it is a matter of law that a child who is to be adopted must be adopted into the religion of the original parents whenever "practicable." Within the past few years more and more states are eliminating religion as a *major* consideration except in the case of an older child reared within a certain religious faith.

But even in states where the religion of the adopters is not important to a public or nonsectarian adoption agency, it is still a major consideration for a church-related agency. Adoption agencies that are church-related must consider only Protestant parents for Protestant babies, Catholic parents for Catholic babies, and so on. They will require that at least one of you be of the faith under whose auspices the individual agency operates.

As for residence requirements, they are there for the agency's greater efficiency. Most agencies operate within a certain geographical limit. This may be state-wide or within certain cities, counties, or miles. Naturally, it is a saving in time and money if the agency can operate without sending its workers hundreds of miles for interviews, home studies, supervision during the probationary period, and the completion of the legal adoption.

Suppose that you can meet whatever requirements a particular agency demands, and that you yourselves feel that you have a secure home for a child. This is a good beginning, but it is only a beginning. There are many other factors which enter into successful adoptive parenthood.

An excellent first step toward a happy adopting experience is to try to screen yourselves as individuals and as a couple. Of course the adoption agency will help you evaluate your capacity for adoptive parenthood more thoroughly than you can by yourselves, but it is a good idea to apply their standards and see how *you* think you measure up. You probably won't achieve a self-screening equivalent to the one the agency helps the people who apply to it achieve. It is difficult for human beings to be thoroughly objective and clear-sighted about themselves, particularly when the goal is very important to them. But *try*. Be as honest with yourselves as you know how to be. Don't attempt to do it at one sitting; give yourselves enough time to think, and feel, and consider, and consider again.

Even if you fall short of complete objectivity—and you will—you will have learned a great deal about yourselves. And you will feel much more at ease when you first go to visit the agency.

The most helpful initial step in the screening process is to try to get rid of at least some of the very natural hostility that all couples, especially those who are unable to have children, feel at having to *prove* their fitness as parents. The prospect of revealing all sorts of intimate details about your lives and your feelings to strangers—and, what is more, to strangers who you believe at their discretion can keep you from getting what you want most— is one that most people find very difficult to face. But do all you can to understand the reasons behind the questioning and to soften your hostile feelings, for the wall that antagonism builds makes it very hard for even the most perceptive worker to see the real you behind it.

It is not the agency's role to judge your capacity for adoptive parenthood. The agency helps you do this for yourself. Keep in mind that once your application is accepted, the adoption agency fully expects and *wants* to place a child in your home. The worker will do all she can to help you achieve that end: she is your help-mate. Even if you have problems, she will bend over backwards to help you work them out.

In the case of infertile couples, the aspect of natural hostility which is closest to the surface expresses itself this way: "If we were having a child of our own—a dozen children—we wouldn't have to talk to anyone first. It just wouldn't be anybody's business but ours!" At the bottom of this feeling, unexpressed, lies the deepest-rooted resentment of all: the fact that you and your husband *can't* have your biological children, through no fault of your own. It isn't fair; you have done nothing to deserve this, you feel, and it doesn't help any to think of the people you know who have more children than they want, or at least talk as if they did. The desire for children is one of the strongest of human drives, and it is to be expected that its frustration cuts very deep. Facing the reality and accepting it is, however, an essential first step in preparing yourselves for adopting.

Time is one of the greatest single allies on your side. When you first discover that medical science cannot help you to have your own child, the disappointment seems almost too great to be borne, and no couple can be expected to see their lives in any sort of perspective during a period when it still hurts to look at a spanking-new baby carriage or a woman awkward and proud in the last stages of pregnancy. It is a great pity that many a gynecologist, humanely trying to soften the brutal blow he has had to deal, suggests that his patient make an appointment with an adoption agency as soon as possible. Couples who rush from his office to the agency, so to speak (even though the earliest appointment that can be granted them may be several weeks away or more), are in no condition to be judged, or to judge themselves, as adoptive parents. They are in an emotional storm; for the time being, they are two entirely different people.

So if you and your husband have tried all that modern medicine can offer and have been told by a physician who you know is up-to-date in his knowledge of infertility and thorough in his treatment that you cannot have children of your own—and why—give yourselves time to take that in. Several months is not too long in which to let your disappointment and rebellion subside to a point where you can handle your emotions. It may take longer, or it may not take so long; some people are more elastic than others.

This is, however, knowledge that must be lived with for a while before the two of you can be sure how or whether you can work through it to an adjustment as sound as that you had before. For the whole pattern of the way in which this infertility is faced is considered by people experienced in child placement to be a very important indication of readiness for adoptive parenthood. So examine together, when you are ready to do so, your feelings about the cause of your childlessness. In most cases both man and wife, given time, become truly resigned to their infertility; they know it is something that cannot be helped, not something to be ashamed of. But if one of you still feels strongly that adoption is just "second best," that having to adopt is something to be apologetic about, perhaps something even to be concealed if possible, then you are not ready for it.

Let us examine the contrasting case histories of two sets of would-be adoptive parents. One couple eventually adopted a child, the other did not. All the names and identifying data have been disguised, of course, but the situations are typical.

The *A.'s,* he 30 and she 28 years old, had been married five years and had been unsuccessful in their attempts to have a child. They appeared to have a good marital relationship and were warm and sensitive people. They said they both had had some treatment, that the problem of infertility was with Mrs. A. and that it was doubtful that she could conceive. Even though they both spoke freely about most things they did not seem to want to go further into this matter of infertility. They seemed uneasy and eager to go into something else. Mrs. A. was altogether silent on this topic even though she took the initiative when other things were discussed.

The doctor's report (nearly all agencies require that applicants submit a medical report) indicated that Mr. A. was mainly responsible for their inability to have a child. When this was discussed with the A.'s, they stated that they had not been completely certain about the exact reasons for the infertility and felt that they would rather not know, since there then would be no reason to blame each other. This was something they just did not talk about very often.

It became plain that Mrs. A. tried to conceal her own feelings and that she believed she was protecting her husband by telling friends and relatives that she was unable to have a child. Mr. A. was relieved at his wife's willingness to take the responsibility. To them this seemed the best way to handle the situation. Throughout the several interviews there was no change in their attitude. They needed to continue to evade the problem and to conceal the truth about Mr. A.'s infertility. They were comfortable about the way they were handling it.

It seemed quite possible that the A.'s inability to handle this problem and their need to evade it might be indicative of the way in which they handled other difficult situations.

There were many strengths in the A.'s relationship and they gave a great deal to each other. It was certain that they could have been good parents to a child of their own. It was likely, however, that adoption could create a serious problem for them as well as for the child. The frustration and unconscious hostility on the part of both would be projected onto the child, who would become a constant reminder of the one thing they were trying so hard to forget.[1]

The key sentence here is: "It was certain they could have been good parents to a child of their own." They could have been better than most, perhaps. They had a deeply loving and satisfying relationship—if you look at it as involving only their own child, or, failing that, only each other. But do you see them as parents happy and relaxed with somebody else's child? Not with Mr. A. so deeply disturbed by his sterility that he can't admit it even to himself, not with his wife so willing, from the depths of her love, to help him maintain his self-deception that she would have to act as a buffer between him and the child for the rest of their lives.

1. Florence G. Brown, "What Do We Seek in Adoptive Parents?" *Social Casework*, April, 1951.

Now to consider the R.'s, faced like the A.'s with the undeniably traumatic fact of sterility, but handling it in an entirely different way:

The R.'s presented a positive picture all through many contacts with them. Mrs. R. was thirty, Mr. R. thirty-six, and they had been married for two years when they applied. The intake worker and family study worker noted their warmth and flexibility and their deep respect for each other. In every interview the security and depth of their relationship was brought out. Mr. R. was the sterile one, and they had explored their own feelings about this before coming to us. Mr. R. was shocked at learning of his sterility and at first could not discuss it with anybody. After living with this knowledge for a while, he was able to face this as a reality that he could not help, and was even able to discuss it freely with his friends and family. Mrs. R. had also been upset at the beginning and was disappointed in learning that they could not have their own child. However, as they thought it over and began to plan toward adoption, she recognized that motherhood could be achieved without pregnancy and that it was a child that she wanted most. They both felt that a child was what was important whether or not it was their own.

Mr. and Mrs. R. had had experience with children and were able to individualize children and their needs. In telling of some of their experiences in caring for their nieces and nephews, as well as friends' children, they showed considerable sensitivity, warmth, and understanding. This was also shown in discussing their readiness to inform a child of his adoption. As individuals, the R.'s were well-adjusted and mature. Mrs. R. was an outgoing and vivacious person, while Mr. R. was more serious. They complemented each other very well and demonstrated many positive qualities in their relationship. We felt certain that they could offer a great deal of emotional security and a child was placed with them.[2]

Let us suppose that you, like the R.'s, have been able to adjust yourselves to the fact of your infertility, can discuss it without bitterness or condescension, can face it, and are ready to go on from there. The next step is to ask yourselves whether you still feel

2. *Ibid.*

that you *must* have a child, that without one your life is meaningless. It is to be hoped that both of you can honestly say you do not. The people who feel that a marriage without a child is only half a marriage usually make sorry parents. Actually they are asking the child to do for them what they cannot do for themselves. It is an unfair task to set any child, and a hopeless one, too. A man and a woman who are emotionally mature and have achieved a satisfying relationship to each other can work through their disappointment to the realization that life is not over just because they may have to remain childless. They have each other. They have their common interests and hobbies and friends, they have a home and can plan for a dream house, they are free to travel, they can be active in civic and community work and so help many children instead of one or two. At first all these may seem to them flimsy substitutes for the deeper sense of fulfillment a child would bring them; but lives can be full and happy and unselfish without children to share them.

Why do *you* want a child? What for? The answer to this one may not come to the surface immediately, if only because children are part of the accepted pattern for couples. They're the next step in living. And the motives of nearly everybody are a mixture of selfish and unselfish, of conscious and subconscious desires. But you must be sure that you *both* truly want to be adoptive parents of an adopted child, and that basically neither of you wants this child for any of the wrong reasons, which are many, and no simpler than the right ones.

It is not unusual to find that the desire for a child of one of the partners in a marriage is a bit more intense than that of the other. Often it is the woman who finds in herself a more wholehearted sureness about adoption. Sometimes it is the man. In either case it is not important that there may be a difference in degree of enthusiasm. But it is very important that neither husband nor wife be reluctant, secretly burdened with reservations but going along with the idea just to please the other.

The results of this mistaken unselfishness can be tragic in the extreme. One of the most pathetic women I have ever heard of is the mother of a seventeen-year-old adopted daughter, a wealthy woman, exquisitely dressed, still beautiful in a haggard sort of way, but desperately unhappy. She has given this child every advantage, she points out—expensive camps and schools, trips to Europe, a summer at a ranch, the prettiest of clothes, the best in music and dancing lessons—and what is her reward? The girl says she hates her mother; there are whole days when she refuses to speak to her, and she is resolved that as soon as she is able to earn a living, she'll leave home and lead her own life. This has been her attitude for a number of years now, and it seems impossible for her to relax her smoldering sullenness.

Of course many adolescents turn against their parents, and wound them deeply with their expressed hostility. Properly handled, the stage is outgrown. But adolescent turmoil did not explain this child's bitterness. Another factor did.

At the time of the adoption, this woman had not really wanted a baby. Basically, she was not dissatisfied with her state of childlessness; she liked her life the way it was. If she had had her own child, perhaps it would have worked out better. However, when she found that through no fault of her own she couldn't, she had secretly felt relieved. The pressure of her husband's desire for parenthood was too much for her to withstand, however, and so she talked herself into a wish to adopt that she did not honestly feel.

It was evident that the girl had seen through her mother's pretense at a very early age. It was perfectly obvious to her that the camps and boarding schools were devices to take her off her mother's hands, and that the fine clothes and lessons and treats were in actuality sops to her mother's conscience. The child was rejected and knew it. She feels nothing but hostility toward her mother; she loves and respects her father, but he has withdrawn from the family more and more in his disappointment over his wife's selfishness and her coldness toward the child. So there they are, three people imprisoned in misery because one of them let her pride get the better of her judgment. Her motives were admirable, some might say—she didn't want to let her husband down. But if she had owned up to her real feelings, after a time of adjustment they would have made a far happier life together than they have now, and in some other woman poor Dorothy might have found a mother who really wanted her.

I was told about another instance in which the father was the reluctant party to the adoption. He wanted children very much, and had tremendous pride of family. The cause of the childlessness was his sterility, and he had not come to terms with this when, at his wife's insistence, they adopted privately a baby girl of sound, healthy stock. This man felt so strongly about taking into his home a child whose blood was not his own that he always introduced her as "my adopted daughter" and frequently referred to her in conversation, and in her hearing, as "not my own, you know." This little girl is now five and for the past year or more has presented appalling behavior problems. She has nightmares almost every night, bites the children at nursery school, and at the height of her frequent rages kicks and hits her father, on one occasion deliberately slamming the front door on his hand. The counseling service where they have applied for help is trying to get the father to accept the adoption fully, the first step in winning back the child's affection, but it will be a long, slow process, if indeed it can be accomplished at all.

To get back to our question, "What do you want a child for?"— it is certainly to be hoped that you don't want one in order to keep the two of you together if your marriage seems about to fail. Men have been known to urge adoption on a discontented wife to keep her busy, "give her something to do." Women have been guilty of adopting because of a forlorn belief that a baby would "keep him home more." It won't work: a child can't save a shaky marriage, even if it were fair to ask him to.

Do you want a child to take the place of one who died? Really take his place, perhaps look quite a bit like him or at least be similar in appearance and in personality, and in his love for you? That's a pretty exacting role for a child to be expected to play. It's hard to say whether it would be better for him to be quite a lot like your Johnny or diametrically opposite. Either way he's probably licked before he starts.

Would you like a child to carry out your own unfulfilled ambitions? To be the surgeon you wanted to be when you left college to take over the family hardware business? To be the concert pianist you would surely have been if you hadn't married? If so, you are risking unhappiness for yourself and for him. If he turns out instead to be a born salesman, who can't pick up anything smaller than a fountain pen without dropping it, you may always feel cheated. And no matter how much he loves you, he will always feel that he has failed you.

Do you want a child to cuddle and fondle, to dress up and show off? It is surprising how many people seem to forget that a child is alive and a person, that a child gets dirty, talks back, hates as well as loves. One man asked by the agency worker why he wanted a child said, "You know, Helen sews beautifully, and I've just bought her a new sewing machine, the best on the market. She would have fun making pretty dresses if we got a little girl for her."

People who want not a flesh-and-blood child but a plaything are familiar to all agencies. Their story nearly always runs like this:

"What we want is a little girl, not more than a year old, with blue eyes, blond curly hair, and of pure Nordic stock. She must be pretty and appealing, and come from intelligent, healthy people. And we're both musical, so it would be nice if there were some music in her background somewhere."

This is not to say that a large black crayon mark is ticked off against your name if you express yourselves as having always admired blue-eyed little girls: most people do! But an insistence on certain specifications, as if the agency were a firm of architects and the child a house that was being commissioned, may indicate very inflexible parents who would bear a grudge against their sunny elfin toddler if she showed signs of growing up into a brown-eyed Brunhild, tone-deaf in the bargain.

Agencies feel, too, that an insistent preference for a boy rather than a girl, or vice versa, on the part of the adoptive parents ought to be looked at carefully. Often there are valid reasons for it which the agency will respect—a family whose relatives have run pretty steadily to boys might feel, and with reason, that a little girl would have to face less competition than another boy would, that her acceptance into the big family would have a sort of special flavor. Many people who at first think in terms of a baby boy for themselves, say, rather than a baby girl, on talking it over together and with their worker find that they don't really feel strongly concerned about the sex—what they want is a baby. But a couple who refuse even to consider any baby except one of the sex they have set their hearts on probably still have some conflict about adoption itself.

Let us assume that you don't want a child for any of these mistaken and selfish reasons we have mentioned. Again, why *do* you want one? Very few people can come up with a quick and complete answer—the tendency is to gasp and sputter and say, "Well —well, we've always wanted one!" As a matter of fact, most people don't really know all the reasons why they themselves want children. In general, they feel that a child will make a richer and better life for them, and that they will do the same for the child— a mixture of self-interest, altruism, and conformity that characterizes most adoptions.

How many children do you want to have? This is a far more important question than it used to be, for it is being realized more and more clearly all the time that the occasional disadvantages of being an only child may be more burdensome to an adopted son or daughter. It is better to think about having two or more, if you are financially able to.

Perhaps you and your husband already have one, two, or more children and are adopting because you want a larger family. Maybe you are unable to have another child; maybe you have two boys and want a girl; maybe you don't want to add to the population explosion. Any of these motives are usually highly acceptable, and of course the situation makes it easier to assess you as parents. But you must ask yourselves some special questions.

Are you sure you could love an adopted child—as much as you love your biological children? Can you be, feel like, see yourself as a parent to a child not born of you? Will you favor your biological children or over-indulge your adopted child in an effort to "make up" for the fact he's adopted?

Now let's look at your marriage as a marriage. Is it a solid one? Is it going to last? It is presumed that you have been married long enough to be sure of this—in fact, many agencies will not accept couples who have been married less than two or three years, on the theory that a man and woman will not have had time to settle down to each other in a shorter period. (It would be well to note here that a former divorce is not in itself as a rule held against you. Several divorces, however, or divorces on both sides, must be looked at carefully to make as sure as possible that the present marriage is a strong one, for the divorce of his parents can be a highly traumatic experience for an adopted child.)

Is your marriage a mutually satisfying one? Are you able to say that each of you accepts the other as he is? Accepts him as the person his life has made of him, with all his assets, his liabilities, his quirks and his talents, his insights and his blind spots? Accepts his needs? Tries to meet them? Are you both fairly tolerant, fairly flexible, yet capable of being determined and aggressive when the need arrives? In other words, would you say that you are mature people?

Of course nobody in this world is completely mature, and it would probably be impossible for the average human being to live with him if he were. Maturity is nothing more than a social and personal goal which we are all trying to achieve with greater or less success, and workers interviewing would-be adoptive parents expect perfection in this field no more than in any other. But they do know that people who are less mature than most, who are too

dependent or too aggressive, whose egos need continual bolster-
ing up by one means or another, have all they can do to handle
their own lives. They're just not equipped to take on another. They
aren't able to grow and to change as a good parent must.

This is the why of a certain line of discussion that to the thoughtless sometimes seems a ruthless and unreasonable invasion of privacy. It is for your ultimate happiness and for that of the child you
may be given that questions like the following are put to you and
your husband. It will be good preparation for you to ask them of
yourselves, together and honestly. Is your marriage a partnership?
Do you plan together, work out compromises in cases of conflicting tastes? Do you spend and save on a basis that you both have
decided is the best for you? Are you sexually compatible?

To the sympathetic worker your answers, both spoken and un-
spoken, are necessary to illuminate her picture of you, for all
these things are factors in successful parenthood as in successful
marriage. Yet the answers can be "yes" to all of the questions just
asked, without insuring a happy outcome to the adoptive parents
or to the child whom they take into their homes. The worker
needs to know still more.

A good parent, and above all a good adoptive parent, should be
a person who relates to grown people and to children on a warm
and responsive basis. This does not, of course, mean that agencies
are looking for people who are gregarious, who are not happy
unless they are in a group nearly all the time. Quite the contrary,
for no one with real depth and maturity is without the need for
times of aloneness, even from wife or husband. But couples who
find it difficult to make new friends, who seldom need or want
anyone's company but their own, who have no small talk, who can
never remember the names or ages of their friends' children, are
not really interested in anyone but themselves. With them a child
would feel like an interloper, meeting with their approval only so
long as he conforms to their placid ways.

The agency knows it is wise to make sure that the adoptive
family is warm and outgoing, and so your worker may ask ques-

tions like: Was your childhood a happy one? Were you an only child? If not, how did you get along with your brothers and sisters? How do you get on with friends? With relatives? With in-laws? With employer?

If you are a single adult—unmarried, widowed, or divorced—and are thinking of adopting, you must do some especially serious self-examining. Why do you want to adopt a child? The agency will want to make sure you are not adopting a child *only* to satisfy your own selfish needs for love or companionship. A child has needs, too. He needs a parent to love and to be loved by, to care for him, to be proud of him, to take pleasure in his achievements, to depend on. The agency will give special attention to your readiness to love and to give to a child without the need to over-possess him.

Are you mature? Can you assume total responsibility for another person? Do you have the capacity to provide the security, stability, and love a child needs without the support of a mate? If you are a single woman are you strong enough to cope with those who would infer that your adopted child is actually your biological child born out of wedlock? Are you comfortable in your role as a woman (or man)? Are you accepting of the opposite role?

How well do you get along with other people? This question is particularly important for a single adopter. The agency will want to make sure that you have enough social contacts to provide a child the opportunity to develop meaningful relationships with other adults of both sexes. They will want to make sure that the child will have an opportunity to associate with other families and with other children.

Do you have relatives or close friends who can provide family ties and support for your adopted child as well as help in case of a crisis? Do you have someone in mind who could care for your child while you work?

It is extremely important that you question yourself thoroughly. Raising a child is difficult enough today when two parents share the job. Raising a child by yourself is bound to be particularly difficult. Adoption agencies recognize this. That is why most agencies hesitate to place children in single-parent homes unless it appears that no other home is available for the child.

For every prospective parent—married or single—it is important, and sometimes a little difficult, to judge how easily you can relate to children. It is especially difficult for you to evaluate your own readiness for long-term parenthood. Bringing home a *baby*—yes caring for babies—takes time, of course, but if Ellen can do it so can I, you say, and presumably with love and common sense and the aid of books we'll work out the rest as we go along. And so you do—nobody is a born parent, though some people have more of an "ear" for children than others. But now, while there's time, while you're still trying on adoption for size, give serious thought to what will be required of you after babyhood days are over.

This darling little infant, with the solemn eyes and the incredibly small fingernails, will grow into the active four-year-old who may loudly label you a "dirty rat" right in the middle of the supermarket. He will grow into the boisterous ten-year-old who insists that he and friend and dog must wrestle on the living-room rug just before the dinner guests arrive. It will happen more than once that he is flushed and cranky at the point of the family's departure for the lake: is he sick or isn't he? Will you go or will you stay home? He will elect to wear a leather jacket on an Indian summer day, then want to set out for school in a cotton jersey when the forecast is for rain and possibly snow. If it's a girl, the pretty dresses you made will hang unworn in the closet until outgrown while the fad calls for fringed bell-bottoms and sweat shirts. Either sex will sooner or later tie up the telephone for hours talking with a friend last seen no longer ago than this afternoon.

And there will be spells of budget trouble too. Sneakers overnight pop holes in the toes, music lessons and piano tuning get squeezed in somehow, and just when you think you've caught up, there's the class ring and the Sunday suit whose sleeves seem to have shrunk two inches overnight.

So much for the annoyances. There'll be serious illnesses, with their worry and heartache. There'll be the uncertainties of dealing with an adolescent, and the many wakeful hours when your child is old enough to have the family car. There may be very real concerns about his development: is this or that behavior a "stage" or does it represent a problem, and if so what should you do about it?

Of course the inevitability of these crises, big and little, does not deter anybody from having children, adopted or otherwise. They all get dealt with somehow, and fortunately they never have to be dealt with all at once! But the problems will be there. And although nobody can possibly estimate how skilled he or she may become at handling them, how relaxed he or she may come to be, now is the time for the adoptive parent to take a good long look at them, at the craggier side of the years ahead. That there will be plenty of rewards and plenty of joys in nearly every day of those years you may be sure. But if the prospect of these worries and crises shakes you, if you find yourself more apprehensive than anticipatory, think about it some more. For you, unlike biological parents who are confronted by these same problems, should be prepared to meet them with an extra gram of wisdom, just because your child is adopted. He must be made *more* secure than his friends. You and he may indeed have your special problems relating to his adoption. And so, while you are entitled to a little natural trepidation, if your doubts are deep-seated, make sure now that you are ready for adoption in every sense of the word.

Actually, in very few cases do serious doubts arise, and as we have said they are more likely to do so in people who just happen to have had little to do with children. It is more difficult for them to screen themselves adequately in this field. The agency's worker, however, who is a skilled listener and a good judge of character, can, if you are honest and natural with her, help you add up your strength and your potentialities pretty well.

The agencies have no fear that applicants will "bone up" so as to have the right answers glibly on the tongue. They are eager to have correct information about their standards and their ways of working disseminated as widely as possible. For if people cheat, they are cheating nobody but themselves. And it is comparatively easy for a worker who sees hundreds of people every year to discriminate between the real and the artificial answer, the real and the artificial attitude. She is trained to listen to the dialogue of the subconscious.

Remember always that by no means do the agencies expect those applying for adoption to be perfect. But they must and do look for certain basic attitudes without which the relationship will mean only unhappiness for everybody concerned. There will always be those whom adoption agencies must reject—the maladjusted, the selfish, the unhappily married—in order to protect the future of the child. The agency tries to do this by helping such applicants come to the conclusion themselves that adoption is not for them.

Working with people is not and can never be an exact science; agencies have made mistakes, for workers are, like ourselves, only human, and in the past have often been too arbitrary in their selection of parents as well as too insistent on trying to "match" child to parents. Much of this has changed. The tremendous increase of our knowledge in the fields of psychology and genetics, and above all our much deeper insight into the psychology of the child, have meant radical shifts in adoption practice as they urge those responsible for child placement into constant re-examination of time-honored policies.

In most agencies this has resulted in still more liberalizing of their approach to prospective parents, in speeding up of adoptions, in placements of babies at a much earlier age than formerly, in placements of many children who in years past were not considered "adoptable": the physically, mentally, or emotionally handicapped children, and in ever-increasing placements of children who traditionally have had a difficult time being placed: the older children, the children of minority groups, and the children who have sisters or brothers to be placed in the same home.

2 What You May Know About the Child

Taking stock of yourselves as potential adoptive parents has been a first step, and a big one, toward the goal of a child for you. Trying to screen yourselves as experienced social workers would screen you has undoubtedly thrown new lights on your personalities and your relationship to each other, revealed to you strengths—and weaknesses, perhaps—you never knew you had. This sort of knowledge cannot but be helpful to you in your marriage just as much as in the adoption process. And it is invaluable in the latter. But it is not the whole story.

There will be three people in this new relationship if it comes about: the two of you and the child whom you will bring up as your own. So you will want to start thinking now about the kind of child he will be, to find out what you expect of this new human being, whether there are certain things you would demand or hope for if you could screen the babies as you are to be screened. And in so doing you will discover still more truths about yourselves!

First of all, how particular *can* you be about the baby you may get? If you have honestly faced your situation, have truly accepted the fact that you are not to be biological parents, you are inclined to come up with few, if any, rigid specifications. Already you have come a long way toward the surest of philosophies for *all* parents: whatever he turns out to be, he will be yours and you will love him. On the other hand, you are probably assuming that it is not standard practice for the adoptive parents to shut their eyes and count "eeny, meeny, miney, mo" over three babies about whom they know absolutely nothing.

So leaving for later examination the important questions of how particular you really want to be, let us find out just what a couple customarily knows about the baby offered them for adoption. If you are like most would-be adoptive parents, certain questions pop into your mind, no matter how undemanding your attitude. Where do these babies come from? How many are there? Are they practically always born out of marriage? What is known about their parentage? What are the adoptive parents told about them? Where are they kept before they are placed in the new family? What happens to the mother? Is it certain she will not know where the child is?

There were 169,000 children adopted in this country in 1971 (the latest year government statistics are available), according to the figures of the United States Children's Bureau. Of this number, slightly more than one half were taken by relatives; the rest were adopted by persons who were not related to them. Over three-fourths of all non-relative adoptions were arranged by state-licensed agencies; the rest of the children were privately adopted. Eighty-seven per cent of the children referred to agencies for adoption were born out of wedlock, the remaining 13 per cent were children of married parents. There can be a variety of cogent reasons for a child's being surrendered for adoption and many of these operate in marriage as well as outside of it.

To answer some of those other questions—all very natural ones—let us assume that you will be dealing with an agency, and let's follow a roughly typical agency placement. The story begins in an average college town in a midwestern state where Jeanne Martens had come to attend college. Like many other girls in her dorm, Jeanne was glad to be free of parental pressures and discipline for the first time in her life. She was anxious to try her new freedom— to experience life.

Although she had dated some in high school, Jeanne wasn't popular. During her freshman year in college she was pleased to learn that the guys liked her and thought her attractive. She never lacked for dates. For the first time she learned she was capable

of causing passion in men. Jeanne was fortunate in that the men
she dated never took advantage of her, but respected her for
her innocence.

Early in her sophomore year Jeanne met Ted—a tall, slender,
tanned, sophisticated junior at the same college. Ted made Jeanne
feel beautiful and intelligent. He took her to nice places and introduced her to people he was trying to impress. He told her he loved
her and even talked about marriage. But it was not until she found
a baby on the way that she learned the flat truth that Ted would
never be her husband. He didn't want to be tied down. In despera-
tion Jeanne turned to her parents.

Although Jeanne loved and respected her father, she had never
gotten along very well with her mother. As she expected, her
mother yelled about how much Jeanne had hurt her—and the
shame of it. Her dad just asked how she could have let it happen.
To Jeanne's surprise her mother wanted her to get an abortion.
After thinking it over, Jeanne decided she just couldn't. She found
out later her dad was against it, too. Her parents arranged for her
to live with an aunt and uncle in Los Angeles. Their minister put
her in touch with an adoption agency there.

When Jeanne first entered the building, she of course felt very
frightened and very much alone. The agency worker, Mrs. Beckett,
was friendly, sympathetic, and very patient, and it was not long
before Jeanne felt that here was the real help she needed. Arrangements were made for medical care, and with Mrs. Beckett's en-
couragement Jeanne decided to enroll at UCLA to continue her
education and help pass the time while she waited for her baby's
birth.

Then began the first gentle searching toward an eventual solution of her problems, the sympathetic exploration of her real feelings about whether she would want adoption or some other plan for
the baby that would arrive in about four months. Jeanne was sufficiently intelligent and sensitive to understand and appreciate
the social worker's suggestion that for her to solve her problem in
a constructive way, a way that would give her real peace of mind,

she must consider her choice of courses from every angle. She would be given emotional support and wise, practical guidance, but she must herself assume her share of the responsibility. It must be her decision.

At times Jeanne desperately wished she could keep her baby. But to live at home with the baby, even if her parents would want her to, would be nearly unbearable, for she well knew that in spite of their love for her their disappointment and reproach, whether silent or spoken, would be a burden. On the other hand, if she went out on her own, how could she manage to give her child the kind of life she would like him to have? She would have to work to support both of them, so she wouldn't be with him during the day. At night, after working all day, she would probably be tired and crabby. If she was forced into a job she didn't like, she would probably resent it. And could she make a real home for the child— be a mother and father both? It seemed to her that in most ways adoption was the best plan she could make for her baby. But she agreed with the worker that as long as she had some reservations, she ought to postpone the irrevocable decision, attested to by the legal surrender, until after the baby was born.

Meanwhile, she had given her worker all the information she could about her background and Ted's, although she soon realized that she knew very little about Ted's people—really only that his father and mother were both high-school graduates and that his dark eyes came to him from the French grandmother on his mother's side. At the same time she was trying, with the worker's help, to know and understand herself a little better, to lessen her own feelings of shame and guilt, and to draw from her experience the strength which might be its only lasting reward for her. Little by little she was able to see that it was not innate sinfulness or no-goodness that had made her, a respectable girl of respectable family, enter into the illicit relationship with Ted, but rather her naiveté and a need to feel loved.

When the baby girl was born, she was a fine, healthy eight-pounder crying as loud and looking as red as all the other babies born in the hospital that day. Her mother gave her the name of Mary Ann, and as Mary Ann she would be known until her placement. After she had had time to recuperate fully from the birth, Jeanne and the worker discussed again the question of whether she wanted to give Mary Ann up for adoption or keep her. Jeanne went over it all again in her mind and in her heart, and although it was much harder to contemplate giving her baby up now that she had held her in her arms, her decision was all the more valid for that. She knew she truly felt that Mary Ann would be better off loved and cared for by a whole family than by half a one. And so the surrender was signed not long after Jeanne left the hospital.

Pending placement, Mary Ann had been put in the care of a foster mother who was devoted to babies and who had looked after many of them with love and with skill. Here the baby would stay until the agency staff, working as thoroughly with groups of prospective parents as they had with Jeanne, found a couple who they knew would love Mary Ann as much as her birth mother would have and care for her better than she might have been able to.

Jeanne's contact with and knowledge of her baby—except for some non-identifying human-interest details about the adoptive parents which would be given her after the baby was placed—was now ended. She went home, more serious even than before, perhaps, but with a new fortitude and with the comfort of knowing her baby was in good hands. Mary Ann thrived with Mrs. Butler, who kept the little house in Anaheim as tidy as a pin and who fell just as much in love with this baby as she had with each of the fifteen others who had been entrusted to her by the agency. Mrs. Butler fed and clothed and aired her according to the instructions of the agency pediatrician, brought her to the doctor for medical checkups and tests, and gave her plenty of love and cuddling, besides.

When the baby was nearly five weeks old, several couples among the many whom the agency had been getting to know in the meanwhile seemed to be especially likely candidates for mother and father to Mary Ann. Jeanne's baby was healthy, blond, with dark eyes, and apparently perfectly normal. An easy baby to place. And it was not a question of matching child to parents and vice versa, for this agency, like many others, has in recent years become much less rigid about this "matching" idea which most of them once fostered. No longer do they tailor the child to the parents like trying to match plaids in a slip cover: so much Scottish ancestry here fits with so much there, only a blond baby here because the Joneses are both fair; there a baby with a tall, thin body build to match the lanky Warrens. There is still some emphasis on matching, but today agencies look not so much for similarities in appearance and background but instead try to match the problems and needs of the individual child with the ability of the prospective parents to meet them and still fulfill their own needs.

The way a family is selected for a child will vary somewhat according to the adoption agency—its size and its policies. In selecting a suitable child for an adoptive home most agencies are guided more by the personalities, expectations, and preferences of the adopters than by a policy of matching details. Adopters vary in their ability to accept differences. Some couples want a child who is very much like them. Others can easily accept and identify with a child who is totally different from them—even one who is of a different race. This is taken into consideration. The agency selects a child who will be comfortable with the adopters and with whom they will feel a genuine kinship. This allows for quite a lot of leeway, when you come to think of it.

And so the agency was by no means planning to postpone Mary Ann's placement until they found, for example, a couple acceptable by every standard and in addition possessing fair hair, dark eyes, and a nationality background which combined Jeanne's ancestral blood with a dash of French! All they wanted to be sure of was which of several couples was the best one for this particular baby. The Randalls, the Greens, and the Espositos all had much to offer: a good husband-and-wife relationship, flexibility, security, and lots of warmth. It narrowed down to a choice between the Randalls and the Greens when it was realized that another baby just ready for placement, a black-eyed lively boy of Italian parentage, was exactly right for the very dark, vitality-charged Espositos. The Randalls and the Greens differed in only one thing that might affect the placement: the Greens inclined just a bit more toward boys because there weren't any in the big family circle to which they belonged. And so the Randalls were called up about Mary Ann, and the Greens put on top of the list for the next boy baby to come along.

Before they saw the baby, the Randalls were given in a somewhat lengthy interview all the information that was available about her: the background as far as it was known, the birth history, the health record, and the details about her experiences, personality, and development thus far. Mr. and Mrs. Randall were asked to give special thought to how much, if any, it mattered to them that most of the paternal background could only be guessed at. Then they were taken to a sunny little room where Mary Ann was waiting for them and were left alone with her for a little visit before they went home to deliberate for a day or two—routine procedure—before notifying the agency of their decision. In their case it didn't need much mulling over; they were enchanted with the baby, and felt that everything they had been told about her was to the good. It was possible, they knew, that somewhere back in her double heritage there might be, just might be, genes that had combined in her in some very special way which could mean a physical or mental handicap showing up later on. They knew, too, that this could happen with a child of their own. They wanted Mary Ann just as she was. They wanted her to be their own Susan Randall. And so in a few days they took her home to their little Cape Cod house with its newly-papered nursery, to love and care for her while they waited for the year that must pass before the adoption could become legal.

And so—if you are dealing with an agency—you, like the Randalls, may expect to be told about the baby's physical inheritance (sometimes with details of special talents on one side or the other), his birth history, his health history, and possibly, depending on his age and background, the results of infant testing. Of course there are many cases which are not as clear-cut as that of Mary Ann and Jeanne. Often nothing whatever can be ascertained about the father, and in the case of foundlings nothing about the mother either. Sometimes the heritage on one side or the other is questionable. Sometimes the baby has a handicap, a minor one like a slight club foot which may later call for an operation and, briefly, a cast, or a major one not correctible by surgery. Sometimes he fails to a greater or lesser degree in the customary responses of babies on the testing table.

The prospective adoptive parents are always told the baby's story and are always asked to talk and think together before coming to a decision, with very special searchings of their real feelings about any deviation from the norm which the baby may show or any doubtful areas in his heritage—any known factor which might mean that more than the usual risk *may* be involved. Most couples who are ready for adoption would feel as did the Randalls —that the gap in their knowledge of Mary Ann's inheritance was nothing to worry about, that they in fact could comfortably meet many challenges more serious than that one. For they would not assume that the Randalls are assured of a thoroughly healthy, intelligent child simply because what is known of Mary Ann's heritage is good. Even if there had been as much knowledge of Ted's background as of Jeanne's, and it, too, was good, they would realize that no guarantee could come with Mary Ann. They know that even had she been their very own child and they able to show strong, healthy parents and grandparents—there is *still* no guarantee!

Does heredity then count for nothing, environment for everything? Not quite. Although geneticists are still and perhaps always will be exploring some still-uncharted parts of this enormous field, man's environment and his heredity so interact upon each other that it is almost impossible to draw a dividing line between them. Scientists do know that many abnormalities are inherited, especially structural ones. They think that certain other variations in structure may be inherited too. And they suspect that some characteristics of personality are likewise due to heredity—but this is the part of the field wherein opinions differ widely, simply because it is impossible to prove, for example, exactly how much of an inactive child's lack of energy and/or initiative is due to his inheritance and how much to the way in which his mother handles him: her treatment of him, of course, being conditioned by his make-up. So who is to say, when he is two, and six, and nine, and twenty, just how much of his personality is constitutional and how much acquired?

But the people who have learned about the ways of genes will counsel adoptive parents not to worry too much about heredity. Many of them, in fact, are adoptive parents themselves. For they know that, while they are taking a chance of a sort, it is no more of a chance than they would be taking if they were to have children of their own. As Dr. Amram Scheinfeld points out in his book, *The New You and Heredity.*

No one can predict to what extent a child will be genetically like or unlike its parents. True enough, we can make some forecasts about physical characteristics and here and there about defects. But no one can predict the character, disposition, mentality, or behavior of any given child of *normal* parentage. These factors are determined or influenced by such a multitude of genes, interoperating with so many environmental factors, that as individuals we can't possibly expect to reproduce ourselves.[3]

(The italics are Dr. Scheinfeld's.)

Anna Perrott Rose makes an interesting comment about heredity in her book, *Room for One More,* the story of her foster children who came from every sort of background. "Heredity gives you something," she says, "and your environment makes you use it, misuse it, or throw it away." Thus her Joey's real musical ability might never have been put to use without the recognition and training they gave him. And Jimmy John, with an unusual mechanical

3. Amram Scheinfeld, *The New You and Heredity* (New York: J. B. Lippincott Co., 1950), p. 565.

bent which perhaps he inherited from his toolmaker grandfather, might with a different upbringing, have turned into a skilled safe-cracker rather than a good mechanic. The love and respect and gentle guidance that the Rose family gave these boys provided an ideal climate that brought out the best in them and redirected the worst. But as Mrs. Rose points out, no amount of love or training could have made a mechanical engineer out of Joey or a musician out of Jimmy John.

And so you and the Randalls and the geneticists and the thousands of other people who adopt each year are taking some chance on heredity. But all these adoptive parents are probably taking less chance than biological ones. For adoptive parents do not have to accept a baby with brain damage or serious physical defects apparent at birth, as do biological parents.

Ah, yes, "apparent" you say. How do they know? And what if they don't? Is this where the infant testing comes in? What are the tests, and what do they prove?

These tests for small babies, called developmental studies, measure in a very simple way the baby's reaction to certain stimuli against a norm which represents findings over a long period of a large group of babies of the same age. The infant's use of his body and other responses in given situations are tested by means of simple tools used with great skill by highly trained examiners. The average sixteen-week-old baby, for example, will try to move his eyes and head, his arms and shoulders, toward a ring that is dangled in front of him, whereas at four weeks he only stared at it. By the time he has reached the ripe age of twenty-eight weeks, he will want to, and will be able to, grab the ring with his hands, to handle it, to put it in his mouth. Between four weeks and twenty-eight weeks, he has been developing his motor abilities, his "adaptive behavior" (in lay language, finding out what hands, fingers, mouth can be used for), his "speech" (from crying to babbling to crowing), and his behavior with people (from unawareness to various degrees of awareness). The normal development in these four areas does seem to proceed in a very definite pattern. But it must be remembered that it is only a pattern: that *most* babies do such-and-so at so many weeks of age. Some babies may reach this stage sooner, some later, and still may be said to be proceeding at a pace that is normal for *them*.

At one time developmental tests were widely used by adoption agencies. They were considered a good way of predicting a child's future intelligence. Infants were rarely placed in their adoptive homes without being thoroughly tested and evaluated to be sure they were "normal," thus "adoptable." A child's placement in his adoptive home was sometimes delayed until he was four, six, or eight months old. It is now well established that with current methods of testing it is not possible in the first year to accurately predict a child's future mental development.

Today there is much less use of developmental testing in adoption. Most experts believe it unnecessary to delay placing an apparently normal infant until he can be studied and evaluated. They consider it much more important for a child's emotional security and physical well-being that he be placed in his adoptive home as soon as possible after birth. As a result, nearly two-thirds of the children who are placed by social agencies are placed before they are three months old; some are placed directly from the hospital.

Although it may seem to you to be far less safe—this practice of placing babies without testing them—it is not as haphazard as it sounds. Even in the days when developmental tests were widely used, they were only *part* of the total "study." The examiner weighed the test results and interpreted them in the light of his knowledge about the whole child: whether the prenatal history was difficult or smooth, whether his birth was with or without complications, whether the health history of his biological family could possibly affect his development. The decision as to a child's readiness for placement was a relationship-centered judgment rather than a test-centered one. The test itself was only *one* of the tools used.

Adoption agencies are still very careful about evaluating the children they place. Before a child is offered for adoption he is examined by a pediatrician alert to genetic and developmental disorders to determine if he has any physical or mental abnormalities. His individual history is taken into consideration by the examiner. If a child's background is poor, if brain damage is suspected, or if the child seems in any way abnormal, he will be observed and studied for a while before he is placed. This is where infant testing now comes in. Developmental tests still have a very important place in adoption. They are an accurate, helpful way of appraising an infant's comparative normalcy of development as of the time when examined. They are useful in diagnosing mental retardation, neurological problems, and defects in sight, hearing and co-ordination.

Agencies go through a great deal of trouble in order to protect the future of the child as well as that of the adoptive parents. If it is discovered that the child has a problem, or that there is even a slight chance he may develop one in later life, the prospective adopters are advised. There is practically no chance of unknowingly adopting a child with any abnormality whatever when adopting through an adoption agency. Those who adopt a child with a physical or mental problem, do so willingly and from choice.

In most instances adoptions of infants in the early weeks of their lives work out very well. Studies indicate that the best adjusted adopted children are those placed in the first two months of their lives. It works out well for the adoptive parents, too. Most adopters wish to love and care for their adoptive children as soon as possible after birth. Although there may be slightly more risk involved in these early adoptions, most adoptive parents are willing to accept the risk. They realize that adopted children, like biological children, come without guarantee.

There is the very occasional placement where study, observation, and testing have failed to forecast a severe abnormality of some kind which develops after the baby has been in the home for some months. Here the adoptive parents are in the same position as biological parents to whom this can also happen. They must, with the friendly aid of the agency and perhaps also with psychological counsel, decide what is the best solution of the problem for them, for the baby, and for other children who are now or may become part of the family. Much depends on the kind and degree of abnormality the baby shows and the flexibility as well as the financial position of the parents. The adoptive parents may decide that it is better to give up this baby and ask the agency for another in his place.

In such cases the parents are not letting the baby down. They do not feel lesser people just because they are not and cannot be the best parents for this particular child. Somewhere in the world there is a set of parents who are the right ones for him, and with care and patience they may be found. Many handicapped babies find their niche with parents who for one reason or another are people who can do more with and for such a child than with a normal one. A mother who herself has learned to live with a bad heart, for example, can take a similarly afflicted child with every chance of success, whereas the adoption of an energetic normal child would probably be a bad thing for her and the child both. An orthopedic surgeon and his therapist wife might make ideal parents for a baby who turned out to have a severe crippling ailment. If, then, your baby should turn out to be unadoptable— at least unadoptable by you—there is no reason to feel guilty about giving him up. It is a hard decision to make, and there's bound to be a certain amount of heartbreak. If you should be one of the rare couples faced with this situation, be sure to get all the help you need in thinking your problem through. And remember that if relinquishing the child is the best thing for you, it is the best thing for him, too.

It is good to know that agencies, by constant revision of their procedures, have so speeded up their programs that they can do everything they must in the line of checking on parents and babies and can do it faster. This is why some babies are placed very young. Of course there are many couples who want a very young baby—they feel that the tinier the baby, the less they will miss of parenthood. This is true, of course, and the feeling understandable.

It is to be hoped, however, that you do not feel insistent about the baby's age any more than you do about the sex or the color of his hair. For what you want is a baby—and when one remembers that the task of the agency is not primarily to find you a baby, but to find for each baby the right set of parents, it becomes clear that the agency staff is there to place the baby when he is *ready* to be placed.

Oftentimes the baby is ready at a few weeks of age, but for various reasons may have to wait awhile. Sometimes a baby needs special medical attention to remedy a condition that is transitory but demands hospitalization or too much care and expense for most new adoptive parents to undertake successfully. Sometimes he must be observed for a while before it can be determined whether some handicap is temporary or is one which may make him subject to very special care in placement. Sometimes the mother is unable to decide for many months whether to give him up. For all these reasons and others, there are many babies who do not become adoptable until they are five, six, seven months old or more.

But does it really matter to you how old your baby is when you get him? If you are truly ready for adoption, it doesn't. For what you want is a baby who needs a father and a mother. To be sure, if you get a tiny one, it may make you feel like a biological parent a bit sooner. And there is no denying that in the very beginning it is a little easier to give security to a small baby than to one who, though he can have no intellectual understanding of the fact that he is leaving his foster home for another, he has learned to recognize his foster mother's face. The older baby does present more of a challenge—but he's more interesting too, and more immediately rewarding. His smiles of recognition, now given to his foster mother, suggest the hit that you will soon be making with him. Then, also, you know a little more about him and what makes him tick than you know about a brand-new baby. But it really doesn't make too much difference: either way, you will feel just like parents— like *his* parents—in a very short while.

Many readers will be thinking about now, "If these tests aren't all-important, then, and if the agencies are sometimes placing babies right out of the hospital, what's all this fuss about agency adoptions? If you're taking chances anyway, why go to an agency? Why not adopt privately?" This is a question that people ask over and over again, even though the publicity about black markets in babies has sensationalized the many risks that parents and babies both may run. And it is natural that they should, for there is no denying that there have been, and will be, many successful private adoptions. Almost everybody has heard of at least one. And as for the tragedies, the human tendency is always to think, "That was sheer bad luck—it wouldn't happen to *us!*"

Let us distinguish first between the two kinds of private adoptions—the black market and what many people call the gray market. The latter term we may use to cover those adoptions which are arranged for a couple by an interested and well-intentioned friend such as a doctor, a nurse, a minister, a friend or relative of the "birth" mother, usually without fee. These people simply want to bring together a baby without a home and a couple without a baby, from the best of motives and without knowledge of the risks that may be involved.

In the black market money is the main objective, and good intentions seldom, if ever, enter into the picture. The link between homeless baby and childless couple is nearly always an unscrupulous individual (or group of individuals) who loses no sleep over the fact that his profitable racket exploits the deepest of human emotions and gambles with the lives of at least three people. When couples desperate for a baby cause word to be spread around that they are in the market for a baby, they are natural setups for the racketeer. It is not too hard for him to find several frightened pregnant girls. He pays them each a couple of hundred dollars (or less, or nothing), gets the babies to the waiting couples as quickly as possible, and charges each couple all that he thinks the traffic will bear. In a few months he may have cleared anywhere from five to twenty thousand dollars.

But it is not solely the amount of his earnings that society objects to, and certainly the parents who so desperately want a baby are not complaining about his fees. The point is that the black-market operator hasn't time or freedom enough, even if he wanted to, to investigate the birth mothers' backgrounds or the physical condition of the babies, let alone size up the parents. Haste and secrecy must be his watchwords. Let 'em squawk later. Never mind if in his haste he sometimes leaves a pretty readable trail from mother to new parents—if she turns up and wants the baby back, let them worry about it. He'll be gone, cleared out, operating under another name in another part of the country.

All this sounds melodramatic, extreme—and it does paint the baby market at its most lurid. Not all its operators can be totally without heart, and, after all, by the laws of probability some or even all of these babies may fit into their new families perfectly and safely and permanently. But the fact remains that this kind of adoption can mean a big gamble. There have been tragic outcomes, such as the cases where desperate couples have paid huge sums for babies born, say, of a mentally defective mother and a criminally insane father. Or the cases where mothers have changed their minds and taken away the baby whom the adoptive parents had loved for ten months or more, sometimes even after legal adoption. The babies take a big chance too: many of them have been given to parents who are alcoholics, criminals, or psychotics. As long as the parents have the cash, they're all right in the racketeer's book.

Thirty years ago, when adoptable babies were scarce and agency restrictions formidable, illegal black marketing of babies flourished. In recent years, as more and more children became available for adoption and agency requirements eased, black marketing was believed to be reduced to a minimum. Now, for the first time in years, adoption officials fear that the black marketing may pick up again. If the current white baby shortage continues, it is inevitable that more and more agencies will have to stop accepting applications for these infants. Adoption officials are fearful that many couples, desperate for a baby, will feel driven to the black market rather than risk long years of waiting and possible disappointment.

To a great extent, the risk encountered by a couple adopting in the so-called gray market is less than that run by parents who take a black-market baby. The unselfish interest of most of the intermediaries in these cases is bound to give just a bit more margin of safety. A doctor bringing together a childless couple whose sterility he is unable to correct and the illegitimate child of one of his patients, with the kindly idea of helping people out all around, is likely to look the baby over pretty carefully first and to take thought if there seems to be anything wrong with it. Then, too, he probably believes sincerely that he knows the adopting family pretty well, perhaps also the baby's mother and family. And a minister performing the same function, though he may not be capable of judging the baby's soundness, is likely to know something of the backgrounds of the people concerned. Minister or doctor would probably seek the advice of a social agency rather than carry through on his own responsibility, if he suspected anything really disturbing about the baby or his heritage. Therefore, the chance of acquiring a heartbreaking misfit is perhaps less in this sort of adoption. But these people are not experts in child placing and so a great deal is left to chance.

Perhaps the biggest single risk that parents run who are adopting in this way—and the most serious—is their lack of protection. It is comparatively easy for a licensed agency, with governmental legal resources behind it, to obtain a valid legal surrender from the mother and to protect the anonymity of both the mother and the adoptive parents. It is far harder for individuals to carry out these tasks successfully, particularly the latter. In any private adoption, even when the case is handled by a lawyer, the adoptive parents do run the risk of having the biological mother turn up at any time before the baby's legal adoption, which may not take place for six months or a year, and demand to have him back again. (It has happened that the courts have ruled that the baby be returned to the birth mother even *after* the legal adoption.) She can say she was too ill to know what she was doing when she signed the surrender, or that she signed it under duress. She can say that now that she is married she can give her baby a home. The chances are that she will get her child back, leaving the adoptive parents heartbroken but helpless before the law.

Naturally, such tragedies do not always come about in private adoption. And it is undeniably true that agency staffs are only human, not omniscient. They, too, from time to time have been responsible for unfortunate placements. But agencies will take back a baby who turns out to have a previously unknown mental or physical handicap, and either find a special family for him or make arrangements for his care at public expense. They will find another child for those parents as quickly as they can. Moreover, the records seem to show that case for case there are more successful agency adoptions than there are private adoptions.

In a famous study made in 1948[4] the late Dr. Catherine Amatruda of the Clinic of Child Development at Yale University examined the placements of two hundred adopted children. Half of these had been placed privately, half through recognized agencies. Among the hundred private placements Dr. Amatruda found seventy-five pretty good couples: stable, secure, loving, happy. Twenty-five other families could hardly be called good adoptive-parent material: the marriage was broken up or about to be, some of the parents showed signs of serious mental and emotional disturbance, and in a very few cases alcoholism, prostitution, wife-beating, drug addiction, or prison records took form in the home background. Oddly enough, exactly seventy-five out of the hundred privately placed babies were reasonably good placement

4. Similar results were found in a much larger study by Helen Witmer *et al.: Independent Adoption—A Follow-Up Study* (New York City: Russell Sage Foundation, 1963).

risks, and twenty-five were found to be poor risks for one reason or another, although some were assumed to be capable of improving under better conditions. Now if the seventy-five "good" babies had been put into the seventy-five "good" homes, that would be a very fair score. But they had not been. On the contrary, some of the most promising babies had landed with the drug addicts and the drunkards, some of the most promising parents had got the mentally retarded or otherwise defective babies. In only forty-six instances did Dr. Amatruda find the good family and the good baby together. In twenty-six other cases she felt the placement was marginal and its success unpredictable. (In most of these the difficulty seemed to be that the adoptive mother hadn't quite caught on yet to being a mother, was not at that time, at least, able to love the child in the way he needed to be loved. Perhaps some of these couples had adopted before they were emotionally ready for it.) In the twenty-eight remaining cases the baby and the family together were obviously an unworkable combination, creating a situation so bad that termination of the adoption was recommended to the state authorities.

Now what about the hundred agency placements which Dr. Amatruda looked into? Here she found that seventy-six placements were good. Seventy-six thoroughly adoptable babies had found homes with seventy-six warm, loving, well-adjusted families. Sixteen other placements corresponded with the twenty-five marginal cases in the private placements: in most of them it was a question of whether the family would be able to overcome its own difficulties sufficiently to give the child real emotional security. In eight cases the situation was very bad, so bad that termination was seriously considered, and was in fact resorted to in two out of the eight.

In Dr. Amatruda's study, the total showing of agency placements as 76 per cent successful, private placements only 46 per cent, certainly makes it plain that even though agencies aren't infallible, their methods and knowledge mightily reduce the chance of failure.

Another interesting insight into the efficiency of agency procedures is furnished by the study published in 1951 by the Child Adoption Research Committee of New York called "A Follow-Up Study of Adoptive Families."[5] Instituted by a single private big-city sectarian agency in the interest of adoption procedure everywhere, this presents a much smaller sample than the Yale study and covers only adoptions made by the agency itself. It represents an earnest effort to evaluate thoroughly and from every viewpoint the success of fifty agency placements. The staff was assisted in this project by Dr. David A. Levy, a well-known psychiatrist, who served as advisor and consultant, and also by trained case workers from other agencies who read all the reports and helped in making impartial evaluations of the degree of placement success. While the fifty adoptive families are too small a sample to furnish statistical proof of anything, the study as a whole is illuminating and raises many provocative and subtle points in the adoptive relationship.

As we have indicated, this material, covering as it does 150 pages which represent many months of work, is fairly complicated. We shall not attempt here to go into all of its philosophy or its findings. A few of the latter, however, show that here, too, in spite of mistakes honestly made and honestly admitted, there is a surprisingly large preponderance of successful adoptions. Of the fifty placements studied at a time when the children had been in their adoptive homes from twenty-six months to three and a half years, twenty-six were judged to be "successful," eighteen "fairly successful," and six "unsuccessful." It is important to know that the standards of success seem to have been very high—indeed, it is my guess that these same standards applied to a cross-section of fifty biological families would result in a much lower score! In spite of this fact, be it remarked, not one of the six adoptions considered "unsuccessful" constituted an impossible situation or one where termination of the adoption was even thought of. None represented parents grossly unfit for parenthood or babies grossly unfit

5. Similar results were found in a much larger study by Lillian Ripple: "A Follow-Up Study of Adopted Children" (*Social Service Review,* Vol. 42, December, 1968).

for adoption, but simply situations which obviously fell short of ideal when they were compared with the successful and fairly successful homes.

So when we consider Dr. Amatruda's findings of seventy-six good agency placements, sixteen marginal, and eight bad out of one hundred, and add to those the Child Adoption Research Committee's findings of twenty-six good out of fifty, eighteen marginal or better, six questionable or bad, all the signs point to a pretty good batting average for agency predictions. All parenthood is a risk, to be sure, but it is understandable that adoptive parents who work with an agency may feel a little more secure.

The work that agencies do costs a great deal of money. The adoptions arranged by those agencies which are supported by public funds usually cost the adoptive parents nothing—except, of course, indirectly, in taxes. But many private agencies, depending for their income on endowments helped out by fund drives, must and do ask parents to pay a fee. Agency buildings have to have clinics and examining rooms, waiting rooms, consultation rooms, nurseries, kitchenettes. Agency staffs, besides the clerical workers, are made up of highly trained social workers, assisted by a full- or part-time staff consisting of pediatrician, psychologist, perhaps a psychiatrist. Then, besides salaries and rent and heat and light, the agency must support the expectant mothers and the babies in the homes of the foster mothers. Sometimes, too, large sums have to be expended for special medical treatment for mother or baby. And so it has become an accepted practice, a practice which is understood and even welcomed by most parents, for many agencies to charge a modest fee. This usually is based on a percentage of the applicant's income, and in no case does even the highest fee completely cover the cost to the agency of placing one child.

Now, suppose that being thoroughly persuaded of the value of agency placement, you go to an agency but you don't get a child.

What should you do? Should you wait and apply again? Should you go to other agencies? Should you give up and try to adopt privately?

These are hard questions to answer. But there are certain courses for you to consider. If the agency you've contacted is not accepting new applications at this time for the kind of child you have in mind, you can wait for a time when new applications will be accepted, you can try another agency, or you can give some thought to the possibility of adopting a child who is different from the one you originally thought to adopt—a child who desperately needs and is presently waiting for a home and a family of his own. This child may be one who is older, one who has a handicap, or one who is of a mixed or minority race. The adoption of an older child or a handicapped child are topics discussed in Chapter 7. Let's take a moment here to discuss the needs of the many mixed- and minority-race children who are waiting for adoption.

In the past, children of mixed or minority race were placed with adopters of the same mixture or minority. Because of the shortage of these applicants in proportion to the great numbers of children available, many adoption agencies have in recent years been encouraging white would-be parents to adopt these children, too; otherwise many of them would spend their entire childhood in foster homes or institutions. Increasing numbers of whites, realizing that race is only one of the many differences that can be recognized and dealt with in adoption, are offering their love and their homes to these children.

The decision to adopt a child of a different racial heritage is a serious one. It requires careful self-examination and thought—especially as to motive. Although these children are in most desperate need of parents, their need alone is not sufficient reason to adopt; while the child's needs are met the adopter's needs should also be fully satisfied.

Raising a child of a different racial heritage is bound to involve problems and difficulties that will require great strength, maturity, and flexibility on the part of the adoptive parents. Many parents are coping with apparent success. Needless to say, interracial adoption is not for everybody. Is it for you?

If you think it may be, it would be well to read about the experiences of others who have adopted interracially—their motivations, the procedures, the consequences. David C. Anderson's *Children of Special Value; Interracial Adoption in America* describes the case histories of several such families. It would also be a good idea to read the chapter on interracial adoption in *Adoption—Is It For You?* by Colette Dywasuk. The author examines interracial adoption from every aspect and helps you evaluate *your* capacity for such an adoption.

Another course you should investigate and seriously consider is the adoption of a child from overseas who desperately needs a good home and a loving family. More and more children, particularly from Korea and Vietnam, are becoming available for adoption. If you think you might be interested in such an adoption, you'll want to read Frank W. Chinnock's *Kim—A Gift from Vietnam*. It is the heartwarming, tender story of one family's experience in overseas adoption.

To learn how to go about adopting a child from abroad, contact Friends of Children of Vietnam, 4568 Beach Court, Denver, Colorado 80211; Catholic Committee for Refugees—United States Catholic Conference, 201 Park Avenue South, New York, New York 10003; Holt Adoption Program, P.O. Box 2420, Eugene, Oregon 97402; or International Social Service of America, Inc., 345 East 46 Street, New York, New York 10017. These organizations can provide you with the necessary information.

It is up to you to decide the kind of child you can accept for adoption. If in spite of your best efforts, enduring patience, and many inquiries, it appears unlikely that the child you want to adopt will be available, if no agency is encouraging about your chances of ever getting the child you want, then it behooves you to take long and careful thought before you decide to try adopting privately. In the meanwhile there are many ways in which you can come to the aid of children who are not up for adoption but who desperately need help. In every community people who are intelligent, warm, and sympathetic and who have a little spare time, can be of tremendous use in working with retarded children, crippled children, or mental-health groups in the many activities carried on largely by volunteer workers—of whom there are never enough.

And private adoption? Is it a never-never? Well, no. If you must, you must—and you may very well have a happy adopting experience that way. It has often been done. But if you *do* try to get a baby privately, observe for the baby's sake and yours a few common sense precautions. Talk to a lawyer whom you know and can trust. He will know first of all whether private adoption is illegal in your state, as it is in Connecticut and Delaware. Then, if you and he work together, he will make sure that the surrender of the child by its mother or parents is in proper legal form before you take the child into your home. He will see to it that the adoption itself, when it is time for that, is legalized. He will work from the beginning to keep the identities of all the parties secret. He can perhaps—and will try to if you make it clear that it is your wish—see to it that the natural mother is given enough time to consider her decision and that the baby is examined by a pediatrician before you assume any responsibility for it. And he will see to it (if the laws of your state permit it, and those of most states do) that the court hearings are private, that the records of the adoption are kept confidential, and that your child's birth certificate is no different from the one he would have received if he had been your biological child.

Prospective adoptors are finding that they have to wait longer than in previous years to get a child or find out that a particular agency can't help them. Agencies have been working continually to try to speed up the adoption process without tossing overboard the practices and standards which have enabled them to make so many successful placements in the past. The more they reduce the waiting period, the less the chance of prospective parents becoming so discouraged that they abandon agency help and seek out the black market. Up to now their efforts have been extremely successful. But recent changes in social patterns are steadily reducing the pool of adoptable babies, while the number of those hoping to adopt continues to rise. Agencies hope for more widely spread knowledge of how they work, so that more pregnant mothers will come to them, fewer fall into the hands of the black-market operators.

There is only so much the agency can do to speed things up. They can't manufacture more babies even if they wanted to, and they can't rush too much the very processes which have been responsible for their overall success in finding the right home for every child that comes to them. They can't hurry the natural mother; for the sake of everybody involved, she needs time to make up her mind. And neither can they push too fast the "getting-to-know-you" sessions with the would-be adopters or the careful and skilled evaluation of the baby's health and personality potentials. But if you want a baby very much, you won't find it too hard to wait. After all, it takes nine months for biological parents to produce their child—sometimes even more months than that elapse between the wish for a child and its conception. And so even though during the waiting and hoping time you feel a little helpless, a little frustrated, this natural feeling doesn't last long. It vanishes like smoke as soon as you get word that *your* baby needs you.

It is exciting to think that somewhere your baby is waiting for you. Perhaps he's being born this minute. Perhaps he was born the vacation night you were driving through the mountain pass and is just now learning to do without his night feeding. Maybe his eyes are blue like yours, or maybe he's still too little for anybody to be sure yet what color they'll be. He could have a cowlick like your husband's. He could be the only redhead in the family. Maybe he'll be a live wire, maybe placid and easy-going. He could be President someday. Or a scientist. Or a baseball player.

Whatever his looks, whatever his temperament, you are prepared to take him as he is. You haven't spent all this time hoping and waiting just to acquire a lump of clay to be shaped and molded into your idea of what a child ought to be. What you really want is a small human person to live with you and be your own, while you love him and care for him—and enjoy with him the great adventure of watching and helping him grow in his own way; helping him to learn little by little how to achieve the best that is in him.

II Living Together

3 The Beginning

Let us suppose that you have achieved some real progress toward your goal of adoption. You have screened yourselves as fairly and honestly as you could, to help yourselves along the road of readiness for adoptive parenthood. You have made application to an agency. You have filled out all the agency forms, have been interviewed a number of times, and have at long last been told that the agency feels you will make good parents and that in due course you will hear from them.

What then?

Well, you go home and wait. Sometimes you will wait only a few weeks, often much longer. But don't expect to hear right away. Maybe your friends Susie and Joe did get a baby almost immediately, and you hear nothing for months and months. That doesn't mean that the agency is playing favorites, or that Joe and Susie are world beaters as adoptive parents. It just indicates that not only were they the right parents for their particular baby but also that that baby happened to be ready for placement at just about the time the agency had approved them. Usually things don't jibe quite that neatly. And so you need patience—lots of it. It doesn't do any harm at all to call the agency occasionally and remind them that you are there, for slip-ups can happen in any organization. But persistent nagging can't speed matters up, and it may raise legitimate doubts as to your flexibility. So don't indulge in any temptation to badger.

This, of course, is very easy to say. The waiting itself is hard. You will find, though, knowing as you do that immediate action is out of the question except in one case in a million, that life goes on as usual and you fill in your days much as you always did. Meanwhile, there are some things you can and should do that will be of constructive help to you. First, you and your husband would do well to take advantage of this lull to give yourselves another emotional orientation. It is true that over a period of months you have accepted the fact that the child you adopt will not be of your own blood and have planned lovingly and carefully for the child you may someday be given. You are confident, and rightly so, that you will love him just as you would your own. But when a woman is bearing a child, Nature has nine months in which to prepare her emotionally as well as physically. Although it is by no means true that all women are turned into gifted mothers by the very fact of birth, it is undeniably the case that the physical changes of pregnancy, the very bulk and weight and the viability of the child, prepare both parents psychologically for the fact that on or near a certain day they will actually be able to touch and to hold a little red squirming mite that will be a newborn baby.

Adoption is different. For one thing, of course, it is much more sudden! Although agencies are trying all the time to speed up their waiting periods, they cannot and never will be able to set a deadline, as Nature does. So no matter how intensive and self-searching your preparation, the whole idea of a baby in your house is actually quite theoretical. You don't even know the age of the baby that is waiting for you! And if you did, you probably couldn't visualize just what he might be like and look like—unless you have a large acquaintance among babies. He could be a very new one or he could be two months old. He may have had six months or more to develop a personality along with bones and muscles and to form something of an idea of the world around him. Unless he is pretty new, he may be surprisingly heavy and possibly wriggly. His care will, of course, differ according to his age: his food, his naps, his clothes. He'll be *real!*

If you are like most couples, when you reach this point in thinking about your adoptive parenthood you are bound to own up to just a twinge of apprehension. Of course you still want a baby. Of course you are delighted that you are going to get one! And of course you must be considered good parent material or you wouldn't be waiting! But you don't know exactly what to expect— and you do know you are about to take on a large responsibility. Sinking feelings, flutters of stage fright are much more usual than is often supposed. To talk about these feelings is better than to stuff them down inside and try to pretend they aren't there—because the less you acknowledge these tiny misgivings, the more likely you are subconsciously to count on the fact that when you see your baby you will then feel exactly as you imagine adoptive parents are supposed to. That very moment just must, you assume, bring with it the unalloyed delight that you have been waiting so long to experience.

Actually, as many couples have discovered, it may not happen that way. No matter how much you want this baby and no matter what he looks like, your reaction on meeting him may very well be quite different from what you both think it will be. And so you and your husband would do well to spend this little breathing spell between your dream and its realization in preparing for the natural shock to your inmost selves that this first sight of the baby so often brings—perhaps more so for you, the mother—especially if you are childless and unable to have children.

For hiding well below the surface, no matter how much you have tried to take it out and air it, is the knowledge that by no amount of wishing are you and your husband to become parents in the way in which most people do. You have talked that out and you have accepted it. It is a fact. But at the moment when you first set eyes on him this baby will be a personification of that fact. Momentarily, your deepest feelings may rise up to "deny" him at the same instant you are reaching toward him in love and thankfulness and affection: at the same time that you are going out to him you are pulling away from him. And there is no reason to feel ashamed of this or guilty about it once you understand the reason for it. That feeling of love and sadness mixed, of tears wanting to come through, is natural. Part of it is the beginning of your real parental love; part of it is pity for this helpless baby and the mother he had once; and part of it is the finality of this last step in facing your own sterility. If you have truly accepted the fact that you cannot physically produce your child, and if a child is what you really want, then this involuntary withdrawal, if it does rise all the way to the surface, will quickly pass.

To a few, this sort of emotional thundershower occurs even before the actual sight of the baby. One of the best and most relaxed adoptive mothers I know, who is bringing up two wonderful boys, confided that she started crying the day before the appointment and couldn't stop for hours, to the bewilderment of her poor husband. In her case it relieved her tension so that at the particular moment of meeting the baby she was relaxed and happy.

Perhaps it ought to be said that occasionally very intense reactions of this kind take place on seeing the child. This may mean that the man or the woman—or both—is not really ready to accept this kind of parenthood, even though he thinks he is. Perhaps they have lost a baby, which understandably adds another ingredient to the emotional brew. It could mean that they need to seek psychological help before they continue with the idea of adoption. Or it may mean simply that they need to take a little more time. Perhaps this is not the right baby for them. If the parents have formed the kind of relationship with the worker on their case which most do, it is certain that she will have the warmth and understanding to accept their feelings and to realize that this is a difficulty with which the agency can help. It is rather risky not to own up to these feelings of hostility when they are marked. For if these parents are, in their hearts, still not quite reconciled to their sterility, and take the baby home with them from motives of pride, or a guilty feeling that they will be letting this baby down if they don't take him, or fear that they must take this baby or none at all, they are handicapped from the start. And so is the baby.

Don't forget—social workers are human, sympathetic, and understanding. Over and over again they have introduced new and green parents to mature babies. If the parents are not happy, it is certain the child won't be, and so if only for that reason they want you to feel warm and easy in this relationship from the first. It happens not infrequently that parents can feel this with one child and not with another. That is why agencies as a rule notify parents they have a child for them to "consider" rather than saying "We have a baby for you." They have seen babies turn down parents as well as the other way around, and so if you know you are both completely sold on adopting but just don't warm up to this particular baby, they are likely to understand and to look for another one that you *will* warm up to!

Besides giving yourselves an emotional reorientation, there are some specific preparations you can make for the baby's arrival. You can get his room ready, redecorate it if you like, and you can get a crib, a high chair, and a baby's toilet seat if you want to, for you will be using them sooner or later. But since you don't know how old or big your baby will be, there are lots of things it might be a waste of money to invest in ahead of time. A "hospital" mother knows, for instance, that she will get enough use out of a real layette and bassinet to warrant their purchase. But our kind of mother may come home with a big fourteen-pounder five months old who wants room to kick in his crib and who couldn't even get into one of those stamp-sized shirts. Many adoptive mothers therefore feel that it is best to buy very little until they know what size baby they are getting, and then when they do, borrow as much as they can from friends and relatives. Babies over the infant size grow like weeds—so borrow clothes, borrow all of the equipment you can, such as sterilizer and bathinette from friends who have retired them for the moment. Have your fun buying the things you can't borrow and let the baby's doting relatives and friends, if they want to shower him, give him pretty blankets of all weights, crib toys, sheets, sweaters in the year-old size or even bigger, electric feeding dishes with bunnies on them, and so on. And the diaper service is a wonderful gift from grandparents who really want to splurge!

Another very useful thing you can do during the waiting time is to select and even get acquainted with a good pediatrician. Now is the time to get a line on the one who is best for you. If you live in a neighborbood where young mothers abound, ask your friends who have babies about their pediatricians. And *listen.* After you have been listening for a while you will have a pretty good idea which ones are rather rigid, which are sympathetic and open-minded. Naturally, you want first of all an able doctor and one who is not so far away as to be useless to you in an emergency. But many authorities feel that it is even more important for adopted children than for biological children to be under the care of a physician who believes in giving their emotional needs as much attention as their bodily ones. Your adopted baby will in all probability have been separated twice from a mother. In most cases the babies are so tiny when they leave their birth mothers that this break leaves no scar, but practically all the babies miss their foster mothers and really suffer from the separation. Outwardly they recover within a few days; inwardly, it may take them a little longer. Consequently, these adopted babies have an even greater need for security and approval than do other babies. And so a doctor who appreciates the importance of meeting the emotional needs of every infant will realize what this shift in homes has probably meant to your baby. Such a doctor will know that your baby is going to need more attention than most, more sucking time, more time in which to learn. He will be most unlikely to slow up the baby's emotional growth by insisting on early or abrupt weaning, strict toilet-training, or inflexible routines of any kind.

And you, the parents, need the support and reassurance that this kind of doctor offers just as much as the baby does. For if you are like most adoptive parents, for a little time you will be somewhat overanxious, overconscientious, even a bit on the defensive. You will worry just a little more than biological parents, will be more inclined to blame yourselves if he doesn't drink every ounce of formula or insists on a night feeding for longer than your friends think is proper. So pick your doctor with care, and when you go to see him, tell him yours will be an adopted baby and that you know he will agree he is a bit special for this reason. Doctors are very busy men with lots of people's problems on their minds, so you may have to remind him of the adoption factor from time to time. But if you can find a doctor who understands the special quality of your baby's needs, you will have gone a long way toward easing the early months for all of you.

Another good way for you to put some of this waiting time to use is in going out evenings while you may! And by all means get to know all the babies you can, helping with as much of their care as their mothers will let you, just to get in practice while you are standing by for that glad news.

One fine day you *will* get word! At last something will have come of all the waiting and the thinking and the hoping. A letter or a telephone call will come from the agency, telling you that they have a child they would like you to consider. It is more than likely that this will happen when you least expect it, and no one, least of all the worker who calls you, will be surprised if you can't take it in at first. Most people are incoherent to the point of stammering. One woman I know (she did have the additional excuse of the temperature that accompanied her case of influenza) immediately called her husband at his office to tell him the news, and only when he inquired whether the baby was a girl or a boy did she realize she had quite forgotten to ask!

Whatever you are doing—elbow deep in suds, painting your nails, reading, or cooking—you lose interest at once in the task. There just seems to be no point in doing anything that is not directly connected with the baby. You want to rush to the agency and bring him home that very instant.

As you know by now, it hardly ever works that way. The program may vary a bit with different agencies, but as a rule the worker has called to make an appointment for a few days later for you to come to the office to talk about the child and then to see him. This is the talk we have previously mentioned about the child's background and history, his general appearance and personality, the results of any tests he may have had, and the reports of the agency's pediatrician. Meanwhile, the baby, who has been brought to the agency by the foster mother—or sometimes by one of the agency's workers—will be waiting for you in one of the rooms. In you will go to see him, to begin to find out whether he wants to belong to you and you want to belong to him.

After the interview and your getting-acquainted session with the baby, you will consider everything you have been told about him to make sure you have no feelings of reluctance or uncertainty. If you have not, of course you let the agency know, and a time will be set for you to come to get him and take him home. You will be told what clothes to bring, what will be needed for his feedings, and so on. Unless there are special circumstances, there is some leeway about the date of the big event, and the agency will not think you don't really want the baby if one day is truly better for you than another. For example, I know of a couple who had planned a good-sized party to honor the engagement of the husband's cousin, who was in town with her fiancé for two days—and everybody had been invited, of course, for the very day the agency suggested. A bit red-faced, fearful lest they seem to be putting parties ahead of babies, the couple explained the difficulty to their case worker, who was only too glad to make the homecoming arrangements for a day or so later. The baby was spared a parade of noisy grownups past—or even into—his new and unfamiliar nursery, the parents were far more relaxed, and the party itself gave an occasion for all their friends to hear the good news that the hoped-for baby was nearly there.

Another acquaintance was obliged to postpone the baby's homecoming because between the initial visit and the day the agency set the husband was called away on business for four days. As most agencies believe it is extremely important for the new parents to bring the baby home together, the staff cheerfully made new plans. This is not to say that dates are to be shuffled about for any passing whim. Neither the agency nor any of her friends had much sympathy for a woman who suddenly decided she wanted to go with an aunt on a ten-day cruise to Bermuda and asked if the agency would mind holding the baby until she got back. The staff can hardly be blamed for deciding that others on their list wanted a baby more than she did.

Another matter to consider about the homecoming and the first few days is how much family you want to have around. It isn't uncommon for new adoptive parents to assume, simply because the mother of an adopted baby has not undergone the physical ordeal of giving birth, that bringing home the baby and organizing his routine is a fairly cut-and-dried affair and that they can all carry on as usual. As a matter of fact, there are big adjustments to be worked out on both sides. Parents are nervous and unsure, babies don't know what to expect. As a rule the babies cry and cry and cry, and the parents blame themselves and rush about wringing their hands, forgetting that the baby must do some grieving for his foster home.

The adoptive father of a baby boy wrote to their worker about how the homecoming made them all feel. He says:

David has been with us a little over four months now and has in all but documentation become a member of our family. I thought that as the father in the picture I'd like to write a note at least of my own satisfactions. You have no doubt realized that our life with David has been remarkably smooth, to a very large degree thanks to David's flexibility and amazing sensitivity. I look back to the first five days of his mourning here. These were times of great sadness for us all, for we realized that they were unavoidable for him and that we could do little to help him with his grief. In retrospect I am very glad to know that he was able to grieve, that he had had the kind of foster home which permitted him to establish real ties of warmth and security. The evidence of that is not only in his early behavior just described but also in all the later expressions of feeling. I am glad that he is able to feel things deeply, painful and otherwise.

Even though they knew the *why* of the baby's crying and knew that they could do no more to help him than to accept and respect his grief, those first days were obviously difficult ones for these parents as for many others. In a number of cases the change is not quite so upsetting to the baby, but some long crying spells are almost inevitable. The parents, even when they understand the reason for it, can't help feeling a bit dismayed and frightened. So usually the couple and the baby can weather these first days more easily if they are alone, or perhaps with a practical nurse who offers a helpful hand but little emotion. Though several mothers have told me that they did not know what they would have done without their mothers or their husbands' mothers to help them, others resented the well-meant advice and the criticism that sometimes went with it. One who had not too wisely but with the best of intentions invited both sets of in-laws for family dinner that first day "blew her top" even above the baby's screaming and asked them please, please to go home and come back next week! Another, who has two adopted children now ten and eight, says she has never forgotten her own mother's tact in going away for a little trip just before the arrival of each baby. "At first," she said, "I was a little hurt that she didn't want to help out. But afterward I was so glad we were alone—at least until we had a little confidence in ourselves!"

Lucky are the adopting couples of whom one or the other partner has grown up in a big family in which there always seemed to be a "lap baby, a porch baby, and a yard baby!" They have their hands in, so to speak, even though their experience may have been a long time ago, and they have at least a rough idea of what babies at different ages are like and what their needs are. That is why it is such a good idea to use your waiting time in getting acquainted with all the babies you can. Couples who haven't done this and who have had no babies around them to learn on are likely to doubt their capabilities when it is up to them to change, bathe, and feed this active and maybe good-sized baby with a will of his own. And while an adoptive mother isn't faced with the additional handicap of not being physically at her best, she still finds that the full care of a baby can be an exhausting job until one gets the hang of it, which takes a little time.

If you can afford it, it is not a bad idea to get some help for the first week, preferably somebody who is more familiar with babies than you are even though you may want her to help with the housework rather than with the baby. A practical nurse can be fine. So can a child's nursemaid between jobs, or an agreeable mother's helper who is fond of babies.

Unless your baby is just out of the hospital, however, don't get a registered nurse who has specialized for years in handling only newborn babies, each for two weeks at a time. Friends of ours did this, and while the nurse was a thoroughly agreeable woman and excellent at her own job, I shall never forget the red-faced frustration of that active eight-month-old baby in his play pen, rendered completely helpless by the nest of soft cushions and bed pillows in which she had placed him "to support his little back and keep his little head from wobbling!"

The actual arrival of the baby is of course a very important event, and parents wish to let their friends know about it as soon as possible. You may be able to find special adoption announcements that are now on the market. If not, you can use regular birth announcements. In the space that says "Born" put his birth date. Underneath you can add, "Arrived at our house" and put the date you brought your child home. The two dates tell the story and let your friends know that the baby is being adopted.

People who have lived in a community for some time and whose close friends are for the most part neighbors often don't send out announcements in the mail, but tell their friends about it at once, and let the good news spread, writing letters to relatives and those friends who live far away.

Once you have definitely been told all about your baby, be sure to give very careful thought to what you will tell your relatives, friends, and neighbors about his background. For if you don't, in the first excitement you may impulsively blurt out details that you may in later years regret having given. It doesn't matter so much as you might think whether such details are "good" or "bad"; what does matter is that people's memories (including your own) are fallible and short. The version you tell now of why your own child's mother decided to give him up or who his father was, may come to his ears at a later date in some distorted form. It is, after all, nobody's business but his and yours. So if you make up your minds in advance simply to say that he is a fine baby of healthy parents and that you are completely satisfied with his background, you will safeguard yourselves from any possible unpleasantness and keep what detailed information you may have where it belongs—in the family. It is good to know that no one is going to be able to shake your child's security even temporarily with words you may yourself have used. It is good to know, as time goes on, that no outsider is in possession of any fact unknown to him.

Another project to which you can give thought before you bring the baby home is the plan for the beginning of your family picture book. I don't mean a "baby book," though you may want one of these, too, especially if you are bringing home a very new baby. As a rule, however, these listings of the ounces and pounds gained, the first tooth, the first step, the first word are of primary interest only to the doting mother and father, and even to them they don't seem to have much interest afterward. In many cases they are not kept up. But even when they are, the subjects themselves, at most stages of growing up, are embarrassed when the volume is brought out. My idea is rather a book of informal snapshots which, shown often to your child even when he is very small, will be the story in pictures of how you became a family together.

"See, here you are the day we brought you home—here's Daddy holding you while Mommy took the picture. Here you are in the play pen we got for you. And this is you looking at your first birthday cake—you wanted to grab the candle! And here's your party when you were three years old, remember?" And so on. Of course such a series of pictures is a wonderful thing for any family to have, well worth the time and effort and forethought involved, but in the case of the family that grows by adoption it plays a subtle but important part in giving your chosen child the sense of having belonged from the very first. So have your camera ready for that big first day and keep it handy—and loaded—for other occasions, not only for festive events but for casual family outings, visits from grandparents: a running record of family "togetherness." It is important to keep the collection simple. Select just one or two of the clearest and most interesting taken at each time, and put them in an accessible and convenient form: a smallish album that little hands can manage is fine and so is one of those spiral-bound folders of transparent plastic envelopes.

One of my adoptive-mother friends told me that she and her child have found a great deal of pleasure in a collection of another kind: a large scrapbook started before Elizabeth came to them, in which had been pasted wedding announcement, newspaper clippings about the ceremony, snapshots, wires of congratulation, Daddy's "greetings" from the President, and so on. To those were added from time to time the things that especially concerned Elizabeth: telegrams of congratulation on her arrival, cards that came with gifts ("to our darling Elizabeth from her aunt Julia"), and various mementoes of the little girl's own life and times, from the kindergarten "report card" to the strange squiggle dated "three years old" and labeled in accordance with the artist's instruction, "A knife, a fork, and a lady." Elizabeth does not find this as interesting as the picture record and so it is not gone over nearly so often, but she knows it is there and very occasionally asks for it. It seems to give her satisfaction to know that long before she can remember it was taken for granted that she belonged in the family scrapbook.

Dozens of parents have helped their adopted children to grow up happily without scrapbooks or albums, of course, but many of these have told me they wished that they had had them, and especially that they had thought at the time to make a picture record of the real beginning—that "wonderful day we brought you home!"

And to most parents it *is* the real beginning—the day they bring the baby home. Even though they know they must wait for six months to a year, depending on state laws and on the policy of the agency, before the adoption can become legalized, they feel that their family started that very day. The legal adoption, important though it is for the protection of the child and the parents, as far as feelings go is only the icing on the cake. Most parents, though, are a bit curious about what happens between the homecoming and the adoption, about just what kind of "probation" they are on. All that rather grim term really means in adoption is that the agency continues to be the guardian of the child until it is certain that the adoptive parents who have been selected for him are the right ones. Most of the "proving" has really been done in the initial screening. Occasional telephone calls, letters, and a visit or two as a rule serve only to confirm the worker's belief that this couple have the makings of good parents for that child.

The system for making sure of this varies from agency to agency. As a rule the practice is for a worker to call on the family at least twice during the interim period. Nearly everybody has heard tales of how in the olden days these visits used sometimes to be pretty awesome affairs. The worker was supposed always to pop in without notice. The house would therefore be at its worst, the baby colicky, and the mother distracted; whereupon the worker would grimly go over the rooms like an inspecting general armed with white gloves: flip the cushions over, run a finger over the moldings, peek under the beds, and flounce out! I don't believe that this was ever true. Certainly it isn't now. But apparently the hangover from that particular bit of folklore is still strong enough to give otherwise steady parents the jitters.

Don't worry: nowadays the worker almost invariably lets you know she is coming, just as any polite friend would, and, in the second place, what she wants to see is a home, not a "model house." She is not interested in whether your tables are nicely waxed and your ceiling corners without cobwebs. She wants to know how you are getting along, and she wants to help you if you are having any difficulties. She knows you may have them—many people do—and she is there not to sneer at any she finds, but to

see if a little detachment, a little sense of humor, a little short cut
you may not have thought of won't straighten them out.

She doesn't expect a saintly baby or even a totally relaxed you,
for she knows that no matter how well you know her or how good
a parent you are, you are bound to feel some strain just because
you are making this trial run. This tension you probably cannot
help; so admit it to yourself—and to her if you want to—and then
forget it. Prepare to do likewise for the baby. For it is simply
amazing how much these scraps of humanity can absorb of the
tense feelings that surround them even though they cannot know
the cause. At least there often seems to be no other explanation
for the sheer number of times when the social worker's visit coin-
cides with the "acting up" of a perfectly happy and well-adjusted
baby. The one that can't yet walk or talk picks this as his debut
for a first try at finger-painting himself and his crib and the walls
with the contents of his diaper. The toddler who has often proved
himself so happy just to be with the grownups and bang "his" ash
tray against "his" saucepan while enjoying a brief period of
living-room society, will select this afternoon (and no other for
months to come) to stand scowling in the corner and hurl object
after object at caller and mother indiscriminately. (Or perhaps just
at caller!) The happy, hearty eater will surely choose this time
to spit out all the vegetables and indignantly refuse the cup he
has for weeks insisted on.

If you are prepared for this sort of thing, as the worker is, it will
upset you far less and the baby will revert to his normal attitudes
much more quickly. The thrown ash tray, the spit-out spinach will
not disturb the worker provided she can see that while you are
human enough to wish she could observe the way your baby be-
haves most mornings, you understand that your tensions and his
have come to an inevitable boil and that you do not hold this
against him. There are a very few parents, you know, who would
without realizing it score up this sort of action against their baby,
would feel that in behaving this way he was letting them down,

spoiling their picture of themselves as parents. It is this attitude which, for the child's own sake, the worker must guard against. When she does meet it, as sometimes she does, it is fairly unmistakable. No amount of acting can cover up the hostility of the parents who feel their child has failed to learn his lines in their play about the happy home. But always when you are truly happy with your child and the reality of having him, and can understand that somehow or other he feels as much on trial as you do, you will accept his reactions for what they are—just as you helplessly accept your own perhaps too rapid and too high-pitched conversation as you invite the worker into your living room. Look on it all as stage fright, nothing more.

When the end of the probation time approaches, you will have word from the lawyer whom you have engaged (or the lawyer engaged at your request by the agency) of the date that is set for the legalization of the adoption—a brief but dignified court ceremony. From society's point of view this step is the beginning of your parenthood. From now on you are his and he is yours in the eyes of the law. The adoption completely severs the relationship between the child and his birth parents and the agency ceases to be his legal guardian. The inheritance laws of your state now apply to your child exactly as they would if he had been born to you, and no natural relatives of his may inherit through him. Likewise from now on, until he is of age, you are responsible for him and for his actions just as you would be if he were biologically yours.

In other words, the solemn courtroom language puts the seal on the parenthood you assumed when you carried your baby out of the agency waiting room. It is a moving and majestic moment, but if you are like most parents it only affirms the reality you have known all along: This baby is yours and you are his.

4 Telling Your Child He Is Adopted

Telling. That one word could stand all by itself as a title for this chapter. A discussion of adoption, therefore a discussion of "telling"—so aware are people in general of this particular dilemma of the adoptive parent. When people learn that a friend or a neighbor is bringing home a baby for adoption, the first thing they speculate about, as a rule, is whether and when and how the parents are going to tell the child that he is not a blood member of the family with which he has come to live. Of course, for workers experienced in the field of adoption and child psychology, for many doctors and lawyers and ministers, there is no question of "whether." They know that although the "how" and the "when" may vary, the child must be told if you want him to have the foundation for a sound personality. They have seen too many cases in which concealment of the facts has led to unhappiness and even to tragedy.

Yet nine times out of ten the first question their friends ask of an adopting couple is, "Are you going to tell him?" And if new acquaintances learn of an adoption of several years' standing they almost always ask, "Does he know?" So deep-seated, so almost instinctive is everybody's consciousness of this particular "differentness" of adoption, that the verbs in their questions seem to need no objects.

It is gratifying to note that a change in emphasis has taken place in recent years. "Are you going to tell him?" used to be put with an intonation that plainly said, "Surely not!" And the new friends

would have whispered their inquiry. "He doesn't know, of course?"
—if indeed they had been let in on the "secret" at all. Nowadays,
however, because of many more adoptions and because of more
widespread information about adoption, far more often the implication is, "Of course, you're going to tell him." What today's in-
quisitors really want to know is the "when" and the "how"—because even though the situation is outside their experience, deep
down inside they are aware that it must be fraught with emotional
overtones. They wonder how *they* would feel in your position. They
are curious to know whether you are at ease with the necessity of
letting the child know he was not born to you, whether you will
find it simple or difficult, natural or uncomfortable.

As we have said, most people today do realize that the "telling"
is essential. So strongly do agencies believe this that nearly all of
them not only require the adoptive parents to sign a statement
promising to inform the child as soon as he is able to understand, but also discuss with them their feelings about it and ways
of handling it, in order to try to smooth the way for them as much
as possible.

Almost all workers in adoption can tell you heart-breaking
chronicles of the disasters or near-disasters that have been brought
about by the tardy discovery of adopted children that they were
not born into their families as they assumed they had been. A
friend, now married and the mother of two little girls, who was
told of her adoption wisely and understandingly at a time when that
procedure was not common, has never quite been able to put out of
her mind a girl of twenty whom she came upon in the washroom
at the department store where they both worked, crying so hard she
was nearly hysterical. She had come across an old letter and
through it had discovered for the first time that she was adopted.
She was hurt and bitter. She had no idea who she was or who her
people had been, but she was sure her background must have been
a very bad one—why else should they have kept it from her? At
the very bottom of her misery was the to her inescapable conclusion
that her own mother hadn't wanted her enough to keep her. The

night before she had been a whole and happy person; this morning a search for a bobby pin had thrown her world into chaos. In two minutes twenty years of security seemed to slide away.

The other girl listened to her, comforted her, let her cry and talk and talk and cry until she couldn't do either any more, and then told her, "Why, I'm adopted, too! What of it? I *like* it!" Very simple, very superficial, as she herself realized, but it did help the girl over her first shock, if only by making her realize that she was not the only foundling who ever came into the world. Other talks on other days seemed to bring relief to the girl, and eventually she appeared to have worked through her problem. How successful she really was in absorbing the experience is not known, for the two are not in touch any longer. Whatever the outcome, it was a fortunate thing for her that in the crucial first hours of her discovery she should encounter not only a warm-hearted girl of her own age, but also one who, like her, had been adopted, one who knew whereof she spoke—and spoke happily.

The world wars saw many instances of such belated revelations. Over and over again boys about to go into the Army and in search of a birth certificate they might never otherwise have needed found out for the first time that they had been adopted as infants in the years when matters like birth certificates were handled more casually and less understandingly than they are now. In cases where they were referred to the agencies by their dismayed and helpless parents, almost without exception they were deeply disturbed. Some seemed stunned, some were poker-faced, many were bitter and resentful. Most wanted the agency to tell them everything that was known about the biological parents— and it was obvious that they braced themselves for revelations that would be sordid and worse. All of them had been confronted with the totally unexpected and shocking news of their adoption and, in most cases, their illegitimacy just when they were having to mature at an accelerated tempo to face war, the first challenge of their new manhood. They desperately needed and were grateful for all the help they could get from the understanding social workers whom most of these were lucky enough to encounter. Since private adoptions were commoner then than now there must have been many more who got no such help.

One must remember that not all the tragic load in such cases falls on the shoulders of the children. The parents suffer, too— from bewilderment, from self-reproach, from remorse and guilt. Sometimes the relationship can never be made whole again. Sometimes it can be patched up so that the crack hardly shows: if the child has been deeply and warmly loved, if he has been helped to believe in and to respect himself, and if he happens to be blessed with a little surplus strength.

A worker told me of just such a case: a boy who was in search of a birth certificate so that he and his wife could go to settle in Israel. He called the social worker on long distance within an hour after his parents of necessity broke the news to him that he had been adopted. He wanted now not only instructions on how to get the necessary papers, but also all the information on his background that she could give him. She told him that his parents had not been married, that after his mother's death his father had accepted but not legally adopted him. She told him that while he was still very small his father had been killed in an automobile accident, and that after the illness of the grandmother who as long as she could did her best to make a home for him, he had been placed for adoption with the couple he now knew as his parents. She was direct and blunt and unemotional, as she knew she had to be, but it was painful to have to give him all this at once, and over the telephone at that. She did what she could to reassure him. To her surprise and relief, he accepted the story with admirable strength and resilience. He eased still another of her worries by telling her that he felt the first thing to do was to tell his wife the story. His next thought was to reassure the distressed parents who, with the best intentions, had for twenty-two long years pretended he was born to them, and for whom he had only the most sympathetic understanding. Though he may have had miserable hours later when the first numbness wore off, he apparently was able to meet the situation without panic or despair. And generously, for one of his main concerns, before he said good-by, was to comfort the social worker and to assure her several times that "everything was all right."

That worker still gets letters from him about the new lives he and his wife are building for themselves and for their small son. Whatever chaos his parents may have unwittingly created for him by concealing his adoption as was then the custom, they had in every other way so supported and loved him that they had equipped him somehow to weather it.

An interesting case about parents who so far have been, and may always be, able to maintain the line of concealment they have chosen appeared in a moving letter written to an "advice" columnist. This is the letter as it appeared in the widely read column in the Long Island paper *Newsday*.

Dear. . . :

Why do most people consider it necessary to tell an adopted child she has been adopted? Our oldest daughter is 16, and we took her when she was a month old. At that time the doctor told me it would be impossible for me to have children of my own. Then later we had two others, a boy four years younger and a little girl two years after. We are one happy family, and I can truthfully say that I love them all equally, and so does my husband.

We have never made the slightest difference between them, but if there were a difference, it would be in the older girl's favor, for we were so happy to have her, and lavished all our love on her. She is very well adjusted, and I don't think it has ever crossed her mind to wonder if she was adopted. We moved to Nassau from another locality so that there would be no question of the neighbors knowing and dropping hints. Nor is there anybody in either my husband's or my family to bring the subject up.

There is only one reason I bring up the problem even now. My daughter confides a great deal in me. The other day she came home and told me that one of her friends had just found out that she was adopted from a relative of the family. She is terribly upset about it, and talked it over with her friends, including my daughter.

Although the girl was perfectly happy until she learned the truth, she is now looking back on every incident of her childhood and seeking an explanation of why she was treated in a certain way at a certain time. She thinks of course that her mother and father were unjust or slighted her because of the fact she was adopted. So I asked my daughter what she thought about it. She said, "I just think she's making up things because she feels kind of let down that her parents never told her. All the girls thought it was sort of mean for that aunt she never did care much for to throw it up to her that she was adopted." Then she went on to say how happy she was that it didn't happen to her, and that she'd tell people they were crazy if they said her father and mother weren't her own.

I felt I had to say something right away quick. So I said that if there was anything like that in our family I would have told her before someone else had the chance. She was happy and very affectionate. Do you think I did wrong? You know, I never even think of her as adopted.

Distressed Mother.

In this case one would be obliged to consider the child and the family very fortunate indeed if, having chosen this course, the parents can manage to keep the secret always, and it looks as though that were possible and even likely. Perhaps the mother, as times go on, can relax and stop torturing herself with the fact that she has taken a just-about-irretrievable step in assuring her daughter that had she been adopted they would have told her so long before. Let us hope that no stranger-than-fiction accident will disclose the facts to the girl, at least until she is mature enough to handle the double shock of such a revelation. And let us hope too that when the child volunteered that she would "tell people they were crazy if they said her father and mother weren't her own" she meant just what she said and no more. Let us hope she wasn't hinting, wasn't desperately trying to have her mother deny some telltale childhood memory.

There really isn't any need to labor the point that the adopted child must be told of his adoption as soon as he is old enough to understand. There isn't any other way to build an adoptive family that's strong and stable, to give your adopted child a happy and sound personality. And if you don't arm your child with this information that rightfully belongs to him, that is a part of him, then every day of your lives you will be in fear that your child will find you out. If that happens, you bear a twofold burden. You will know that you have made it much harder for your child to assimilate his history without damage to his self-respect. And there is a chance that you will have lost his trust and confidence forever.

Or if being aware of the serious dangers of concealment you see to it that your child knows he is adopted but feel so ill at ease in the situation that from then on you try to ignore it and evade discussion of it, you are in all probability endangering his future happiness by instilling the idea that being adopted is a misfortune, something better not talked about.

In addition to the warmth and stability of the family that is built on the complete acceptance by all the members of the adoptive relationship, there is the enormous peace of mind that comes from being able to behave naturally in occasional situations where the adoption must be brought to the attention of others. For instance, it may be that the doctor to whom you take your child knows of his adoption and has for some time. On the other hand, it is quite possible that the man you and your child are facing across his office desk has never seen you before. Your child's "history" for purposes of record may be quite brief and uneventful, and it may not occur to you to mention that he is adopted. In fact, you are probably not even conscious of the adoptive relationship at the moment. You feel like, and you *are* like, all the other mothers in the waiting room. But suppose that as the questioning goes on with reference to the child's current difficulty the doctor pauses in his note-taking to ask, for instance, "And how about you and his father? Are either of you subject to any allergies that you know of? Either of you ever have any asthmatic attacks like his?" How much better all around if both you and your child are so at ease about your special situation that you can casually and smilingly say, without fluster, "Well, no, Doctor, but it wouldn't prove anything anyway, because our boy is adopted."

A trivial thing, you say, and it may be, more or less so depending on the age of the child. But while it is true that the words the doctor is using and the implications behind your answer—that your child's genes and your own have nothing in common—have no meaning to a young child, the degree of relaxation with which you speak can mean a great deal to him. And so, for your sake and his, he ought to be used to hearing the word "adopted"—to hearing it used in just as warm and matter-of-fact a tone as that in which you say, "Dickie's five, Doctor—he'll be six in September." My belief is that if this is your feeling about it, as it should be, the information may as well be given to the doctor at the beginning of the history, of which it is a part, just as much as the vaccinations and TB tests.

Many parents ask me whether the school should be told that the child is adopted when he first attends. Opinions differ about this, but I am inclined to agree with those authorities who feel that whereas the adoption is an integral part of the physical history which the physician needs and is entitled to, this is not true of the school. Your child's birth date goes on the record, as does his residence, and his previous school attendance if any. The fact that he is adopted does not belong on that record. Why label him? The teachers and office workers who would instinctively or by training appreciate the significance of his adoption in terms of his handling do not need it; they would be warm and sympathetic to your child as to all the rest. For the others, it only sets him apart. The information would be of possible benefit to the school staff only if there are behavior difficulties. If there are none, so much the better. If they arise, it would be natural in discussing his problems with the teacher, the principal, or the school psychologist, to mention that he is adopted, in case that fact might have some bearing on the behavior, in just the same way anyone might mention that a brand-new baby brother or sister was making things temporarily difficult for him. Here again, it is a protection for you both if you are accustomed to using, and he to hearing, the word "adopted," and if he knows what it means.

Before we get to the how and the when of the telling, let us try to discover why the anxiety of parents is so strong about this task they know lies ahead of them, and by doing so perhaps relieve the tension a little. It does go back, once again, to the fact that you may still feel somehow *lesser* parents just because your child is not your biological offspring. This has nothing to do with reason or common sense—only with emotions.

If you are unable to have children, it is doubly hard. You know it has not been easy for you to accept the fact of your infertility; in fact, you may still be trying to. But the knowledge that you must somehow inform your child of it and in doing so must make *him* accept it, and accept it happily, is another and a higher hurdle. You can't help wondering if you are capable of being sufficiently sure and confident when it comes actually to talking about it with your child.

It is natural that you should feel some constraint, some worry, no matter how much you have endeavored to work through your feelings—just as almost all parents, no matter how modern in their thinking, cannot help feeling a little constrained when they deal with sex information in talking to their children. Intellectually they are adequately prepared; their emotions, however, take over and make their voices tight and a tone higher than usual, cheeks a bit pink, pulse speeding up be it ever so little. Emotions govern you in telling your child about his adoption in exactly the same way and for the same reasons, with the additional factor that in this area practically all adoptive parents feel more self-conscious than others. Then, too, they know that the way in which they handle it is much more important to the future well-being of their child than is the handling of even such a significant matter as sex information with a child who was born to his mother and father. Don't, then, feel guilty or ashamed because you are self-conscious and a little afraid. That is only natural. But remember that these emotional associations, these feelings of embarrassment, are yours and yours alone. Your baby, even your child, has not one of them. It is *your* fears that make you tense, not his possible reaction to what you are going to say—for what reactions could he have? It is your—adult—interpretations of the facts that disturb you. It is your awareness—not his—of the social and personal implications underlying the facts that makes you apprehensive.

All he knows is that you two are his father and his mother. Because you are there he is warm and dry and happy. And so in the beginning all he needs to know about "adopted" is that it is something good to be. It may help you and it won't hurt him if you use the word very occasionally—*not* constantly—in your play with him, in bathing and dressing and loving him. He certainly won't know what it means, any more than he knows the words "little imp" or "butterball" when you are rolling him over and laughing and playing with him. But he will know that his mother and father like little imps, and butterballs, and adopteds. They like *him*. The word will have pleasant associations for him, the important associations of safety and approval.

As he gets a bit older and you talk to him in sentences, when you feel like it—and only when you do—you may say, "We're so *glad* we adopted you!" or "Aren't we lucky we have you!" You may tell him once or twice the story of his adoption in its simplest terms: how you and Daddy wanted a baby so much and you didn't have any, so you looked and looked to find a baby that needed a daddy and a mommy—and you did!

The words you use don't matter much; they will be your words used in your way. What *does* matter is that his hearing the words in happy and relaxed situations will not only help him to continue associating "adopted" with love and approval, but will also help you to soften any self-consciousness you may feel. The earliest years are the easiest in many ways where telling is concerned, because as far as your baby knows *everybody* is adopted. He doesn't know that there is anything different about it. So by all means, but without overdoing it, without ever harping on it, get yourselves and him used to the mention of "adopted" every now and again, always with overtones of matter-of-fact pleasure.

It will certainly be helpful to you in these early years to have on hand two books which deal most understandingly with many aspects of telling the child of his adoption. One is *The Chosen Baby,* by Valentina Wasson, and the other is *The Adopted Family* by Florence Rondell and Ruth Michaels, published in two slim volumes. Of these latter books which tell in pictures and brief text the story of how adopted babies join their families, one is intended for the parents; the other, for small children. *The Chosen Baby* is also a picture book for very young children telling the story of one baby's adoption. Either or both of these books will go far toward providing you with the reassurance that all adoptive parents need.

As we have indicated up to now, your small child knows he is adopted, but since he doesn't know what the word means, that has been only a preparation for your explanation of what adoption is. When do you take the next step? How old is "old enough to understand"?

It is impossible to give a firm and definite answer to this. Children differ. Some at an early age are alert, observant, and soak up information like sponges. Some are dreamier; their gaze is oftener directed inward. They accept rather than question, and it is hard to be sure what they really want to know and whether or not they are satisfied with your answers. When your child is three or four, however, you will want to be prepared for the first step whether it comes this year or next: the honest answer to "Where do babies come from?" Not brought by the stork, not out of the doctor's black bag, not under a cabbage leaf, of course. If ever those answers are unwise—and they are—they are truly dangerous to use with an adopted child. Your stake in being honest with him, particularly about this, is enormous. But, as so many adoptive parents have complained, it is much, much easier said than done!

It is hard enough for ordinary parents to know just when and just how to present this basic information. Your task as an adoptive parent is doubly difficult because the information you present must go a giant stride further. You must first explain that babies grow inside their mothers; then you are obliged sooner or later to make it clear to your child that he didn't grow inside *you,* but inside another woman. It's not only hard to explain—it's hard to say. But being prepared helps: getting ready for, but not on edge about, this first conversation. And remember, you are not alone in feeling a bit apprehensive; the books I have mentioned, plus many articles, plus this chapter, would not be printed unless there were thousands of people in need of a helping hand.

An excellent book to keep on hand for the time when your child begins to question more deeply the various aspects of adoption is *And Now We Are a Family,* by Judith Meredith. This book, meant to be read aloud to young, adopted children, explains clearly and beautifully what adoption is, how babies are adopted, why parents adopt, and why some people must make the decision to give their child up for adoption. Written by an adoptive mother for adoptive parents, this book is meant to be a beginning, a tool to help you talk to your child about his *own* story.

The first talk may come about in a number of ways. The pregnancy of a friend or relative may give you a good opportunity to open the subject. You may have a cat heavy with kittens, or perhaps a neighbor's dog is about to have puppies. Make any of these situations serve you if you can. For it is always better to lead into the discussion by way of a natural situation which almost automatically inspires children to questioning, rather than to seem to make an occasion of it.

You will explain how Aunt Laura, or the cat, or the dog, is getting big because the baby, or babies, inside are almost ready to come out, to be born. You will explain that all people and most animals are born this way, that they stay in their mothers' bodies in a special place where they are warm and protected, until they are big enough to come out, to be born. This probably will be enough for your child at this time. If it is, he will show it. If it is not, he will almost inevitably ask, "Did I grow inside you, Mommy?" In that case, there are just two things you don't want to say. One is "yes," and the other is "I'll tell you about that some other time." For you do not want to lie to your child and have to take it back later. Nor do you want, by postponing the discussion, to give him any notion that it is something you are too busy or too uncomfortable to talk about. When the direct question comes, you need to answer it. And it is easier when you are prepared. So you will want to be ready with the next step, whether it is needed at this moment or some months later, because when your child asks that question, that is the time when he must begin to learn the meaning of adoption as it applies to him and to you.

Here again, there is no formula for what you say next. Emotional readiness on your part is really the basic need here. For there is no single set of words guaranteed to do the job for any parents and any child. The words are not so important anyway: better wrong words in a warm and natural voice than right ones rushed through with stiffness and embarrassment. It's not so much what you say that matters; it's how you say it. A certain amount of tension will be there, but keep remembering that it's *your* tension. Your child will have none unless yours is strong enough to infect him. Your love and pride in him will come through as you explain that it just happened that babies didn't grow in your body, and so you and Daddy went to see a lady who helps find babies for people who don't grow any. It took a long time. She looked and looked, and finally she found *him!* And she told Mommy and Daddy to come and see him; and you did, and you loved him the minute you laid eyes on him. And you took him home so he could be yours and you could take care of him always. And you bought bottles for him, and a crib for him to sleep in, and blankets, and toys, and so on.

This is the story that breaks the ice—for you as well as for him. You will want to take it slowly and easily. You will take your cue for the amount of detail you give him from the degree of his interest. You will tell him whatever you tell him unhurriedly, with love, with warmth, with physical cuddling if he is in the mood for that. You know that whatever your choice of words, you want to try to get across three things: that babies grow inside women's bodies, that no baby grew in you so you looked for a baby, and you were so glad when you found *him!*

You will be prepared to repeat it all at a later date, probably more than once, for children forget and then, too, they often like to hear about their babyhood over and over. As time goes on and your child's understanding increases, you will want to enlarge gradually on this information. Not long after your telling the story of his biological birth—or perhaps at the same time depending on his age, his interest, and his questions—you will want to tell him that a man and a woman start every baby, and that the baby then grows inside the woman's body. If you overlook this for too long, a child is likely to get the idea that only mothers perpetuate the race, that fathers are just to work! And for adoptive children even more than biological children, a deep and sound father-child relationship is essential. Here again, once he understands that he had two other parents before he had you, who are his *real* mother and father, you ought never to let him feel that these first parents failed to take care of him because there was anything unlovable about him.

When he asks, as he eventually will, *why* no baby grew in you, you will probably say that sometimes that just happens—people don't always know why. He may ask then, or at some other time, "Why didn't the other woman keep me?" and you may say, "Whatever the reason, it must have been a very good one, because I am sure she loved you and would have kept you if she could." This will be enough to satisfy your child for a while.

Another thing you will want to do, and this before school age if possible, is to enlarge your child's experience with adoption, lest he get the notion that he is the only "adopted" in the world. You can tell him of friends you know who have been looking for a baby to adopt and have found one. You can tell him which of your friends' children are adopted. If you know any grownups who were adopted, by all means tell him about it, unless by some mischance they are unsympathetic or sensitive about it instead of warm and outgoing, as they must be to make the acquaintance a valuable one for him.

Some parents have told me that they thought it helped them and their child at this age to let him undertake a personal bit of "adoption" himself: a kitten, a puppy, or a doll. In the cases I have heard of, it happened to work out very well, but I can't help feeling that these parents were just lucky. It's a long, long gamble. What if the puppy dies? What if the kitten runs away? What if a few months later the child breaks the doll or leaves it on a bus? It's just possible that the child might well suffer from a mistaken sense of guilt, ashamed that he had treated his "adopted" dog or cat or baby in a way he knows was not loving even though he hadn't meant to do it. Worse yet, it might awaken in him the fear, sleeping deep down in almost every adopted child, that some accident, some desertion, some separation, may happen to *him.*

These things may never come about, but there is no way you can guarantee that his personal experience with this "play" adoption will be an absolutely secure and happy one. You're the grownups; to you belongs the responsibility. Just keep on adopting *him,* and let him enjoy his pets and his toys as friends and playthings, not as symbols.

An important guidepost along the path of telling your child the adoption story is never to let him sense any resentment or disapproval on your part of his biological mother. You probably have just a little; it's a form of unadmitted jealousy that is very natural. But try to keep it out of your voice and your expression, because for the sake of his peace of mind and his self-respect you want him to feel from the beginning that it was not because he was unlovable or she unloving that she couldn't care for him, but that, on the contrary, *because* she loved him she made a good plan for him to be part of a family that would love him too.

Don't let it surprise you if, after your most careful explanations, your child forgets, is confused, or seems totally disinterested. Take heed of the familiar anecdote about the child who, when asked after a fairly thorough briefing on sex, "Now have you any questions?" said, "Yes! How do they make bricks?" An old, old chestnut that, but a sound one still, for it is illustrative of children's quick shifts in interest, of their acceptance of what they are told, and, above all, of their natural and casual attitude in areas that for grownups are charged with emotional cross-currents. Small children squirrel away all the information they can get about this exciting world, and because they have no built-in tensions, the answer to "Where does a candle go when it burns?" is just as interesting as "Where do babies come from?"

A letter from an adoptive mother to the worker at the agency illustrates the short span of a small child's attention and his inclination to "disremember." The family was in the garden, the mother writes, and the parents were talking about something that had happened several years before when Sally asked, "Was I there?" They told her she hadn't been born yet. "Well, where was I?" She wanted to know. She was told that she was a tiny seed growing inside her mother.

"Inside?" was her incredulous reply. "How did I get out?"

"God provided an opening when it was time for you to be born."

And Sally's answer to that was, "Oh, Daddy, look at that airplane! Was that the kind you were on?"

So ended these parents' "first experience of facts-of-life questions."

A few weeks later they again mentioned something that had happened years before, and again Sally said, "Was I there?" Here we go again, they thought, and once more said, "No, you weren't born yet." This time Sally said at once, "I know. I was a seed growing in the garden and I got up and came in the house and you washed me off."

As the mother so understandingly puts it, they don't know what kind of ideas Sally is forming but they will just go along with her and answer as truthfully as they can. Already they foresee the question about "Whose tummy did I come out of?" and the mother writes, ". . . as I see it that will be a difficult part for her to under-stand, but we shall see. . . ."

I have read many letters and heard many questions from adoptive parents who, just like you and Sally's mother, are apprehensive, if only a little bit, as to how all this is to be made clear. There is no question that this is one of the most demanding jobs adoptive parents have to tackle. But it is a comfort to know that nearly all the others—and there are many thousands—are anxious, too. And it is a comfort, too, to know that it is not a do-or-die matter. There is ample room for the mistakes we cannot help making, as long as your child knows he is warmly loved and fully accepted.

Although it is difficult to be concrete about just what to do and say, it is possible to point out a few pitfalls that are easy to avoid. First, when you are talking with your child about his birth, it is best not to use the term "your real mother" or "your own mother." Or father. *You* are your child's real parents, his own parents, in every sense except the biological one, and you don't want to imply other-wise. When you want to refer to the biological parents in any dis-cussion, it is perfectly all right to say "your first mother" (or father) or "your first parents." It is true, and the word "first" has no dis-turbing connotation to a child. He is used to talking and hearing about "the first time we went to the park," his first tooth, his first friend on the block. "Your other mother" has been used by some, but this word, "other," it seems to me, unfortunately hints that the biological parents are available somewhere. It seems to make them about as real as you are, but removed only in space.

Second, don't wait too long to tell the basic adoption story. The earlier this story becomes a part of him, the more secure he will be. Then, too, you don't want your child to be helpless, frightened, unprepared if a playmate taunts him with "you're adopted!"—as children sometimes will. You don't want him to overhear a neighbor whispering to another, "He's adopted, did you know?" and to won-der what's wrong with *that!* All your talks and your warm men-tions of the word will help him, of course, but he must also be forearmed with such of the facts as he is old enough to understand.

Then if he has any doubts or misgivings arising from episodes like these he will not hesitate to come to you and ask you—if only indirectly—to straighten things out for him.

As he gets older, and as both he and his friends become more articulate, you may want to be ready to arm him, if the need arises, against the occasional teasing or taunting he may encounter that is couched in terms you happen not to have used with him. An adopted friend of mine says she will never forget the way she felt when somebody called her an "orphan": she knew she was adopted, and would have been perfectly capable of dealing with that particular challenge, but she happened not to know the meaning of the word "orphan." All it meant to her was the grotesque comic-strip child, little Orphan Annie, and she had never dreamed she looked like that!

Surprisingly often a child will provide his own defense against such teasing: many a child without any coaching has won the round with "Oh yeah! Well, they picked *me* out—*your* mother had to take what she got!" or words to that effect. Naturally the more at home the child is with the story of his adoption, the better he can handle himself.

It is too bad, of course, that adoptive children run into situations like these. Certainly there are far fewer instances than there used to be, but ignorance, hostility, and the tendency of little pitchers to have big ears still combine to create difficulties now and then for the little adopted and his parents. Even grownups can be amazingly tactless in this respect. One adoptive mother told me that the woman next door, watching her child perform with unusual grace on the backyard trapeze, remarked in a disapproving manner, "Did you get her from a circus family?" Another parent told me of a neighbor who, rebuking her child for some misbehavior, said to her, "Your mother doesn't have to keep you if you're bad, you know! She can send you back any time!" And there are a few—fortunately a very few—people who don't want their children to "get too friendly" with an adopted child, because "you never know . . ." Let us be thankful that such attitudes are on the decrease, for there is not too much you can do to protect your child against them except to be aware, to make as sure as you can that he will talk to you about them, and bring any hurt out in the open rather than let it fester inside.

On the other hand, you may even be obliged, as some adoptive parents have found, to see that your child doesn't go around boasting about his adoption. It is not uncommon for a kindergartener or first-grader to do this, but it's a form of showing off which, if persisted in, will hardly add to his popularity and should be very gently discouraged.

So far we have covered the early years, the first and the simplest stories you tell your child about his origins. When you have made sure that he knows the facts and is comfortable about them, you have made big strides. But don't forget that, like sex information, the explanation about adoption is never a once-and-for-all matter. A very little satisfies small children; older children need to know more; the sixth-grader still more. And children forget. They also confuse things. No matter how interested they seem at the time and how lucidly you explain, they will ask all over again, or they will show that either then or later they misunderstood or misapplied the information you gave them. There are many adopted children who in spite of their parents' careful explanations persist for months or even years in thinking babies are adopted *or* born, not both. They get it straight after a while, but hardly ever at one hearing, and it behooves you to be ready without surprise or impatience to go over it again whenever questions are raised, as well as to be alert for indications that though direct questions are not being asked you, something is puzzling the child.

Many adoptive parents, like other parents, want to know the best way to give further sex information that is physiologically accurate yet warm and unself-conscious. Once they have made sure their child has a pretty sound understanding of the adoption story as it applies to him and to his family, adoptive parents can, I feel, adapt existing books on sex information for children. This, of course, should be done in such a way that while the child is not allowed to discard his knowledge of the "differentness" of his own personal story, the stress is not on that difference but rather on the wonder of life and growth. The names of several such books are listed in the bibliography; I feel that one of the very best, because it is complete and yet so warm and natural, is *The Wonderful Story of How You Were Born,* by Sidonie M. Gruenberg.

It is comforting to reflect that you are maturing along with your child—that just as his widening experience and growing intelligence lead him to ask more searching questions, so your growing ease in the job of being a parent helps you to deal more confidently with those questions as time goes on. And if you listen as well as talk, you will find that you get guidance from your child. If he shows you that you told him more than he was ready for or interested in, you make a mental note to be sure to review thoroughly when the questions come again. If the number of questions and their trend show he is absorbing the material and is interested in every bit of it, he will be ready for more information next time.

If you are a typical adoptive parent, it is probable that you are apprehensive about the time when your child will ask questions about his biological parents: what their names were, who they were, where they are now. Nearly all the parents I talked to are much concerned about this, even when their children are still small. And over and over again the parents of older children have confessed to their uneasiness, too, saying they wish they had not been given so much concrete information, which they felt had been of no positive help to them. It would be far easier to say, when their children ask direct questions about their backgrounds, "I don't know."

This may be the easiest way out for you, but it would be unfair to your adopted child. He has a right to know about the people who gave him birth. His background is a part of him—his identity, his heritage. The common feeling today is that knowledge of his biological origins is good for the adopted child when it is made a part of his upbringing. It helps the child when he knows about the worth and normalness of his forebears. As an adoptive parent you should, in fact, take great care to find out all that you can about your child's background so that you have the information ready and available for him when he wants it.

There is no reason for you to feel uneasy, embarrassed, uncomfortable, or defensive when your child begins to ask questions about his biological parents. There is nothing against you in his questions. He is *not* challenging your right to be his parents. He knows you are his real parents, his family. He is merely trying to find out about those who gave him life. He has the same curiosity about his biological parents as any of us may have about our grandparents and great-grandparents. The very fact that he is asking demonstrates a great deal of trust and confidence in *you*.

When your child questions you about his origins, answer truthfully. There are no set rules about how to go about this—what to say, how much to tell him. This is, of course, up to you. Each family must do what seems best—what feels most comfortable. Whatever you say should be honest, but don't confuse honesty with total confession; you don't have to go into every detail. Be sure to let your child know that his curiosity is only natural—that he should always feel free to ask you what he wants to know, that you are not offended by his questions, and that there is no reason he should ever feel hesitant or ashamed about wanting to know about himself.

Some children develop a consuming interest in their "secret" background when they reach their teens. Your child should know that if he desires to see the court records of his adoption, that you would consent to it—when he is older. He has a right to know all about his past, including the names of his biological parents. But he should be reminded that they helped create the barriers to his past—that when they released him for adoption they deliberately limited their role to giving him birth. They might not be too happy to have him reappear in their lives after so many years.

Many parents wonder if their child can face the true facts and details about his adoption. Your child, if he is like most adopted children, will go through a period of questioning—a period of turmoil—at some time in his life. There is no way of telling at what age it will come. For one teenager I know, it came when her biology teacher asked each of his students to draw his own family tree. For a little seven-year-old boy I read about, it came when he began to realize that his younger sister was born into his family whereas he had been adopted into it. Each of these youngsters was able to work out his frustrations and resolve his uncertainties because he had the love, the concern, the support, of his adoptive family. And your child will, too.

If throughout the years you have raised your child with love and understanding, if you have made him feel secure and good about himself and what he came from, he will find within himself the means of coping with the facts of his existence and still feel good about himself and his background. He will be able to accept the weaknesses and strengths of the man and woman who gave him birth. He will be able to understand that his mother gave him up because she thought it in the best interest of both herself and him if he were adopted—she was not prepared for parenthood, and hoped others would provide him with a better home and conditions to grow up in than she could give him. He will have the self-assurance to learn he was born out of wedlock without being destroyed by it.

A great majority of adopted children are born out of wedlock. It is highly likely your adopted child will be, too. The questions he will ask about this may seem particularly difficult for you to handle. While it's true that these questions are not easy, it is good to remember when answering them that two people can love one another a great deal even though they are not married—and that morality is not inherited. Fortunately, in today's society, the stigma of illegitimacy is greatly diminished if not totally gone. Even so, your child should be made to understand that although his biological background is a part of his existence, he is a separate individual—a person unto himself.

Alexina M. McWhinnie, a British psychologist who conducted a well-known study into the adjustment in later life of adults who had been adopted as children, believes it is best for a child to be told about his origins. In a paper given at the Annual General Meeting of the National Council for the Unmarried Mother and Her Child in London, November, 1969, she said:

. . . adopted children, as well as wanting to know from their adoptive parents that they are adopted, want and need some information about their biological background and about why they were placed for adoption. Communication about adoption, however, tends to be one-way, i.e. from the adoptive parents to the child, and the child, though curious, will often wait for information to be given about its early background rather than ask for this.

Adoptive parents, however, find it much more difficult to talk about adoption than is generally recognized. This is particularly so in relation to giving information about the biological background of their adopted child. Such children, however, as they grow up, will want to be given such information. The times when they are particularly curious are when reaching adulthood, when asked for a health record, on marriage, or when having children themselves. The kind of information which they ideally would like to have are details of their biological mother and father, their ages, occupations, what they were like as people, their physical appearance and whether they were healthy. If they are not given information, or are given conflicting information, this can lead to fantasies and often to disturbed behaviour. Ideally, these details should be given within the family. . . . One's experience, indeed, is that if communications about adoption break down within the family the adopted person will feel the need to seek this information outside. Lack of information can cause the person to suffer acutely from feelings of doubt, uncertainty, and conflict. Such persons talk of feeling 'rootless' and of 'being in a vacuum' or 'being in a flood and clutching at a straw'. Any fiction would be viewed as better than the uncertainty which surrounds them. Some become neurotic about the risks of inherited disease and create fantasies around the few facts they know. . . .

These findings, that adopted children, though viewing the people who brought them up as their parents, need factual information about the parents they were born to, are confirmed in the few other reported research studies which have concentrated on the adopted person. Rosner in *Crisis of Self-Doubt* (Child Welfare League of America, 1961) when doing counselling work with adopted adolescents describes how once the flood gates were opened, questions about origins came flowing out. Hagen in the research study 'The Adopted Adult Discusses Adoption as a Life Experience' (Lutheran Social Service of Minnesota) found similar attitudes and needs. Clinicians involved in therapy with disturbed adopted adolescents find this questing for identity is frequently an acute symptom. Psychotherapy with adopted children shows this clearly (James B. McWhinnie, 'Psychotherapy with Adopted Children in Adolescence.' Paper presented at Seventh International Congress on Mental Health, London, August 1968) with the need to work directly with these problems of poor communication in adoptive families.

Unfortunately, some adoptive parents who are given detailed information about their child's background by the adoption agency either obscure it or withhold it entirely from their child. The fear, the frustration, the uncertainty, such secrecy arouses can best be demonstrated in a letter written recently to Ann Landers, a well-known national columnist:

Dear Ann Landers,
The people who adopted me are the only parents I have ever known. They have been wonderful and everyone tells me how lucky I am.
But there's this big blank in my life. I need to find my real parents. I have to know what the circumstances were that made them give me away. My imagination runs wild when I think about what might have happened that made them abandon me.

I think about these things more and more. It's getting so that I don't think about anything else. I have to learn the truth about myself so I can stop brooding.

Don't tell me to forget it because I can't. I need some advice.

—Confused in Chicago.

Although some of your adopted child's questions may be difficult for you to answer, the more your child knows about who he is and where he came from the less he will feel threatened by "the unknown." Even the knowledge that his questions will be answered as he goes along—that nothing will be kept from him if some day it seems best for him to know—will reassure him. In the long run it is much better for you and your child to learn to live with and face adoption honestly instead of trying to camouflage it. That he is adopted is a fact of your child's existence. He must learn to accept it. You cannot change the fact nor make up for it, no matter what you do—and you shouldn't try.

The particular problem of telling their children about their origins may seem to be one that is faced only by adoptive parents. And of course biological families are not faced with the identical situation. But every child at one time or another questions his antecedents, and it is the rare family indeed that can produce a double set of them admirable in every member. Quite often an alcoholic uncle, an aunt or grandmother who acts a bit wacky, a "black-sheep" brother, make biological parents uneasy even as adoptive parents, wondering whether and how to come out in the open about it, how much to tell, what effect the disclosure will have on sensitive budding personalities. There is at least one skeleton in every family closet: sometimes the children know or suspect it, sometimes not. Sometimes they worry and are fearful about it, sometimes not.

The real meat of the matter is this: the child who feels unloved and unworthy, whether he be biological or adopted, cannot rest as long as there is anything for him to be anxious about. If there seems to be nothing, he will find something. But the child who feels loved and worth-while, biological or adopted, can and will take on his family's liabilities as well as its assets.

And so in this respect, as in many others, the task of the adoptive parents is, after all, not so very different from that of biological ones. If you yourself have fully accepted your child's adoption, you will be able to make him accept it, fully and happily. You may have qualms—it would be odd if you didn't—especially in this undeniably difficult area of "telling." But you love your child without reservation, and he knows it. You like the kind of person he is and he knows that, too. This being so, you are altogether likely to have smooth sailing even in these waters. And if you do, your trials and his in the latter part of his growing up will be far fewer and far less upsetting. You will have set the best course for his future.

5   How Will
He Feel About It?

You are so happy in your baby, so proud of him, so overflowing with love for him, so conscious each day of your own good fortune in getting him. You mean to be, you want to be, such good and loving parents to him that he will always feel as glad as you that he was given you for his mother and father, and never question that your love for each other is or could be any different from the love of all other parents and their children. Thousands and thousands of adopted children have grown up secure in this happy and rather special kind of closeness. And yours will, too. For you will remember, as adoptive parents should, that the happiest and best-adjusted "chosen" child is confident always that he is loved for himself, loved just as he is. Even during the storms and stresses of adolescence, with its tormented questionings, that child doesn't *really* wonder, deep down, whether he is actually a disappointment to his parents, whether if they had to do it over they would choose differently. He knows that he *was* wanted and *is* wanted.

And how do adoptive parents go about achieving this state of affairs? How can they insure that their child never feels inadequate, unadmirable, perhaps unwanted? They can't, of course—not all the time. And they would be giving him very faulty preparations for living even if they could. But with insight parents can minimize a child's self-doubts, and with foresight they can avoid at least some of the situations which help bring them about.

All children suffer from time to time from the gnawing worry of somehow not measuring up, or of being overlooked, or left out. Biological children are no exceptions. They have these feelings too, and they cope with them as best they can, usually successfully, sometimes not. But if you are the parents of an adopted child, you will be prepared to be more on the watch for signs of such feelings than a biological parent, for here, as in other areas, your child is just a little more vulnerable. He may—not will, but *may*—depending on his temperament and his situation, be more susceptible to self-doubt just because he is adopted. But of one thing adoptive parents may be sure: if their child does feel that he is failing to measure up, if he has any doubts at all that he is lovable and that he is loved, he is bound to be wounded more deeply than a biological child in the same position. Especially because he is adopted, he needs to know that he is wanted, that he is acceptable, that the kind of person he is, is a good kind to be.

"... that he is lovable and that he is loved." How can he think otherwise, you ask yourself. How can he fail to know that he is the most precious thing in the world to us? He does know it, of course, and it is a tremendous help to him. But it can't always be everything, for he must make his own way in his own world, from kindergarten to wage earning. He doesn't have to be liked by everybody, but he does need to know that he's pretty well thought of by most of his contemporaries as well as by the grownups who mean something to him. And if he isn't, or if he imagines that he isn't, the adoration of his parents won't help—enough.

At first glance, this possibility may seem terrifying to adoptive parents, so very many of whom are a bit frightened and even— they have told me—somewhat on the defensive about their ability to perform the task they have set for themselves. If our love isn't enough, they ask (out of the deep-buried hurt of the non-biological parent), what then? We can't go around making people like him —do all adoptive parents start out with a strike against them? Are biological children automatically provided with insurance against this kind of defeat?

The answer of course is "No!" No parent, biological or otherwise, can control and manage and direct everything for a child, even if it were desirable to do so. Like all children, your child will run into many situations that are not built to order for enhancing his own personality. He may feel temporarily inferior because he is undersized for his age, because he doesn't shine at baseball, because he has to wear glasses. He may imagine a brother or sister to be more a family favorite when such is not the case. He may have got off on the wrong foot with a rather intolerant teacher. If you and your husband are active extroverts and he is a dreamer, or if you are readers and he is far better in sports than in English, he may wonder, even though he knows that you love him dearly, whether all the same you don't wish now and then that he were different. Up to here, the adopted child's problems are the same as those of any biological child under the same circumstances. But the adopted child, especially at adolescence and pre-adolescence, can hardly help going a step further in his wonderings about himself. Consciously or otherwise, he is nearly always inclined to ask himself, "Is all this maybe because I'm not much good anyway?"

And this is where adoptive parents need a little extra insight, a special awareness. Of course they love him—more than ever. And because they do, they stand by to help him at times like these. They can't take his glasses off, they can't cause him overnight to feel the magic in a De la Mare poem, but they can try to make sure that the wonderings he may have as to whether he is stupid or bad or unlovable are not being turned inward and brooded about with the fact of his adoption assuming more and more unhealthy importance in his mind's eye.

Everybody feels unloved at one time or another. No parents can prevent it, and in fact parents have their turns at feeling unappreciated or misunderstood often enough by their husbands or wives, by their children, by the boss, or the new neighbor. Most of us, unless we are very insecure, can jog along just the same and work our way through or around these feelings, with us they are usually temporary. But a child has no perspective about them. If they come too often, and if the parents who should be loving and understanding don't even notice, take no steps to reassure him of their love and of his worth-whileness, those feelings will put down deep roots inside, as fast-growing as a cancer—and as destructive. So with your adopted child you need to be aware—ready to recognize the call if it comes, ready to give extra support and understanding if they are needed.

This is not to say that you must constantly be apprehensive about his mental and spiritual health, that you must dig up his personality once a week to see if its roots are thriving. On the contrary, if you show concern and anxiety you are quite likely to bring about the very feelings you don't want him to have. He will start to wonder what can be wrong with him that you can't take him for granted. Children, both biological and adopted, like plants, thrive on a certain amount of being left alone to grow.

A confident, serene love is what he needs and what you will give him. Not suffocating love, not blind, sacrificial love that wipes out your own personality, or the sort that wraps him in cotton wool, but just plain, outgoing love of your child himself because he is what he is and because you're glad he's yours. With this you will start him off on learning to form happy and secure relationships with other people.

In the first years and months of his life, when his parents are the people he knows best and looks to for everything, there are many ways of managing day by day so that your love spells for him appreciation and understanding as well as attention to his physical needs. How lucky the parents who are adopting in this era when fathers and mothers are told not to be afraid of loving their babies! Who knows how many children have had somehow to persuade themselves of their parents' love just because they grew up in the days when the sagest advice was to "let him cry it out! Don't spoil him!" Those children had toilet training forced upon them whether they were physically and emotionally ready for it or not. Their bottles were snatched away and cups substituted willy-nilly. No night lights helped to keep the shadows in their places. And what cuddling they had their mothers often felt uneasy about giving them lest they be spoiled. Now, fortunately, the pendulum has swung the other way. Parents are reminded that what the hospital nurseries call "T. L. C."—tender, loving care—is just as important as the formula and the vitamins, if not more so. Demand feeding, new babies rooming in with their mothers, a relaxed attitude about toilet training, and weaning by easy stages are signposts down the new road.

In many small ways you can see to it that the work involved in the baby's physical care doesn't shut out time for loving him. Don't make yourselves slaves to his routine. Formulas must be made, bottles sterilized, washing done, and there's no denying it takes time plus a certain amount of scheduling. But don't be afraid to alter or interrupt the routine. It won't hurt him a bit to skip his bath for the sake of a little extra playtime with Daddy. On the contrary. If you can be relaxed from the beginning about how he eats and what—and, above all, how much!—it will pay off in big dividends later on. As for weaning him from his beloved bottle, just put yourself in his place. If you do, you can imagine his hurt and bewilderment when this comforting mainstay that has meant a full, warm stomach to him ever since he was born suddenly vanishes and the good milk that he learned to get from its satisfying nipple now has to be got at by way of a cold, hard cup. Don't give him cause to associate *you* with this unhappy turn of events, but instead go from bottle to cup by easy stages. And when he starts to feed himself and messes with his food, remember that he has to, that it is part of his physical and emotional development to squeeze, to splash, to grab. Don't rush his toilet training just because Mrs. Butler's baby is "completely dry at ten months." Think to yourself that Mrs. Butler may be singing a different tune when her baby is a few months older, and make up your mind that *your* role is going to be that of an amiable helper while your baby trains himself in his own good time. All of these things and more the new books about child raising and baby care will tell you, and it is well to give yourself a refresher course from your books occasionally. But you don't need books to remind you always to love your baby, cuddle him and smile on him, laugh with him, and show him that you enjoy just being with him, that you think he is the nicest baby that ever happened.

On the other hand, keep in mind that you can't possibly love him 99 per cent of the time or even 95 per cent—and it is foolish to expect that you will. When your baby is still small and helpless, it is comparatively easy to think of him lovingly just about all day long. But when he gets the power of locomotion, when he discovers the delightful fire power of a loud "No," when he does something he knows he shouldn't just because it's fun to get Mommy mad—at such times the knowledge that this, too, is part of his development will not automatically sweeten your disposition. You will frequently be impatient with him. You will even be angry with him to a degree that may surprise you. Especially if you are a mother. Fathers can and do get exasperated too, of course, but it is Mother who is with this little jumping jack all day long and has to try to keep him in line without squelching him altogether, at the same time coping with the shopping, washing, ironing, and so on. Often a mother who has been relaxed in the care of her infant takes a little while to get her bearings when overnight her cuddly baby seems to have turned into a person, with a powerful will and mind of his own. Sometimes she may even be shocked by the intensity and the suddenness of the hostile feelings she may have, and then on top of her natural irritation she tries to shoulder a load of guilt. She doesn't need to. In the first place, she is not alone in having these angry feelings—all mothers do. Biological or adoptive, they are people before they are mothers. And during. And after. In the second place, although the baby needs appreciation and affection, he would grow up with very false ideas indeed about this world if he never saw his parents anything but sunny. They just wouldn't be real! If they are loving and accepting most of the time, it will do him good to learn by degrees that they are people too, that they have their rights just as he has his, and that they won't *let* him walk all over them or anybody else.

As your child approaches school age and his world expands,

the situations multiply in which he may feel different, inadequate, or in some way less acceptable. Some of these we can do nothing concrete to prevent; we can only watch to make sure the effect is not lasting. But we can try to see that no such situations arise in our family living through our own shortsightedness or unawareness. Illnesses and operations, a different school or a new home, a baby in the family, are examples of the kinds of situations we all must meet in which our deep concern for his ultimate well-being or that of the family may so absorb us that we forget to give our child the extra loving he especially needs at such times.

There are a few pitfalls awaiting all parents which adoptive parents particularly are wise to avoid. For example, your child even more than a biological child needs to believe that when you and his father assure him something is, it is so. His trust in you is essential not only for a good family relationship, but also for his untroubled acceptance of the adoption story—*his* story—as he learns it through talking with you. This doesn't mean being the sort of prig who would rather hurt somebody's feelings than lie about her unbecoming new dress, or that you and his father need to be solemn and didactic as judges every moment of every day. It just means that when he is earnestly in search of information, give him seriously as much as you feel he wants to know and can handle; don't fob him off with teasing or sarcasm or "cracks." He needs to know that he can reach you when he wants you.

You need never be afraid to say you don't know. Far better, in fact, to say that than mask a guess with an air of authority and be found out later! And the parent who says, "I don't know, but let's find out," does much for his child. At the same time that he is opening the door to interest and the ways to satisfy it, he is demonstrating that he is warm and human, not an all-knowing and all-powerful being whom it is easier to be in awe of than to love.

Speaking of truth and honesty between parents and child, let us consider a universal question which perhaps concerns adoptive parents just a bit more than others. And that is the answer to "Is there really a Santa Claus?" All parents do a good bit of worrying about this, and rightly so. Many authorities have speculated as to whether it is a wholly good thing to foster in their children too solid a belief in a living, white-bearded saint who comes down chimneys to leave presents for good little boys and girls. This is because the ultimate revelation that he isn't real is such a shock to a few children. Parents and grandparents get so much pleasure out of the game that they are likely to postpone the inevitable enlightenment too long and sometimes even keep on reassuring when playmates have already planted doubts. Many, many children seem to be only slightly jolted by the disillusionment; other sensitive ones take it quite hard, and with these the disturbance appears often to be caused as much by the fact that it was the *parents* who deceived them as by the deception itself.

Just how you handle the Santa Claus story in your family is a matter of preference, affected, of course, by the ages of your children, by family traditions, by the presence of grandparents, by many other things. Certainly to many people Christmas with the children seems flat without stockings hung for Santa's visit. Perhaps the time for the parents and children to share the fun of all the pretending is in the real baby years. But be sure to plant the notion of the symbol, the legend, soon enough, for it is better not to wait until questions are asked. Adoptive parents especially do not want to run the risk of having their four- or five-year-old, already told of his adoption in a loving story, wonder to himself some years later, "Well, they certainly fooled me on Santa Claus. Maybe some of that other stuff is bunk too." Mind you, this isn't likely to happen. But it could, if at eight or nine or eleven your child gets just a bit off the track at school or at home, with himself or with you. And it's one of the risks that can be avoided.

As your child grows more mature, it is easy to let him acquire a "left-out" feeling by not letting him share in family business and family crises. This does not mean to make a crony or a gossip out of him or to burden him with large doses of life in the raw. But it will wound him to be ignored, thrust aside, treated as if he had no eyes or ears and no feelings. If, for example, word comes that Uncle Frank is very ill, tell him so. Be as calm as you can and as reassuring as you can, but don't evade the direct questions he may ask, don't try to conceal your real concern altogether, don't concretely hold out false hope if there is none. The facts will bring their own shocks and fears, and will, of course, upset your child. But with your help these fears can be put into words, and then they can be faced. No matter how tragic the reality, it cannot be half so frightening as wondering what terrible thing can have caused the smothered sobs, the hasty conference, the phone calls, perhaps the sudden departure of Father or Mother.

Talk about lack of money is especially likely to cause children great anxiety. When concerned and sometimes heated discussions about bills and expenses go on between the parents, the child has no way of judging how serious the situation really is. He may imagine that in another day or so there will be no food in the house—no house, even, for that matter. On top of that worry he may feel guilty about having asked for and gotten the expensive bike for his birthday, or about his tonsil operation which is said to have "wiped out the new coat" for Father. So it is safer not to try to conceal all financial discussions from a child. On the contrary, let him participate according to his age. Reassure him if it becomes necessary; tell him that from time to time you *do* get worried about money (everybody worries about money!), but that he is more important to you both than all the money in the world. If the crisis is minor, tell him frankly that the promised croquet set has to be put off for another month because the car needed a new tire. If the family's position is more serious than that, tell him Daddy has to get another job, that you feel sure he will find one though it may take awhile, that in the meantime you will all have to be much more careful about spending money but that you can manage. If the child is old enough to assume some responsibility and wants to, by all means accept with pleasure. Don't take the stand of big shots who will fix everything, even if you feel that way: receive his offer with the respect it deserves. If his newsboy's earnings or a part of them would ease the milk bill and he wants to share, let him. If his desire to pitch in outruns his abilities, help him think of a real contribution that only he can make—as, for instance, watching the baby so that Mommy can type the job letters for Daddy.

Just how much detail you give your child in any of these situations depends on how old he is, and how mature, whether he is fairly secure or rather dependent, whether he is practical or dreamy, whether he is the only child or one of several. If you must eliminate some factors as too frightening, too much for him to handle, stick as close to the truth as you can: don't embroider with things you may have to take back. In general, it is better to err on the side of telling a little too much than to brush his questions aside or tell him he is too little to understand. He understands a whole lot more than you have any idea of, and he worries. He worries for his parents and for himself. If you refuse to let him share, he thinks maybe it is because *he* is no good, or maybe that the worry is in some way connected with him or even caused by him. So while he must be shielded from panic, he does need to know what has happened to upset everybody. He can even stand it to know that you feel like crying, that you are worried, if he can see that you know what to do next and are going to do it. Don't lay your burdens on him and don't say or imply that in order to help he must assume an adult role. Reassure him, and encourage him to talk his fears out with you. Then he is comforted; he can wait with confidence until the bad time is over. But when instead the fears go underground, they may months and even years later crop up in some seemingly unrelated form, by then so deeply rooted that it may be very difficult to dig them out.

Oddly enough, you will almost certainly find that in any of these family crises, especially the big ones, thinking how to help your child helps you. Calming yourself so you can sort out what you want to tell him and talking to him about it will soothe your own fears and strengthen you, let you go on from there with more courage than you thought you were going to have.

Almost all of us can handle times of crisis better than we can the petty moments when the strain of daily living frays one's good will. Sometimes admonition, "pushing," gets to be a habit. It is all too easy to plant unsureness, a feeling of unworthiness, in a child by always tweaking at him, whether with words or with hands. So remember not to nag at your child, at least not more than you can help. Don't nudge him to say thank you to Johnny for the nice present. Don't remind him again and again to be sure when the party's over to tell Mrs. Adams he had a good time. Don't get in the habit of saying things like "All the other girls came out of the gym five minutes ago! Where were you?" The implication behind all this well-intentioned badgering—and it seldom escapes the child— is that you don't have much confidence in his ability to represent the family or even to manage his own affairs, that he is the kind of person you have to keep checking on.

Too much strictness can have a damping effect, too. The little child who is never allowed to eat between meals when his companions up and down the street always catch the ice-cream wagon begins too early to feel rebellion against authority. The boy of ten and eleven who is not permitted to go anywhere even in the daytime unless his parents know exactly where he is every minute is bound to feel resentful of them and distrustful of himself. This is not to say that you should let your adopted child do as he pleases; on the contrary, he, exactly like other children, needs the comfort of some rules and regulations, of knowing that you will not let him do things that are out of line. But remember that children are conformists; they need to do what the others do. If it really seems to you that the school dances end too late for seventh-graders, you can try to work it out with the help of other parents. You will find that many of them are also concerned and worried, but, like you, afraid to stand alone. Parents in many communities have found that a united front, some ingenious planning, and hard work can provide a solution that safeguards the children without seeming to destroy their new-found maturity. But especially if your child is adopted, you don't want to take issue with a whole set of customs and arbitrarily pit your rules against the rules of the crowd. For if you do, you may find your position far weaker when you need to take a stand on something you truly feel you cannot permit. And you just *may* discover too late that your child is converting a natural adolescent straining against authority into resentment against you for having adopted him and against himself for having had to be adopted.

On the other hand, it is easy to be too permissive with your child. And overpermissiveness can be more damaging to the adopted child than to a biological child, because the former a bit more than the latter needs his security reinforced with kind but consistent authority. What *is* permissive? What is *too* permissive? So many parents are bewildered about this, and many have come to grief through misinterpretation of its meaning and its aims. The permissive method of handling children is the reaction to the rigidity of our grandparents' slogan "Discipline for discipline's sake." Its aim is to help a child to grow and to learn and achieve independence while still remaining acceptable to himself and to other people. It makes use of freedom—but of freedom within certain bounds. It is a loose rein replacing the straitjacket of "Do as I say, and do it now!"

The rigid parents plop their five-year-old down at a restaurant table, forbid him to pile up the silver, tell him to eat what they have ordered for him, drink his milk, sit still, and stop playing with the rolls. They ignore the fact that the table is too high for him to reach comfortably, that the "regular dinner" is so big it discourages him, and that it is very hard for a small child to sit still through a three-course meal.

The overpermissive parents, on the other hand, may (if they are sufficiently thick-skinned) enjoy themselves in spite of their offspring whose loud noise, interruptions, and running around the room bedevil the helpless waitresses and the other diners. The first child will feel defeated because it is impossible for him to measure up to his parents' standards. It does not take the second very long to find out that he is no pleasure to anybody, least of all to himself.

The parents who truly accept their child at the same time that they respect their own and other people's rights avoid all this by making sure in any dining room that he is comfortable, that his portions of food are small enough not to be discouraging, that he has something to play with if he needs it, and that he shares their attention but doesn't monopolize the conversation.

This same guide of the happy medium applies to all the child's activities, inside and outside the home. The rigid mother may flatly forbid Mary to play with finger paints because they're messy. Or she may do all the playing for her, showing her just how, being fussy about spilling, constantly criticizing, so that Mary gets neither fun nor a sense of accomplishment out of the paints. Mother does it for her, including cleaning up and putting away afterward.

If Mary's mother is permissive she probably spreads newspapers on the kitchen table and covers Mary with an old smock, she helps her to put the paints in the dishes, and, if necessary, helps her to clean up and put away. Mary's mother does *not* meekly tidy up while Mary skips off to another activity. And should Mary insist that it would be nice to finger paint the wallpaper, she is firmly prevented.

Rigid, permissive, properly permissive, are all just words. "Rigid" can be the word for parents who spend most of their child's growing time in forcing him into a mold of the "ideal" child. They press and shape him with their thumbs until he is smoothed out into a miniature adult—this in the name of love, and with no malice aforethought. Sometimes it is subtly done, sometimes less so. But whether with adoptive or biological parents, the hallmark of the rigid treatment is that the last thing the parents are interested in is the child's own self, either his limitations or his assets.

In the name also of love do the "overpermissive" parents set the stage for their child to be himself at all times and in all places, with the rights of others (including the parents) ignored in the interest of the growth of this small personality. Perhaps these parents lavish on their child the attention they themselves missed as children, perhaps they have misunderstood the modern approach to child raising, perhaps there are other reasons for their indulgence.

Properly permissive parents are by no means afraid to say "No." They say it and say it firmly when the child is about to do something dangerous, something destructive to property, something inconsiderate of other people, something that is not acceptable behavior. Properly permissive parents are not bullied by their children. They do not pleadingly offer choices of action in the hope that the right one will be chosen. They do not tack "okay?" onto the end of every direction. They do not feel they must provide an elaborate explanation for each routine command. They are not *afraid* of their children. The reins are loose, but it is the parents who hold them, not the child.

Naturally you will, because you are human, be both rigid and overpermissive with your child from time to time. Children are fallible and parents are too; there is no reason to suppose you will hit it right every minute of every day. There are bound to be times when you realize too late that you jumped on Jane too hard in order to impress Aunt Judy—or perhaps just because you were angry about something. There will be times, too, when you know you have been too soft with Jane, or with Jonathan. But you needn't—and won't—worry about these lapses if Jane and Jonathan know that not only do you love and accept them but are strong enough to take care of them.

We have been talking about some of the ways in which insensitive handling may make any child, and especially the adopted child, feel insecure or unwanted. There are other situations in which the adoptive parent needs to be doubly wise and doubly aware. These are the special ones which without wisdom and foresight on the parents' part may galvanize a deep though subconscious fear of most adopted children: the fear of being left again.

Nobody is sure how much an infant remembers—in terms not of words but of feelings. From his very first weeks emotions come out to him from his mother, and soon from other people: his father, his grandparents, his small brother or sister, his babysitter. All of these, or the great majority of them, are happy emotions which wrap him in good feelings, feelings that give him comfort. And most of all when he is with his mother. She feeds him, keeps him warm. She cuddles and croons to him with the freest kind of warmth. The very tone of her voice and the way in which she holds him tell him not only that she loves him, but also that she is there to protect him, and always will be. It is not too long before he recognizes her face when she leans over him, and associates it, too, with love and protection.

With a biological baby, his mother will no doubt go on being the first and warmest protector, continuing to represent security to him all through those important first months and years. But many, many adopted babies have had to be removed first from the birth mother and then from the foster mother. Of course it is possible that an adopted baby may suffer some emotional setback from the separation from his birth mother, but this seems doubtful, and one would suppose recovery from it to be rather rapid. But the separation from his foster mother is different. She is the one he remembers as having kept him warm and fed and comfortable. For weeks, and sometimes for months, he has associated her voice, her face, her smile, with contentment and safety. He may be old enough now to feel, though not to know, that this anchor of his days has somehow gone away and left him. We have pointed out how many of the babies must and do grieve for their foster mothers when they first enter their adoptive homes. It is at least conceivable that in later years any threatened separation from the adoptive parents, and particularly from the mother, whether it is real or fancied, might reawaken those fears and feelings even though no actual memory of the foster home may have survived.

This may seem to be an overdrawn picture of infant memories. But here is an illustration from life which shows how far back some of these associations can go to project themselves even into *conscious* memory—and in this case in circumstances not nearly so upsetting as those into which most adopted babies are thrust.

I talked not long ago to a mother whose baby had been born shortly before she and the boy's father were divorced. She had almost immediately to go to work to support herself and the baby, but she was able to leave him daily in the care of her parents and an excellent babysitter. Before the baby was a year old, she met her present husband and six months later married him. Her new husband adopted the child, giving him his name, and proved to be a warm and loving father. But thinking that such a baby could not possibly remember the period when he was without a father, the mother avoided telling the boy about the adoption. Because of her hostility toward her first husband, she was emotionally unable to consider her story from the child's point of view. In attempting to "shield him" she was really trying to shield herself from the questions he might then or later ask her.

When her boy was five, she realized she had not succeeded in shielding him. On the contrary. A very sensitive and also highly intelligent child, he had for some time been anxious and fearful, full of worries about himself. He kept asking, "Where was Daddy when we lived with Grandma?" He wanted her to tell him over and over again that, unlike some of his friends in the neighborhood, he really and truly came out of her stomach and wasn't "adopted." And he was desperately afraid to let her go away from him even for a few hours.

One might guess that though he could hardly have had a specific memory of his biological father, he had feelings about him, that he was worried because although he could dimly recall a good deal about his life in his grandparents' household he could remember no father there. Quite possibly his mother and grandparents, without meaning to, stressed his father's abandonment of him at times when they were caring for him, never dreaming that he would "understand." Understand he did not, in the sense that we use the word. But he might well have "felt" what they meant, and might have remembered with his emotions that something had been wrong before, at a time when his mother wasn't often with him, so that if she should disappear he would be truly lost.

This mother was able with help to see that she must tell her child about her divorce and his adoption by his new father, and she was able also to understand her real reasons for wanting to postpone the revelation indefinitely. Though it was not an easy thing for her to do, she did it. And reported afterward that his face lit up, and that he has acted like a different child ever since.

This mother was positive that nothing could have been said in the new neighborhood to cause him unease because nothing was known, and was equally sure that the family had preserved secrecy as had been her wish. So he must have had just enough memories, both conscious and unconscious, to feel frightened by her evasive answers to his questions and to distrust the permanence of her protection. The simple facts satisfied him and set his mind at rest.

Every child, adopted or biological, needs the physical presence of his mother in his babyhood, and there are stages in his development when he is deeply afraid that she may leave him and never come back. How much deeper this fear of abandonment may be in the adopted child we can only guess. We know it is there, and we can only surmise that it *is* deeper.

In the child whom you take into your family it may well be that because you took him when he was very young, because of an extra dose of stability in his make-up, or for any one of a number of reasons, the seed of this fear is minute. It may never grow, may never come to life at all even at the age of two, when so many children cling to their mothers and are fearful of being left with strangers or even with friends. But since you cannot possibly be sure, you will want to avoid putting him into any situation which might cause that deep-seated fear to stir in its darkness.

This does not mean to pamper and overprotect your child. It certainly does not mean that you can never leave him. But you will want to be careful about the circumstances under which you leave him and the way in which you do it.

Be particular about your sitter: make sure she loves and understands children, and that she is mature and warm enough to be truly comforting in case of need. See to it that your baby is acquainted with her a little before you take your leave. Make your trial flights brief and preferably in the daytime. And if he is to be in bed when you return, make a point of telling him you'll come in and kiss him good night even if he is sound asleep—and keep your word. In the morning tell him how you did it and how it was. And never, of course, steal away without telling him.

For the same reason adoptive parents must be very careful about hospitalization and operations for their young children. Avoid hospitalization when you can; unless the case is serious or the diagnosis uncertain so that complicated tests or treatments must be carried out, the child is better off at home with your amateur nursing than turned over by you to even the best and kindest professionals.

A minor operation such as a tonsillectomy can be an extremely frightening experience for a young child, no matter how well it is explained beforehand and no matter how sure he feels that you will come back tomorrow to take him home. Postpone it if you can until the child is at least past three, better yet of school age. If you can't, try to get the hospital to co-operate in letting you stay with him. In any case tell him in simple language about what will happen: about the enema if he has never had one, about injections, about how his throat will be sore afterward. Tell him about the anesthesia: what it is for and how it is administered (check this with the doctor first), and what he must do to help. It is wiser not to use the expression "put you to sleep," for the idea of being *put* into a "sleep" so deep he can be hurt without knowing it may be frightening to some children. Bring from home a toy that he can keep with him. And tell him over and over again just when and how you are coming to get him.

A little imagination and ingenuity can work wonders. One adopted four-year-old who had to be left at night for an operation next morning could not be consoled. She was a child who could remember two other homes before this, her final one, and it was clear she was afraid that all these goings-on meant her nice new mother was going to leave her for good. She refused to believe in any of the reassurances. At length the mother had an inspiration. She took her driver's license, keys, and bills out of her purse, gave the purse and its other contents to her daughter, and asked her to keep it until she came next day. The child was satisfied immediately. Any little girl knows that no Mommy would ever be without her purse for long! She would certainly come back, just as she said she would.

Starting school is another of those experiences hard on many children which can be particularly disturbing to adopted children. This is especially true if the child is beginning nursery school very young. Make sure, before you enter your child, that the members of your nursery school staff are warm and experienced. If they are, they will be flexible enough to help you accustom your child to being left at school. It may take many compromises as well as time and patience to bring him to the point where he will willingly abandon you for his new friends in the nursery group. You may find that he objects to your leaving. If that's the case, try staying on the scene (inconspicuously) for a few days; or take him home after an hour, gradually lengthening the time he spends in the group. If this does not work, it may be that he is not quite ready for the experience. Try it again in three months or six months.

Whatever you do, don't get emotional about it, don't lose your temper with him, and don't force him. When he is ready and able to do so, he will enter into the activities with the teacher and the other children. If you scold him, yank him, or go off and leave him screaming, it may take weeks or even months for him to get over the realization that you *are* capable of just disappearing and leaving him to the mercies of he knows not what.

As with hospitalization and nursery school, so with those first visits to the barber, the doctor, and the dentist. Here is an opportunity for you to prove you are worthy of his trust and confidence and that you understand his feelings. Tell him at home, a day or two beforehand, casually and not at too much length, what is to happen at the doctor's. Tell him about the dentist's chair, perhaps play dentist with him. And a word of warning about the first haircut: if you can possibly refrain from using an expression that is second nature to grownups try not to say "haircut." Remember that for a long time now you have seen to it that he knows "cuts" and "cutting" are to be avoided. You have cried, "No, no!" to knives and pointed scissors because they'd "cut you." So use the word "trimmed," instead, or "fixed like Mommy's."

It often works wonders to let the child on a first visit to the dentist just get into the chair and be allowed to go up and down in it. Or to watch Mommy while she takes first turn at having teeth cleaned. And it is an excellent idea before his first hair trim to let the child go with Daddy once or twice and watch him get his.

We have written much of this material about the challenges of bringing up adopted children as though 95 per cent of the job were up to the mother. This is due partly to the defects of our English pronouns and partly to the inescapable fact that although this is changing, the mother in our mores is still responsible for most of the daily upbringing of the children. The mother happens to be the one who is at hand when questions are raised such as "Why does Bobby stand up to go to the bathroom?" or "Can I have a rifle on my birthday?" These are questions that you can't cram for, that you and your husband can't consult on beforehand. And they are, as a rule, questions that put all your alertness and awareness to the test because they so often come without warning. You never know what is coming next. An easy one, like "Why does the water make noise when it goes down the drain?" may be followed in the next breath by one like this: "John says his father and mother are getting a divorce. What's a divorce?"

All mothers—and fathers—get these questions and they do the best they can with them. Sometimes one can explain that the question ought really to be brought up in a family discussion, and a promise to do so will suffice, as in the case of the rifle. Others must be answered—and answered honestly—right then and there. Just what you say in reply is not so important as your honesty and your warmth. Some adults feel that such questions as that about the divorce, for example, cannot possibly be answered honestly because deep down they feel it is wrong to imply to a child that grown people can be faulty.

But if you want to be honest with your child, you will make him feel not that you are trying to pull the wool over his eyes, but that you are truly trying to help him understand. And if you can give him the feeling that everybody has problems sometimes—children and grownups too—that they have to do the best they know how and that sometimes they are mistaken, you are laying the foundation for real understanding between you and your child. At the same time you are showing him—and this is very important no matter how small the beginnings—that you see him as a thinking person who, when he has enough information and experience, will be able to form his own judgments.

As we say, it is because the mother is the one who is *there* that she is the one who gets most of the questions, handles much of the discipline, settles most of the fights—and gets days full of rewards as well as days packed with frustration. But your child's picture of life is not complete if the lights and shadows are filled in always by the mother. The father's role is very important with any child, and most particularly with the adopted child, who needs to feel from the beginning that he has and deserves the wholehearted love, respect, and understanding of *both* his parents in equal part. It is therefore doubly dangerous for an adoptive mother to make the not-uncommon mistake of shutting the father out in the first months. But more than this, the closeness of father and child as time goes on should be nurtured. Family togetherness is important always, and the child should frequently have his father all to himself. It is splendid, particularly if they are father and son, if they can do things together, have special interests and hobbies which they share.

To safeguard this closeness, there is one thing the adoptive mother must be especially careful not to do. A mistake that many mothers make is to shield the child from his father's displeasure by giving in to his plea not to tell Daddy. You don't have to threaten to tell on him. Since you're on the spot, mete out whatever punishment may be deserved, if any. And point out that you're not the one who lost the pliers—why should you tell him? But don't promise him you won't tell Daddy if he will never do it again. His honest confession and his promise not to repeat the mistake are really between him and his father; if you show yourself ready to conspire with him to hide the mistake, you are as much as saying that Daddy is an ogre from whom the child has a right to be protected.

One of the nicest things about the adoptive relationship, however, is that there seems often to be an unusually good relationship between adoptive fathers and their children. One adopted girl now in high school told me that she had often thought her friends far less able to count on the understanding of their fathers than she, and she felt that this was largely because she was adopted. A number of young adoptive mothers have confided that they felt their husbands took a much earlier and much warmer interest in the children than did the biological fathers of their acquaintances. Of course, there are born fathers just as there are born mothers, and these would be warm and affectionate parents in any case. But it may be, too, that adoptive fathers feel more needed. It may be that Father and Mother have together gone through so much in the way of hope and hope abandoned, of emotional readjustment, and the long waiting period, that there is a special closeness here. Whatever the reason, it happens sufficiently often so that if you exert every effort to coax it into growth and keep it flourishing, you may count on it as one of the real plus values of adopting.

6 How Many in Your Family?

If your adopted child is one of several children, some of your problems are easier, some harder. In many ways the give-and-take of a larger family group makes for more relaxed handling on the part of the parents, more flexibility on the part of the children. The children in large families—after the first one—achieve independence much earlier than most. They dress themselves sooner, quickly adjust to having chores to do around the house, and like looking after the younger ones to a certain extent. They often render the parents invaluable assistance in teaching one another what is and what is not acceptable behavior. The admonitions of mere parents on such a subject as grubby nails count for nothing compared to the advice of an admired older sister just starting to date. Not that children of large families don't have their problems too, and some of them *become* problems. But, generally speaking, the atmosphere of the larger family group seems more suited to the growth of children, and particularly adopted children.

Should you have such a family it may help to be aware of the special compensations and disadvantages of the position of each child. The oldest—and this is true of boys especially—is likely to suffer a good deal, no matter what the parents' efforts, from having had to abdicate as "first baby." None of the others will lose what he loses when the next baby comes along, for none of them will have been for many months the only one, the best-loved. And so your oldest may be inclined to be jealous, irritable, supersensitive, a bit selfish, and, unless helped, may have a tendency to boss the younger children more than is good for him—or for them. The child in the middle has a hard row to hoe because the family seldom considers that there is anything special about him. They take him more for granted. As he gets older he may get more permissive treatment than the oldest did, but will also have to get used to less fuss being made over his accomplishments. He is likely to become a bit aggressive in order to protect his rights as the one in-between. Particularly if the family is a warm one, he may end up the most self-confident and the most practical. The youngest has to learn to guard against being considered "the baby" for too long. Or his parents may have to ease him out of babyhood if he shows an inclination to like it too well. Then, too, he may suffer from always having to be the first to go to bed and sometimes from having to wear hand-me-downs he is already sick and tired of looking at. He has to compete with the older children in games, in school, and in everyday living—and this is often very hard, although it will give him techniques, sometimes good ones, occasionally unacceptable, of dealing with those who are stronger than he is.

These "position patterns" are only general guides, of course. You can find families whom they fit and families whom they don't fit. But they do provide a sort of chart for large-family parenthood. And if you know that many, many "own" oldest boys, for example, suffer for years from resentment of the next child to come along, you can realize that such a feeling might well be more intense in the case of an adopted oldest. So if some of your children are biological and some adopted, you *may* have a delicate job on your hands keeping them in equilibrium.

As might be supposed, it is easy for such parents not only to be too much aware of the difficulties involved but also to consider them as of one kind only. They assume that the whole problem is to protect the adopted child from feeling less wanted than the biological child. Often this is so; but it is possible to go too far in this direction and end up by damaging both of them. Consciously trying to "treat them just alike" is a course that may boomerang.

The ostentatious extra helping of love, the conscientious attention, the too-careful dividing of praise, don't deceive the child one bit. The result is that the adopted one feels he doesn't measure up or his parents wouldn't "protest too much," while the biological one may feel justifiably injured because *his* accomplishments don't earn the sincere and special commendation they may warrant. As in the case of Jenny and Lynn, for example.

Jenny was the older child, who had been adopted at seven months. When she was four, Lynn was born. Their temperaments —an important factor in any of these situations—were quite different. Jenny was bright, pretty, and aggressive: what used to be called "pert." Her parents idolized her, and she was made much of in the four years when she was the only child. The parents made special efforts when the new baby came along to insure that along with Jenny's normal jealousy she would not have cause to feel further set aside on account of being adopted. Without realizing it, they traveled too far and too long in this direction. By the time the sisters were nine and thirteen, Jenny was a very trying child indeed. She was bossy, conceited, arrogant. She preened herself on her good looks and her high grades in school. She was patronizing to poor little Lynn, who was pudgy, shy, and had trouble with her studies, so much so that the school psychologist was called in to find out why the child could not learn to read. With her help the parents discovered that Lynn, docile though she appeared on the outside, on the inside was a seething mass of resentment against Jenny and her father and mother. The well-meaning parents, in their zeal to "prove" their love to Jenny, had, with their overpraising and coddling, their extra treats like new chintz for her bedroom while Lynn got along with the old curtains from the guest room, accomplished just the opposite from what they intended.

It does not pay to oversimplify these things; the dispositions of the two children, their relative ages, the difference in intelligence, all had a great deal to do with this problem and has with others like it. It is even possible that the parents were subconsciously trying to make up for a guilty feeling that they really did love Lynn a bit more, and that some of Jenny's cockiness was her defense against a real hurt.

In the adoptive or mixed adoptive family there is the same complex interplay of personality, environment, and position in the family that exists in the biological group—but adoption may complicate these relationships even further. A brighter and younger adopted child may contribute unwittingly to the rejection of the older "own" child. Sometimes the adopted child is so far behind a younger "own" child in intelligence and attractiveness that he feels it is hopeless to compete. It has happened that to an adoptive couple there is born in their later years a child who is outstandingly intelligent and who is the very image of his father. In two cases I heard about, the father's name and the "Jr." had already been given to the adopted child, and it did not help matters any that unthinking friends and relatives deplored this aloud. In any of these situations the child who is not the "star" feels pushed out of the picture, the more so if he is adopted. And if his feelings go unnoticed for too long he may be headed for very serious difficulty.

There is another situation where the handling of adopted and "own" children in the same family can present extreme difficulty. This occurs when the biological parents of an only child adopt a child around the same age as their child. If there is in the adoption a very strong feeling of wanting the child for his own sake, and if the parents are warm, flexible, and experienced with children this can work out well. If the parents are adopting from purely selfish motives, failing to consider the human values involved, the experiment is a risky one.

First of all, the parents are inclined to demand too much of the adopted child, particularly if he is the older. Consciously or otherwise, they expect him to be grateful for the new home he has come into, and to devote most or all of his attention to the child he finds there. They are inclined, too, to want their biological child to be the dominant one, and often compare and take sides unfairly. Much to their surprise, the newcomer may have ideas of his own. No doubt institutionalized or placed in a number of foster homes, this child may have problems which demand patience and forbearance. He will prove stormy in many ways, especially if he is adolescent. The distracted parents may put the whole blame on him and on adoption. They do not realize that all adolescents are disturbed and disturbing. (Their own will be too, but they may not have found that out yet!) They do not stop to think that a child with such a background is bound to show serious problems while he is testing his new parents—and himself—in order to find out for sure whether, at long last, he is really loved and really wanted. Instead of trying to help him, they resent him. He is impossible. He is not the least bit grateful for all that has been done for him. His heredity must be poor. He is a bad influence on *their* child. And so they withdraw, either by shunting him back to the orphanage if they can, or by "putting up with him" in ill-concealed hostility. Either way, they mercilessly ink in the finishing strokes on the poor child's picture of himself as a being nobody could love.

Fortunately, however, most of the good-sized families, either wholly or partly adoptive, turn out well. While serious problems may arise, just as in biological families, they can usually be dealt with by parents who are wise and loving, who take the trouble to go below the surface in case of persistent difficulty, and do not hesitate to seek professional counsel if the problem is too difficult for them to solve alone. Parents of big families have to keep an eye out for quarreling that is too intense and too frequent, for one-sided bullying and picking on, and for persistent attempts to curry the favor of Mother or Father or to divide their authority. Quarreling, bullying, tattling—all will happen in the best of families, but if one child seems always to be the offender (or always the goat), if the children aren't friends after a fight, the parents will do well to set aside a few days for quiet but attentive observing and listening and a re-examination of their own attitudes.

When parents listen and watch with insight, with their hearts as well as with their ears and eyes, what they learn may surprise them. Often they discover that George the bully feels left out and has found that loud aggression will focus some kind of attention on him pretty quickly, even though it's not just the kind he really wants. Has he had enough of his parents' companionship recently?

The undivided attention, without little Susie's horning in? The answer often is "No." Sometimes it may even be that George is actually the goat and sweet Susie the real bully. Without knowing why, or what to do about it, he knows that Susie always manages to get him in trouble while appearing to be as good as gold herself.

It is easy for all of us unconsciously to take advantage of the growing independence of our older children to gain more hours in a busy day. It seldom occurs to us, even if we realize what we are doing, to feel guilty, for are we not using the time unselfishly as a rule—to look after the younger children as well as to do the marketing, cleaning, cooking, laundering, and chauffeuring for all? But sometimes we don't stop to think that the older ones, who gave us more of themselves by learning the things we asked them to learn, get less and less of ourselves in return. And before we know it, these older ones have turned into teenagers whose lives are so full that they need us less than we would like them to. We should try to remember always that each child in the family yearns to be the one that is loved the best. Almost all the time this is what he is trying to achieve by his behavior, even though by adult standards he may seem to be demonstrating how unlovable he can be if he tries.

It often happens that a really good look at ourselves and our children and our routines will show us that we have allowed our closeness to some of these children to diminish to the vanishing point. Sometimes the obvious remedy of giving more time to the unhappy one works like a charm. Sometimes the solution is not so simple. It may be that the renewed welcome into the circle of his parents' love straightens George out into the normal boy he used to be, and everything runs smoothly again. But it may also happen that while George straightens out, Susie, though as much loved as before, may continue her trying ways, teasing, goading, and tattling, while managing to look like a little angel. Maybe she needs more times of aloneness with her father or mother or both. Maybe she resents George's superiority in size and strength and privilege, and needs to be helped in finding her own abilities and her comfortable place in the family. Maybe she has some difficulty too deep for the parents to find, and they may need to seek outside help.

Perhaps the greatest single advantage that the parents of several children have over the fathers and mothers of only children is that the former find it easier, after the first child, to be relaxed. If practice doesn't make perfect parents, at least it soon relieves them of a passion for perfection. Such parents soon decide to winnow the essentials from the non-essentials, to stop expecting the ideal from either themselves or their offspring. They learn to enjoy parenthood, and their children are freer to enjoy childhood. Even though each child learns, and sometimes painfully, that he is not and cannot be the best-loved or the only-loved, it is of some comfort to him to discover that if the parents' love must be shared so must their concern. He sees that the others too must abide by sometimes irksome standards of behavior set up for children; that they, too, have to share their toys, take baths, do their homework, assume some of the chores that keep the house going. Whatever worrying his parents do about the children, he can see that it is diffused. If they flutter and cluck, it is over the others as well as over him.

It is a fairly common thing, on the other hand, for parents of only children to try too hard. They have heard so much about "only-child" difficulties and dangers that they unthinkingly create many of these by sheer force of concentration. And if their only child is adopted, their concern is doubled.

Actually it isn't at all a terrible thing to be or to have an only child. Much is missed, but there are many compensations for both parent and child. The parents can never, of course, provide quite the same kind of closeness, of family solidarity, of learning to get along day in and day out with other children that a flock of brothers and sisters supplies. But the only child has this tremendous advantage over one with brothers and sisters: he knows he doesn't have to compete with anyone for his parents' love. He *is* the best-loved.

It isn't especially easy, of course, to bring up an only child, and particularly an only adopted child. But neither is it as hard as many people make it sound. There is just one danger that parents of only children, particularly if they are adoptive parents, ought always to keep in mind. The single serious handicap of the only child—and this is increased in the case of the adopted one—is his parents' tendency to *hover*.

This is the only child these parents will ever have in all probability, and they cannot help feeling that they must not fail him in any way and that he must in every way be a credit to them. They worry unduly about their child's growth and development, about his eating habits, about each and every aberration in behavior. They anxiously compare notes with the parents of children the same age as their child. They debate endlessly back and forth, trying to decide whether the lying Ellen is now going in for is a "stage" or a "problem." They are concerned out of all proportion over an unfavorable comment on the report card about Ellen's "social adjustment."

If this tendency toward an abnormal tension and anxiety continues throughout the child's school years, the child is bound to suffer. Such a child feels as though his parents' love were a giant searchlight that floods everything he says and does, even what he thinks sometimes. There is no other child on whom the parents' attention can be focused from time to time to leave him in the peaceful dark. There is no brother or sister to deflect some of the watchfulness, some of the training, some of the love.

He does not have to worry about sharing his parents' love, as we said. But, on the contrary, he may often feel smothered by it. He wishes that they would leave him alone more. And this does not mean physical aloneness. He has his room in which his privacy is respected, and he can go there. But he feels that even there the thoughts of his parents follow him—the wonderings whether he is feeling hurt or upset, the concern over whether they should be making him play outdoors this fine afternoon, the overemphatic praise of his good deed or accomplishment, the consultation about whether they are being too strict or not strict enough about the Saturday-night bedtime.

Yes, their love he knows he has. But if he is adopted, he may go a step further and wonder if the constant concern may indicate that he doesn't quite measure up to what they expected, that maybe he never can. Yes, they picked him out—but perhaps they're just bravely making the best of a bad bargain. And anyway, if adopting is so wonderful, why didn't they adopt a brother or sister for him?

The picture I have painted here is fairly black—blacker than normal, for it is not likely that even an adopted only child would have quite so intense a reaction to his situation unless he were facing other problems of adjustment also, problems for which the parents are not necessarily responsible. But it can happen, and it has happened, that the overconscientious parents of an only child in this way unknowingly provide a wonderful culture for problems to grow in.

This unconscious tendency of parents of only children to live in a hothouse instead of a home is perhaps a little stronger in the case of adoptive parents. The best insurance against it is to remember, as all parents should, that you are people as well as parents. Don't focus all your time and attention on your child to the exclusion of the interests that stimulated you before you had him. Of course when he is small you are tied down to a considerable extent, but you do have time to read, to sew, to hook rugs, to take pictures and perhaps learn to develop them, to see friends often, to do all sorts of things that can be done at home. And don't forget that when he is of school age, unlike the mothers that have more babies and toddlers lined up, you have school-session time in which to pursue your outside interests: garden club, PTA work, civic committees, and so on. Make sure, too, that you and your husband maintain certain interests together. You don't want your child to feel that he is the end-all and be-all of life in the home. If you find that after routine homecoming questions are over just about the sole topic of real conversation between you and your husband is Ellen, her achievements, her misdeeds, and whether she finished her prunes—watch out! If the two of you don't expand your horizons, don't find some hobbies together like gardening, amateur painting, collecting plans and clippings for your house of the future—you may find that Ellen will get the feeling you two are always together *about* her if not against her. And that may intensify a feeling which all only children have occasionally, the feeling that you two have each other but she has nobody—nobody, that is, who is *hers*. The more reason to be certain that your only child has frequent times to be alone with *each* parent.

Then there are specific things which parents of only children can and should do to provide for them the companionship of other small fry. It takes only a little thought and a little trouble to provide the only possible substitute for brothers and sisters—and that is to have children frequently in the house, for after-school snacks and games, for supper, often to spend the night. If the branch in your community is active and capably run, Cub Scouts or Brownies are most rewarding for an only child, and the mothers of only children are better able than most to be the ever-needed Den Mother. If, as sometimes happens, the younger Scout groups have not got off to a good start in your town, it is almost always owing to lack of parental co-operation. Maybe you and your husband can do something about that. It is no accident that the parents of the best-adjusted "onlies" are those who are habitually active in work with young people, whether through church, Little League baseball, Scouts, or school. Start to become active in some of these things while your own child is a little young for them, if you can; you will find that just being with groups of children regularly will help you to keep your image of your child from being a myopic one.

Something that must be done, though it isn't always easy, is to see to it that your only child has a share in the work of the house and that he does it regularly. The difficulty here is that in today's homes there are not many meaningful chores. I have heard many a suburban or "apartment" parent, for example, speak enviously in this connection of farm families, where there is real and varied work to do and where every helping hand counts. A farm child can see for himself that his help is needed, and needed every day. In the modern house, there is so little that really cries out to be done, so pitifully few "self-respecting" jobs for children, and particularly for boys. So we have to do the best we can with the jobs we have. Even though some may not seem very creative, we must lead our children to appreciate the fact that they have to be done to make the home run smoothly, that it is a real help to the parents to have them assumed by the child, and that there is always a satisfaction in work well done. Keeping one's own room clean and making one's own bed every morning, for instance, is a real help to Mother, and it is not sissy, as any boys' camp will demonstrate. There are wastebaskets which need emptying regularly, sometimes firewood to be stacked or brought in, occasional errands to run, and often outside jobs like leaf-raking and lawn-mowing. (If, however, parents have been paying outsiders to do these latter tasks they should decide beforehand on a long-range policy about payment to their child if he should take over the whole job. They should ask themselves how much it is fair to expect the child to do "for free" as his share of making the wheels go round, and what part of it he should be paid for as one of his early experiences in earning money.)

Boys do window-washing very well too, and the early teens can do a beautiful job of washing the car. After-dinner clearing away or helping to do so is both a natural and a needed chore. Dishwashing or drying for girls, and for boys if Daddy pitches in too, doesn't seem to be resented if the child's help is appreciated and the specific job varied once in a while. Girls, of course, can help fold and put the laundry away, take on some of the housework on Saturdays, and occasionally take some responsibility for cooking, starting, or preparing part of the meal when Mother is out.

Pets and hobbies are almost "musts" in the case of the only child. Naturally, apartment-dwelling families are more limited in the pet line than country or suburban families. But you can always have something. Cats are good friends, are not hard to take care of or train, and don't have to be walked. Parakeets or canaries are cheerful, are "company," and can become lovable pets. Tropical fish, if they are to be a success, require a bit more of an outlay in equipment than most pets. But once a tank is properly started they need little care, can be left without attention for as long as a week, and are so interesting to watch and to learn about that the whole family becomes absorbed in them. In fact, I know one family where these "pets" turned into a hobby. Father, mother, and child grew so fascinated with the miniature world of their first tank that they built others into a bookcase wall, and before they knew it they were breeding rare jewel-colored fish and even growing microscopic live food for the babies of certain species.

A dog is, of course, the ideal companion for a child. If you have a dog that has grown up with the child, fine. But if you get a dog for a child who is not used to animals, don't get one that will grow to be overpowering. Big dogs, as a rule, can be very patient and gentle with small children, but if they are at all bouncy or noisy they can be terrifying to the young. Remember that to a two-year-old an Irish Setter seems nearly as big as a horse does to us. For a small child, a small dog like a beagle or a cocker or a sheltie is much more companionable.

If you get a dog with the condition that the child will take care of it, make sure that you are not expecting too much of him. He will promise everything, and truly mean it, but to carry the full responsibility is probably beyond him. With a few exceptions—those children who are really gifted with animals—most children under twelve are simply not ready to remember or to carry out the daily feeding, the frequent walking, the brushing, let alone the housebreaking. So as a rule it is safest to make it clear that while you do not intend to assume the entire care of the dog, you do intend to help him while he is learning how.

As we have said, to bring up an only adopted child is no sinecure. But with the love and care that go with any kind of parenthood, plus plenty of good fresh air let into the relationship, it can be done and happily done. And it has so many rewards. Companionship is one of the greatest of these. It is a simple matter for the parents of one child to give him plenty of their time, both separately and together. And the three of them can do so many things—visit relatives, sight-see, "eat out," travel, go to football games together—that the parents who must always consider the feeding and sleeping habits of the youngest child find it troublesome to do. All these things make possible a happy and relaxed companionship between the only child and his parents, one that other parents sometimes contemplate wistfully as they calm down the bickering oldest and think how much they would all enjoy the motorboat show if it were not for the littlest who would be whining to go home ten minutes after they got there. Then too, of course, there is money: however little there may be to begin with, it is easier to afford occasional treats, really good toys now and then, perhaps a bike when it is most needed, if you must buy shoes and sweaters for only one instead of four.

It used to be thought that only children practically had to grow up spoiled and selfish. But recent studies have shown that in general they turn out just about like other children. They have problems, to be sure—but so do the others. They need wise and thoughtful guidance; but so does the oldest of three, so does the middle child, so does the baby. It has been found that only children stack up very well with the others in initiative, in reliability, co-operation, and sociability, in fact, in all the qualities we should like our children to have.

Another sort of offspring who, with their parents, may share special difficulties are twins. In adoption, of course, these are comparatively rare, but it happens much more frequently than you might suppose that the adoptive family has started off with two instead of one infant to be looked after. Naturally, this means not only extra equipment, but extra care and extra planning from the beginning. The physical care of twins is a very demanding job, especially during the first year, and the mother should have help for as long as she can manage to afford it. If she does not, she will become so exhausted from the double set of chores that she will have neither the time nor the energy to give her babies the quiet times for loving and cuddling that each twin needs in a very special way.

The relationship of twins is complex and subtle, especially, of course, in the case of identical twins. But even non-identical twins react in many ways not like two babies but like different aspects of the same personality. Both kinds of twins present a real challenge to the parent. In the case of adopted twins, the adoption itself does not create a problem if they are babies when they are adopted, but it may intensify any difficulties they have later on. If they are accepted and loved each for himself, their closeness will make them more secure; if either or both feels slighted, that very closeness will tend to separate them from their parents and from the world around them. For twins always have each other. This is a very comforting knowledge to live with—but not healthy to retire into.

The special task of the parents of twins, particularly if they are adoptive parents, is twofold. They must be sure that each twin feels equally loved from the very beginning, and they must so handle their children that their innate closeness is neither emphasized nor destroyed, but assumes lessening importance as each twin learns to make his own way in his own world.

Some authorities feel that while there is much in the feelings and behavior of twins that is genuinely "mirrored," a great deal of the likeness comes about because it is fostered by their parents, friends, teachers, relatives—in fact, by the whole community. People exclaim so over the physical likeness if there is one (or over the lack of it if there is not), make so many jokes about telling them apart, ask so many silly questions, that twins feel they *must* play the part that is so obviously expected of them. And then their natural closeness tends to become exaggerated, may even become a serious handicap in their relations with other people.

Twins, after all, are bound to grow up. Each will earn his own living, choose his own hobbies and friends, have his special abilities. Each may be expected to marry and live in his own house with his own wife and children. And so the parents of twins must be ever watchful that each twin has the opportunity to be his own man. Twinship must not be foisted on them to the extent of submerging their individual personalities. And, on the other hand, neither must they be perpetually forced apart, be made to feel that it is wrong to enjoy the aspects of the relationship that fulfill a real need in both.

Love and attention are most important with twins, as with any children. But with twins a really equal sharing is essential from infancy on. That is why the mother of twins needs more extra time and help than are accounted for simply by the arithmetical doubling up of formulas, diapers, and so on. She will have to learn short cuts, ways of keeping one baby contented while she cuddles the other one, taking turns to feed one from her breast while the other uses a bottle for that meal.

A "for instance" that reveals a great deal about the awareness of all babies is told by a mother of identical twins. Blanche Fulton Martin, in an article which she calls "If You Have Twins," says that it took her and her husband a little time to realize that they had a much greater problem on their hands than just supplying two of everything.

What first opened our eyes to this, was the decided difference in personality the boys began to show when they were six months old. The minute we entered the nursery, Johnny would light up, coo, smile. Bobby didn't. He waited almost resignedly until he was picked up. Then he would smile and coo, too. But not before.

When we began to ask why, we found an astounding answer. We thought we were giving our sons exactly the same love and attention, but we weren't!

The two cradles were placed along one wall of the nursery. Johnny's just happened to be nearest the door. We discovered that we had been doing a natural thing—stopping beside him first. Could Johnny have the idea, at six months, that he was the favorite because he always got first attention? We would find out. We switched the positions of the cradles. In one week their personalities had switched! It was Bobby who was lighting up the minute anyone entered. It was Johnny who was waiting resignedly until he was picked up.

That pulled us up short, and we have tried ever since to keep things even. If we give special attention to one, we turn immediately to the other so that no little nose can get out of joint.[6]

Here is the real crux of the problem of having *adopted* twins. An insufficiency of loving and cuddling has been proved damaging to the emotional and physical well-being of all babies and even more damaging to the adopted baby. The average adopted baby, however, even though he may not get every bit of the warm affection he unknowingly seeks, doesn't have to watch somebody else his own size getting it! It is not hard to imagine that adoptive parents who unthinkingly get into a routine of caring always for one twin first because it's easier and more efficient are laying a poor groundwork for the second twin's acceptance of himself as a worthwhile person. And if he grows up with that second-best feeling, how can he help a suspicion that his adoption was perfunctory, that his parents took him only because he "went with" his twin?

As the Martins found out, it isn't altogether easy to avoid overdoing the "just-alikeness" and at the same time satisfy the children's *need* of being alike in certain ways at certain ages. One day, when the boys were two, Mrs. Martin changed the muddy white sunsuit of one to a clean yellow suit, and both boys set up a loud outcry and ran off to hide as if there was something wrong with them. It was not until they were four that they would accept difference in appearance—when they were given white polo shirts just alike except that each bore the name of its wearer in blue block letters on the front. From then on, the parents were able to encourage them to exercise their own choices in what to wear, though plenty of their clothes were alike in cut or color.

Most authorities agree that, whenever possible, it is best to separate twins in school to make it easier for the personality of each to spread its branches out and to lessen the extremely intense competition that often develops between the two. The Martins wisely "planted" this idea while the boys were still in kindergarten,

6. Blanche Fulton Martin, "If You Have Twins," *Family Circle*, July, 1951.

because they knew that their being in different rooms in first grade would mark a tremendous change in their lives, one which might be frightening if they were not carefully prepared. Now that the boys are in third grade, the parents are very glad they separated them. The almost hysterical competition which in kindergarten had led to extreme tension, even to speech difficulties, quickly altered to the pride of equals in each other's accomplishments. Each has his own friends in school, and at home friends and twins mix happily. They have made good starts on their separate ways, and yet they have kept the intense loyalty and closeness that mean so much to them and always will.

7 Adopting an Older Child

Bringing into one's family an older child rather than a baby is another and very different part of adoption. To help a little baby achieve a happy childhood is one thing. To make a relaxed and confident child out of one who is already a person when you get him—and perhaps (though by no means always) an unhappy person—is something else again. It is a real achievement. The challenge is great, but success more rewarding than can be imagined by those who have not done it. Would-be parents who may have to wait a long time to adopt an infant are well advised to consider applying for an older child, especially one of school age, who needs a home. Whereas there are once again many more applicants for infants than there are infants for adoption, applicants for older children continue to be in short supply. There are so many more older children than there are people who want to adopt them, that the requirements are often less rigid. For example, the usual agency rule is to place children only in families where there are both parents—a father and a mother. Yet a single parent—a man or woman, never-married, widowed, or divorced—is considered by many adoption agencies when no other home is available and the child is otherwise likely to be left in an institution or foster home for the whole of his childhood.

This is not intended to imply that practically anybody can get an older child. On the contrary, just because these children *are* older it is harder for them to get used to a new family than it is for an infant, especially if they have been shifted around a good deal, and so they require very special care in placement. They may be said to need stronger and wiser parents than the little babies, often parents with some firsthand familiarity with the ways of children, whether it be from having shared the give-and-take of a large family or from raising other children, their own or adopted. The extra years which have put you out of the running for a little baby may be an asset when it comes to adopting a girl or boy of five or nine or eleven.

What else does it take to be good parents for these older children? Well, it takes just about the same things we have been talking about all along—warmth, flexibility, maturity, and, above all, "acceptingness"—plus a few other qualities often needed in this special situation, qualities which other parents develop but which ideally those who adopt older children need almost right away. Before we discuss what these plus qualities are, let us see first why they are needed. Let's see what adoption means to a child of two or seven or nine, or older.

Although most of us have never paused to do so, it isn't too hard to imagine what a change in home and family means to a child beyond babyhood. The boy who is nine, the girl who is seven, even the smaller ones of three and five, are already people. They have memories—sometimes of their own mothers, and certainly of some years of love and care by the foster mother, of sharing life in that foster home. They have their routines, their friends, their toys, and a considerable amount of affection. But often they are old enough to know they don't really belong. Then they may be afraid to move out of this situation because, imperfect as it may be, it is at least one that they are familiar with. Subconscious and even conscious memories of earlier rejection may make them unwilling to trust. One has only to imagine oneself as a child suddenly separated from one's own family and dumped into another to have some slight understanding of how hard it is for a child to leave a comfortable, loving foster mother for even the friendliest of strangers.

So no matter what his age, it takes great skill, love, and understanding to get one of these children ready for adoption. You might think it would be comparatively easy with the littlest, the toddlers.

In some ways it is, yet workers often spend days in preparing these for the shift, especially those around the age of two, when all children are inclined to shrink away from new people. The older child can often be prepared a little more quickly, for though he must be protected from rejection in special ways and may find the actual adjustment to his new parents difficult, at least he must be consulted, and has enough maturity to know what the step really means. But all these children, whatever their age, need time and love to help them cross the bridge.

The skilled case worker judges according to his age, temperament, and history how much time and how much help a particular child needs in making the change. She knows she must try to get him to understand that it *is* a change he is making. She must help him get acquainted with the new parents. She must let him grieve for his foster mother. Sometimes she needs to give the foster mother, who in most cases has become deeply attached to the child, help in facing up to the situation. She must see to it that the adopting parents recognize that the child has to have difficulties and learn a little of how to help him. And she must be aware of some of the difficulties that the parents themselves may be experiencing and be ready to help them, too.

It is often very hard for the adoptive parents to understand how it may take so much time to help the small child get used to the idea of leaving his foster home to come to live with them. As we have seen, with a baby one visit does it: usually the second time the parents see him it is to take him up in their arms and carry him home. Not so in the case of a toddler. In the best interests of parents and child he ought to be led to understand *before* he goes with them that he must say good-by to his "other mother," that he will not see her any more. He must be allowed, even encouraged, to grieve for her. And before he can replace her with new parents he must be helped to get acquainted with them gradually—not in one visit but in several.

All of this is hard on parents and child alike; the parents feel so sure that if they could just take him home right away he would adjust to them quickly, would soak up their love willingly instead of crying and shrinking away from them as he may have done in the nursery. And this is true of a few children. But years of experience with the idea of enabling the child to participate in the break rather than "just whisking him away" have shown that these painful few days of helping the child *accept* what is happening are likely to make the real homecoming much easier for all of them. Without this opportunity it is possible that weeks and even months may pass in the adoptive home while the child refuses to have anything to do with his new mother or father or even takes out his resentment and bewilderment in the most destructive kind of behavior. It is far, far better not to trick him or belittle his real feelings, but to let him know what is going on and help him get his sorrow out of his system.

Let's see just how a worker, a foster mother, two new parents, and a small girl together make this big change.

It is Friday morning, a busy one everywhere in the agency, and especially in the big sunny room where the boarding mothers and their charges wait their turn, while in another room Dr. Jameson gives each baby and toddler a careful physical examination. Some of the mothers are chatting over coffee and doughnuts, some are giving their babies a feeding, others are changing diapers or tucking the babies away for a nap in the cribs that line one wall. The toddlers are at their foster mothers' knees or on their laps, or are sitting on the floor playing with toys from the toy boxes.

One of the boarding mothers has a double job this morning. Mrs. Dolan has brought in four-months-old Freddy, whom she has cared for since he was two weeks old, to be taken home by his adoptive family, the Grahams. The moment of parting is always hard for the foster mothers, and it is easy to see that Mrs. Dolan is finding it even more difficult than most not to brim over. It's as well she has little Betsy to distract her. Betsy is the toddler just under two. She is about to be placed with the Beckwiths, who have already watched her through the one-way window, and, loving her at first sight, are eager to take her home with them in time for Christmas.

So Betsy is here today to get her final physical examination and to take the first step toward leaving her foster mother.

It is the worker, Mrs. Crenshaw, who translates for us all that happens on the days carefully planned for and allotted to helping Betsy make the move. Mrs. Crenshaw, though Betsy has not known her hitherto, must be the bridge between the adoptive parents and the foster mother, for Betsy's own worker, her familiar friend, has unfortunately had to fly home to be with her ill mother. And so this morning Mrs. Crenshaw slowly starts to make friends with Betsy and to watch carefully her reactions to the departure of her "baby," little Freddy. Betsy, she notices, seems to be at home in the clinic, is willing to say hello to everyone who says hello to her, goes freely to the toy box, takes the toys back when her foster mother tells her to. She's an attractive little girl too, tall for her age, with fair skin, curly reddish hair, and sherry-brown eyes. She is serious, though, and laughs very little. Mrs. Crenshaw notices that she never seems to let her foster mother get out of sight. She knows that Freddy is leaving today and Mrs. Dolan reports that for some days she has seemed a little disturbed about this, rocking his crib and saying several times, "Freddy is going." Today she suddenly misses him. She looks in all the cribs as if hunting for him, then comes to her foster mother and looks earnestly into her face as Mrs. Dolan fights back the tears. When Mrs. Crenshaw approaches, Betsy does not draw away, but does seem shy. After a while she accepts Mrs. Crenshaw's help in taking the top toys out of the box to get at the bottom ones. When they leave, Mrs. Dolan is careful to repeat Mrs. Crenshaw's name to Betsy and to say that they will be back on Monday to play with the toys again.

When Monday came, Mrs. Crenshaw met Betsy and Mrs. Dolan in the clinic room. Betsy paid practically no attention to the worker but, instead, spent quite a bit of time looking at the one small baby who was there. Mrs. Dolan explained that she had been much concerned about Freddy and kept asking where he was. At Mrs. Dolan's suggestion Betsy went into the playroom where Mrs. Crenshaw was waiting for her. At first she hesitated to come in, but finally did, and closed the door herself. But when she was in she just stood still, showing no interest at first in the toys the worker offered her. Finally she did sit down to play with some of them, and later explored the room. When she touched the rocking horse and it rocked, she began to cry. She seemed to be interested in it although afraid of it, and kept going back to it between playing with the crayons and the stuffed animals. Her play was entirely independent, and though she stole looks at Mrs. Crenshaw she otherwise ignored her. Mrs. Crenshaw showed her how to rock the horse gently and later asked if she wanted to get on it. She said "No." And that was the only word she spoke. Then she went back to the clinic to see her foster mother and to get a cookie. She accepted Mrs. Crenshaw's suggestion that they go back to the play-room, but again played independently. Mrs. Crenshaw drew a picture of a house with stick figures of a man and woman and ex-plained that this was her new house and her new Mommy and Daddy. Then she drew a dog in the yard. Betsy appeared to have little reaction to this but her foster mother, who had also been talking to Betsy about adoption and about a new Mommy and Daddy, felt quite sure that Betsy did associate Mrs. Crenshaw with some idea of leaving. When Betsy went back to the clinic, she again became absorbed in the baby. Before they left for good Betsy pulled Mrs. Dolan into the playroom and seemed to want to stay to play with the toys.

On Tuesday they came again. Betsy seemed quite excited. She did a lot of running about and "showing off" and was attentive to everybody except Mrs. Crenshaw. She wanted to go to play with the toys but she didn't want to leave her foster mother, and so she took her along. However, when Mrs. Crenshaw entered, Betsy did not seem to object, and in fact presently began to include her in the play a little, even allowing her to set her on the rocking horse, though she cried and wanted to be taken off in about a minute. She talked a lot to herself, but it was hard to understand what she was saying.

Mrs. Crenshaw told her that today her new Mommy and Daddy

were coming to play with her, and showed her the door that led to the room where they would be, leaving it open. Betsy shut it firmly. Again Mrs. Crenshaw drew the house and the stick figures, and this time Betsy said "bow wow," and pointed to the dog. When the Beckwiths came, Mrs. Crenshaw opened the door again. Betsy came and looked at them, then went back to her play. Mrs. Beckwith got up and came into the playroom and her husband followed. Betsy went on playing with her back turned, and seemed to take no notice when Mrs. Crenshaw left. Watching through the one-way window, Mrs. Crenshaw thought that things were going very well. Betsy appeared to accept the couple's helping her to pick out toys. She did keep running back to her foster mother, but soon got into a sort of game, taking a toy first to Mrs. Dolan and then at her suggestion taking it back again to the "new Mommy." And she did allow Mr. Beckwith to put her on the rocking horse.

After about twenty-five minutes, the foster mother started to get Betsy into her snow suit, and the Beckwiths went back into the room where they had originally waited. It was interesting to see that when it was time for Betsy to go she seemed reluctant to leave. She looked in at the Beckwiths and said "bye-bye," but she seemed uncertain whether to go in to them or to follow Mrs. Dolan down the hall. (To Mrs. Crenshaw she paid no attention whatever.) So the Beckwiths made a move toward her. But this she would not accept. She started to cry and was still crying when she left the building with Mrs. Dolan. She was tired, of course—it had been a busy morning. But it did seem as though she knew a change was coming.

On Wednesday Mrs. Dolan and Betsy came again. This time Betsy made it plain she did not want to go with Mrs. Crenshaw to the playroom; in fact, she pushed her away. But today the boarding mother, though she was obviously finding it hard not to cry, tried gently to encourage Betsy not to cling to her but to go to the playroom, and before too long she was playing comfortably with the worker, asking to be put on the "horsie" and even sitting quietly on Mrs. Crenshaw's lap while the worker talked about the new

Mommy and Daddy and the fact that they were coming today. Several times Betsy made a sing-song tune of the words "Mommy and Daddy." When the Beckwiths came, Betsy would not go into the other room to meet them, but did not run away when they came into the playroom. She played with them as before and allowed them to give her lunch, which was brought in for all of them. She did not cry at all. But later, when she caught sight of Mrs. Dolan in the corridor, she called "Mama!" and ran after her. Then she seemed to get quite excited and tense, wanting, obviously, to be with both Mrs. Dolan and the Beckwiths at the same time. She took her time about leaving the agency with Mrs. Dolan.

The next morning Mrs. Crenshaw, as planned, went to the boarding home to call for Betsy who was all dressed and waiting at the door. Mrs. Dolan was quite choked up. Betsy seemed serious and reflective. She did not object to going with Mrs. Crenshaw but showed no response to her. She did not say a word, but sat in the car limp as a rag doll and finally went to sleep. When they arrived at the agency they played together for about forty minutes, and this time Betsy warmed up to the worker and appeared more relaxed. She seemed interested in the stick drawings and presently made a sing-song of "Bow-wow, Mommy, and Daddy." She knew that the Beckwiths were coming and appeared to look forward to the visit. After a while she got restless and went about the clinic and the offices apparently looking for her boarding mother. She looked in several carriages and pushed them, saying "Freddy" several times.

When the Beckwiths came in, she started to go to them and then ran away and hid herself behind Mrs. Crenshaw. At the worker's suggestion she did let Mr. Beckwith pick her up, though she whimpered a little. Later on Mrs. Crenshaw left and she played with both of them, and whimpered often but did not cry. This time she did not eat much lunch. When it was time to go, she seemed glad to see Mrs. Crenshaw but reluctant actually to leave the building. In the car on the way home she would have nothing to do with her but sat as far away as she could get, and whimpered. Finally she quieted down and cuddled up to Mrs. Crenshaw for comfort. When they got to the Dolan house, Betsy did not want her to leave. She pushed the front door shut and said "No" several times. When Mrs. Dolan picked her up, she punched at her and then dissolved into tears, but Mrs. Dolan was able to soothe her in a few minutes.

The next day Mrs. Crenshaw again called for Betsy, this time to take her away for good. Mrs. Dolan's son put Betsy's things in the car and carried Betsy in. She stood up stiff and straight by the car door, clinging tightly to the doll and the bottle Mrs. Dolan had given her at the last moment, and said not a word. When the car actually started, she uttered a plaintive cry. She stood as far as possible from Mrs. Crenshaw and maintained this position for some miles. Then she gave Mrs. Crenshaw the bottle to hold and after a while the doll. She let Mrs. Crenshaw take the doll's bonnet off. Finally she sat down, but she turned her back on the worker. After a while she turned around and lay down on Mrs. Crenshaw's lap and let her stroke her hair. Her eyes were wide open. She sucked often on the bottle but did not drink from it. Still she did not say a word. Mrs. Crenshaw talked a little about the Beckwiths and said she would be seeing them. Suddenly Betsy said, "No more Mommy." Mrs. Crenshaw picked her up and held her while she talked about how there would be no more Mommy but there would be the *new* Mommy and Daddy.

When they arrived at the agency, Betsy's manner changed from sadness almost to gaiety. She waved and said hello to everyone, and seemed to look for the Beckwiths. Mrs. Beckwith came forward. Betsy tried to run. Mrs. Crenshaw held her hand and Betsy slumped on the floor and cried. Mrs. Beckwith picked her up and took her into a room, where Betsy let her take off her coat. When Mrs. Crenshaw went in to say good-by to Betsy, she let out a scream and kicked and hit out at her, at the same time clinging to her, but was quiet and seemed resigned when the worker kissed her and put her arms down from their clutch around her neck. After the worker left Betsy with the Beckwiths, she could hear alternate crying and quiet, and in about an hour much less crying and much more quiet. At last Betsy had begun to accept her real Mommy and Daddy.

You can see from her story how very gradually Betsy was led into this rather frightening experience. And yet this agency felt as many others would that, ideally, it ought to have been more gradual still. They wished that circumstances had permitted giving her more time to make the move. Each situation is different, of course, affected by many variable factors besides that of the child's personality. In Betsy's case it was, of course, unfortunate that she could not have the aid of the worker with whom she was familiar, but that simply could not be helped. Then, too, with Betsy the boarding mother's emotional make-up required special consideration, for Mrs. Dolan does love her children dearly and truly suffers when they are placed. Some boarding mothers, although they are deeply attached to their children, are able to be more comforting, more supporting, at the time of parting. But while by expressing her grief Mrs. Dolan relieved it somewhat for herself, the overt emotion did put a burden on the child. Then, of course, Freddy's leaving added to Betsy's confusion and sorrow, even though Mrs. Dolan used it lovingly and skillfully to help prepare her for her own.

Here, too, as must happen now and then, the agency had to pick a path between many pressures and do the best it could under the circumstances. Baby Freddy was ready to be placed, and his parents longed to take him home for Christmas, exactly as the Beckwiths wanted so much to have Betsy hang up her stocking with them.

In spite of all these things, the worker and Mrs. Dolan made a successful transfer for little Betsy and showed deep insight into the special problems. Of course, she does seem to be resilient and able to adapt herself quickly to new situations, and the marked warmth of the new parents made the change easier for her too. But it was recognized, too, that for a child of that age she showed almost too much control. One can imagine it might have been quite damaging to her had the separation been made in any way that encouraged her to bottle up her feelings altogether rather than to express them as much as she could. As it was, she seems to have worked things out pretty well for herself, to have accepted the change. She is making a good and quite rapid adjustment to her new Mommy and Daddy.

When one understands what a push and pull of feelings a two-year-old must undergo to make a change in homes it is easy to see how difficult it must be for older children to take this step. This is especially true when, as is often the case, they have lived in several homes without really belonging to anybody. "Will this one really be the last?" they think, hoping so hard that it will but almost afraid to believe. And so these children, too, need special safeguards and special help before they can make the change to an adoptive home, especially if up to now life has kicked them around a lot.

When the placement of an older child is being planned, it is the usual practice to have the prospective adopting parents see him first without his knowledge. It would be a dreadful experience for such a child to be brought to the parents for inspection, as it were—perhaps to realize at once from their expressions that he is not quite what they want! And so it is usual for the meeting to seem accidental. The worker takes the child to the zoo or the park, the parents watch and listen, then, if they are drawn to the child, they enter into conversation with him, and the four become friends. Then there are other park visits, ice-cream treats, and often a weekend stay at the prospective parents' home before the idea of having this couple for a "new Daddy and Mommy" is even suggested.

When it seems sure that the child and parents will take to each other, the worker must prepare the child in the way that best suits his needs and temperament, usually making it clear to him that this isn't just a one-way affair—he has something to say about it too. As a rule he is longing to be their child, but is just a little afraid that he may not measure up. He may show this in different ways. Perhaps he is afraid they will not like it that now and then he wets the bed, and the worker needs to reassure him, to tell him that she is pretty certain they will understand how this can happen sometimes. Perhaps—and especially if he is older—his fears are expressed more subtly, in sullenness or in criticism of the new parents' looks or ways. In the latter case he is probably just getting his licks in first because he fears he may not measure up to the parents, and the worker must build up his confidence and convince him that he is just the kind of boy they are looking for. When all this is done, the child can as a rule make the move from the foster home or institution to his new parents without too much difficulty. And then how rewarding it is to both worker and parents! How touching and gratifying it is to have the little five-year-old who was so timid in the first interview walk proudly into his new house and announce, "I am coming to live with you always!"

But even this auspicious beginning does not mean that all will go smoothly from then on. Depending on the child's age, sensitivity, past experiences, and the strength of the tie to his foster mother, there may be difficulties of various kinds. Often the child, just like a biological child with a new baby brother or sister, reverts to babyhood for a time: going back to lisping, pretending to be more helpless than he is, nearly always wetting the bed even though he may have "outgrown" that some time before. It is practically certain that for some time he will be afraid to be left alone; he needs constant reassurance, in deed rather than word, that the new father and mother—and especially the mother—can be counted on to be *there* with him. All these things the parents who understand will be prepared for and will meet with patience and more and more love, until he feels truly sure that he is there to stay and that they will love him "always."

Difficult as is the adoption of a new home by a small child, there is no doubt that it is still more difficult for a child of eight, or ten. In the first place, such a child has usually known and can remember more than one home, so that he wants an "own" home more and at the same time is reluctant to cast the die. In the second place, arrangements, as a rule, must be made with his knowledge and consent—he must participate actively even in the early stages. It is not always possible, for instance, to disguise the first encounter with the parents-to-be as a casual one. This fact, of course, makes social workers want to be even surer than they usually are well in advance of the meeting that parents and child will take to each other, but the risk is there. Then, too, whatever sordid or hurtful experiences the child has had in earlier homes increase his distrust. If he has known nothing but constant change and harsh treatment, he will be hostile to everyone. If, on the other hand, his most recent foster home has been his first acquaintance with affection and stability, he may be the more afraid to transfer his allegiance.

Perhaps the most serious consideration in planning the placement of an older child is that everybody concerned must be as sure as it is possible to be that the new relationship will work out. If the adoption fails, the damage done to the child may take years to correct. And sometimes there just is no room for a mistake, as, for example, in the case of little Elizabeth, whose early experiences were particularly unsavory—and damaging. She was three when she first came under care, and was placed first in an institution and then in a foster home while her very complicated legal status was getting straightened out. Already Elizabeth showed signs of being a very difficult child. She was destructive, she was spiteful, and, for some reason, she desperately feared and hated any woman— which made matters very hard for the foster mother. A second foster mother, like the first, proved unable to "get to" her and make her feel wanted. When Elizabeth was five, her legal status was clarified and she was free for adoption, but by this time she was so wild and unloving, so hard to handle, that the third of these ordinarily successful foster mothers could not cope with her and was obliged to ask for her removal from the home.

A fourth foster mother was very carefully chosen for qualities of special warmth, permissiveness, and unshockability. To her at last, after six long months, Elizabeth began to respond and to very, very gradually show improvement. It was thought that now she was nearly ready for an adoptive home, but it *must* be the right one.

There could be no failure this time—or Elizabeth would be beyond help. Much time was spent in selecting parents who were flexible, patient, and experienced enough to understand Elizabeth and to accept her.

One crisp autumn Sunday Mr. and Mrs. Jonas met Elizabeth and her worker at the polar bears' cages at the zoo. Together they enjoyed not only the bears but the elephants and the monkeys and the seals. The following Sunday Elizabeth and her worker again ran into the new-found friends near the lions' cage. When the visits to the animals were over, Mr. and Mrs. Jonas asked Elizabeth and Miss Woodward to come home with them for some ice cream. Elizabeth was more than willing and appeared to enjoy talking with the Jonases and seeing their apartment as much as she did the animal crackers and the ice cream. She was so much more at ease than any of them had expected that Mr. and Mrs. Jonas told her they had no little girl of their own and asked her if she would like to come and spend the next weekend with them. Elizabeth accepted with delight. And she enjoyed the visit so much that when Sunday afternoon came and the worker arrived to pick her up she did not want to leave. To everyone's surprise, she seemed somehow already prepared to accept Mr. and Mrs. Jonas as Father and Mother. The worker's suggestion that they liked Elizabeth so much they wanted her for their own little girl was so happily received that in only a few days Elizabeth went to her new parents for good. Although she still needs much loving and tremendous patience, she is making steady progress and there is no doubt that the placement is a good one.[7]

Obviously, much is required of the parents in these cases. They should have all the qualifications any adoptive parent ought to have—perhaps an extra pinch of each—and they must possess heaping amounts of flexibility and patience. Beyond this, they must be able to appreciate wholeheartedly the needs of a child who has been for so long without his real mother. They must be

7. Helen W. Hallinan, "Who Are the Children Available for Adoption?" *Social Casework*, April, 1951.

able not just to *know,* but to *feel* how it can take a child a long time first to believe in them, and then to make sure that they believe in him. They need to know that they can be prepared for almost anything in the behavior line while he is finding all this out. Then, too, they will need to be aware not only of the many times when the child's sense of security demands that limits be set, that he begin to know some discipline, but also of the more frequent occasions when acceptance and love have to come first.

Parents who have themselves been a part of a large, happy family, or those who have other children—biological, adopted, or both—often find it a little easier than childless couples to manage these older children. As with all parenthood, it is easier to be relaxed with a second or third child, and any experience with children helps a great deal. Then, of course, the presence of other children in the home is likely to give comfort and companionship to the new child.

But although it is a help, it isn't absolutely necessary for a couple adopting an older child to have children already in the home or to have had wide experience with children. A more important qualification—and one which ought to exist no matter how well the parents can relate to children—is their ability to provide a rich, full life for the child they adopt. For this child will already have passed through the home-centered baby years when life just means eating, sleeping, playing, and Mother and Daddy. Even if he has been comparatively underprivileged, this child's horizons will already have begun to expand: to school, to friends outside the home, to radio, television, sports. He has started to be a thinking person, to take heed of the headlines, to wonder about good and bad, rich and poor, about love, marriage, the world of today. He needs to be not part of a cozy little circle of three people content with a daily routine, but a welcome new member of a vital, open-minded, busy family whose interests are widespread, who have hobbies in which he can share. He needs a father and mother who have a wide acquaintance with grownups and with children of all ages, who have put down roots in the community. If they are active and well known in the church or school, so much the better, for when he enters these groups he has some standing, perhaps some prestige, to ease his way. In other words, he needs to be able to step into a family where things are going on. If, on the contrary, the family's life is rather empty and sterile, not only will he be handicapped in his development, but also he will be far more likely to suffer from those aforementioned disadvantages of only-childism than one who has been conditioned to it from birth.

Resilience and plenty of energy are two more of the plus factors which are handy to have in this particular kind of adoptive parenthood. For no matter how deep the love of parents for child, no matter how good the placement and how great the chances of success, there are bound to be some very rough times which are hard on the ego and hard on the arches, too. While the child is making his adjustment to you (and you are making yours to him) there will be plenty of times when you wonder, "What next, do you suppose?" And there will be plenty of times when you wonder if your physique can take it even if your emotions can.

It helps a great deal to know what you may expect, and while there are of course dozens of individual variations on the ways in which these children act out their inner turmoil, there are some expressions of their temporary insecurity which are almost universal. One of these is bed-wetting. And needless to say, it is one of the hardest to take. No matter whether the child is six or eleven and no matter what steps you take to correct it, he will stay dry through the night when he feels safe, when he feels at home with you—and not before. Since this is so, there really isn't any point in pushing him by encouraging him daily, by bribing him, by cutting down on fluids, and so on. And don't scold him, punish him, shame, or ridicule him. It will be exasperating, especially when it happens several times in a night, but try your best to let him see that you don't think it's a crime, but that it's something that can happen to anybody.

Another common reaction of "new" children is swearing and

using dirty words. In many cases, of course, the background is largely responsible for this. The child can't be expected to drop overnight the language he has heard around him for years; but just as often the child will indulge in it even though he knows better. What he is really saying with his damns and his hells and worse, is, "Can they take this? Can they take me?" The swearing, like nearly all the other troublesome behavior, is a form of testing. For many weeks and in many ways the child will use first this and then that form of unacceptable behavior to test you, and also, in a way, to test himself. He has to find out—he cannot rest until he *does* find out—whether you want him for himself no matter what, or whether you want him only as long as he conforms to your idea of a "good boy." At the same time he is trying to preserve his own "self," to keep around him the shell in which he came even though he knows it to be a faulty one. While he is discovering whether he will be safe with you, he had better, he thinks, keep that shell: it's all he's got. So with swearing, as in many other forms of upsetting behavior, it is best never to appear to criticize or belittle the home he had before or the people with whom he lived. He is prepared to be aggressively defensive about them and their ways— he has to be. Just explain to him firmly but gently and without hauteur or condescension, "We don't use those words here." You will no doubt have to remind him several times over quite a long period, and you must be prepared, before it takes, to be deaf on purpose some of the time.

A very common reaction of older adoptive children is to sneer at their new surroundings and boast about the old. They'll tell the wildest tales about what they used to do, to the neighborhood children as well as to you. Sometimes these yarns are fantasied extensions of your own home: "Oh, a piano, sure—that's nothin'. Where I came from they had a piano in every room, even in the bathroom." Or he may embroider in the most clashing colors he can find. He drank, he says (and maybe he did!), he smoked, it was nothing for him to go to a night club with another guy a couple times a week. All this is very hard on parents who, while they are hardly looking for expressions of appreciation, can't help expecting a pleased reaction to their pretty home and the new room they fixed up especially for him. But you won't really mind any more once you stop to think that this child is fiercely fighting off pity. He has to show you he's no dog begging for crumbs but that he's just as good as you are. And this too will pass, as long as you don't ridicule his pretendings or call them lies or show him in any way that you think he's a pretty lucky kid and he'd darn well better be grateful.

Plain lying is as common as the fancy kind. Usually it's because he's on the defensive and is afraid of punishment. That's not at all uncommon with biological children too, as you know, and, like them, he will learn as time goes on that the people he admires most are honest and truthful. Meanwhile, you will help him all you can by not putting him in spots where he almost has to lie and by showing him that it is more comfortable to tell you the truth even though sometimes there must still be punishment for the misdeed that sparked the lie.

Spells of whining, tantrums, and frequent crying may be the refuge of younger children who are not used to their new life. So may nail-biting, picky eating, thumb-sucking. And at any age nightmares are likely to recur often, as with all children who are frightened and insecure. All these will gradually dwindle away as the child becomes convinced that here he is loved, here he is safe.

The testing that older children must do sometimes takes a more subtle form instead of, or in addition to, the overt misbehavior we have mentioned. The child may attempt to divide authority or to set the parents at odds against each other. He may demand expensive clothes or more spending money, he may wheedle to have more freedom than he is able to handle. He may manipulate you just as a chess player shrewdly forces his opponent into a losing move. He may seem to take pleasure in poking fun at or ridiculing your ways, or he may engage you in serious conversation on a sub-

ject about which he knows you have strong opinions, like politics
or bingo or church-going, and take the opposite side deliberately.
Unless this sort of thing seems to have a peculiar intensity or goes
on longer than you feel it should, it is no more serious than the
bragging or the tears or the bed-wetting, though it is likely to seem
so to the parents who are undergoing it just because it is so subtle
and because the mental agility that one needs to handle it is somewhat of a strain. But it too can be lived through and will pass when
you remember to handle it as you would handle other kinds of
testing: by loving him, by being firm when necessary, and by gradually building up his sense of his own importance.

About his money and clothes and toys, about the limits he must
accept in his daily routine, you will be firm and unvacillating, provided you feel these arrangements were fairly made in the first
place. But it is well to make it clear that while you are not going
to alter these for a whim, the subject of allowance or bedtime
or whatever can always be reopened at a later date and that you
will be glad to listen to his side. In just the same way, when he
gets into personal discussions with you, you make it clear that
while you are entitled to your beliefs and do not propose to pretend they are what they are not, you realize that he, as a thinking
person, is entitled to *his* opinions whether or not you agree with
them. For this kind of testing usually has a two-pronged purpose:
the child who uses it wants not only to find out whether you can
truly accept him, but he is trying to discover also whether you have
the strength to withstand unreasonable demands.

Much of the material discussed in the following chapter about
determining what may be a true behavior problem will be helpful
to the parent who has adopted an older child. Everything that is
said there about children with problems applies to these adopteds,
too. There is just one difference—a difference in degree only—
and that is that while those parents who are bringing up a child
from babyhood must be cautioned not to assume that every behavior problem arises from the fact of the adoption, the parent who

is taking on an older child may be pretty certain, in the first year at least, that in their case the adoption may well be the focus of the difficulty. Yet, it must be remembered that if the behavior problem persists, or is too much for you to handle, or seems to you to be all out of proportion even considering what he is going through, it is wise to seek professional help before the problem gets worse. There isn't any reason to feel failure if you need to do this. It is not at all unusual for the backgrounds of some children to be responsible for behavior that may be socially just plain unacceptable and that can indicate real disturbance on their part, such as an undue and precocious interest in sex, for example, or excessive masturbation, or persistent stealing. You can't be expected to handle deep-seated problems, problems that may go years back, at the same time that you are trying to help him adjust in so many other ways. And it isn't fair to the child to wait for him to "outgrow" something that, if it is persisted in, will lose him friends and standing in the community. So by all means don't hesitate to get treatment for him if he needs it.

How long it takes all of you to get to the point where all this testing behavior starts to dwindle into the normal up-and-down behavior of a usual childhood depends on his age, his disposition, what he has been through in the past, and, to a certain extent, on you. When he finally feels sure that you love him, that you think he is a worthwhile person, and that you are going to keep him, his behavior will settle down into a more average pattern. This is likely to take *at least* six months.

When, as not infrequently happens, a child is quite slow to feel accepted or has especially difficult behavior problems, parents may want to postpone the legal adoption for some months, or until they are quite sure that ultimately child and family will fit together. The determination to keep him "no matter what" which arises from a real love and acceptance of the child does, of course, make the parents abundantly sure that adoption will be the outcome. All the same, there is no reason to feel guilty about not rushing to the court the first moment you are entitled to do so; on the contrary, where older children are involved, agencies seldom push parents to the final step and often counsel waiting a while—another year, if necessary. Far better to have a placement that doesn't work out than an adoption that can never jell! A word of caution, though: it is just as well to avoid *promising* your child that "a year from today" or "in six months" he will be legally adopted, unless you are 100 per cent certain of this. If it should turn out that you can't keep him, he will be hurt, of course—this you can't avoid. But you *can* avoid setting a date for him to have a family of his own and then canceling it!

If you are seriously considering or have already embarked on the adventure of taking an older child into your home, by all means read some of the heart-warming accounts of the people who have done it—what they lived through in the beginning and what their rewards have been. Their stories will make you laugh, make you cry sometimes, and, above all, will spark your courage and your desire to go and do likewise.

Even though Mr. and Mrs. Rose could not afford to adopt their several foster children because they already had three of their own to clothe and educate, the Roses brought to maturity a wonderful batch of children who were "misfits" to start with, from crippled Jimmy John to the wild little Latvian D.P. for whom bombing and concentration camps had made death a daily commonplace. Mrs. Rose tells what love and acceptance did for them in two books, *Room for One More* and *The Gentle House,* which are a must for adoptive parents' libraries—as they are for the bibliography of this book.

An abbreviated version of an "older child" adoption which turns out to be gloriously successful against heavy odds shows how childless couples, too, provided they have energy, imagination, and abundant love, can make a go of this kind of family. Katharine T. Kinkead, in writing about some of the experiences of the Child Placing and Adoption Committee of the State Charities Aid Association, the biggest and oldest nonsectarian child-adoption agency in New York State, tells of an adventuresome couple, the Adamses. They took on not one but *two* children of school age—and these were generally agreed to be "the worst children the agency had ever placed," as Miss Colville, one of the workers, told Miss Kinkead before together they visited the family nearly a year afterward.

"They were terrors," she said. "Freddie is eleven now and Ellen nine. When they first came to us, their mother had just died, their father was in a state home for mental defectives, and they were restless, irresponsible, and destructive. They competed fiendishly with each other for attention. They went through five boarding homes in three months. After fifteen couples had refused them, we had about decided that an institution was the only place for them when the Adamses turned up and asked for a boy who had outgrown babyhood. They were a relaxed couple in their forties, intelligent without being intellectual, and with a good sense of humor and lots of experience with children through their church work. Mr. Adams was the principal druggist in his town.

"Well, the agency decided, after the usual interviews, that it wouldn't hurt to at least try Freddie and Ellen on the Adamses. It was explained to them that the children literally had no place to go, but we also gave them so graphic an account of the youngsters' behavior and habits that Mr. Adams took us to task for being defeatists."

Quite an assignment for the Adamses, wouldn't you say? But even in the first explosive and frantic meeting with the children the Adamses were delighted with their spirit and soon off the four marched toward their suburban home. One month later Mr. Adams called the agency to say he wanted to apologize. The children, he said, were all that he had been warned they were, only worse. However, they were going to keep them. "I always wanted children I wouldn't have to stick up for," he commented. "Regular American kids who could fight their own way. Well, we got them, but tougher ones than I ever expected."

When Miss Kinkead asked Mrs. Adams how the children had acted at first her face fell. "Awful, just awful," she said. "The first night, they were so excited they vomited in their beds, and from then on, for the first two or three months, there was never a letup. They did bad things, really bad things. They stole, threw stones at trains, punctured tires. It got so I was afraid to answer the telephone."

"They beat up every kid in the neighborhood," said Mr. Adams. "Every night, when I came home from work, some father would be leading his child up the street to our house, to demand an explanation. When the little girl across the way had to answer the question 'What are you most afraid of?' in a psychological test in school, she wrote 'Freddie and Ellen Adams.' Finally, with Miss Colville's agreement, I gave them an old-fashioned walloping, the only thing of that sort they've ever had from us. And, do you know, each looked at me during it and said, 'I still love you, Pop!' I was so sick afterward I couldn't go to church meeting that night."

"But that phase of things is all over," Mrs. Adams said happily.

"Yes," Mr. Adams said. "They haven't done anything really bad since they set the hose to spray into a neighbor's open window last summer. I think the turning point came when we finally made them realize that no matter what they did, we loved them, and that when they did bad things, it hurt us."

"Now," chirped Mrs. Adams, "the neighbors go out of their way to tell us how nice they are."

How long had it taken the Adamses to feel that the children were really theirs, Miss Kinkead wondered, and she asked them. Mrs. Adams said, "The very first day we brought them home. When Mr. Adams went back to work and left me alone with them, they tore around the house wildly excited, pulling out this, opening up that. Everything they did was wrong. They were loud and fresh and boasted about things I knew they had never had or done. I thought, 'Oh, Lord, what *have* I let myself in for?' But they tried so hard to be helpful around the house it was pathetic. Later that afternoon, I put my arm across Freddie's back. He was trembling all over. Then I realized how scared they were and that they were talking so fresh because they didn't know any other way to talk. After they had gone to bed that night, Mr. Adams said gloomily, 'They are certainly two fresh kids, aren't they?' I began to cry, not for myself but for them. And I'm not the crying kind."

"That's when I knew the children were already Mother's," said Mr.

Adams. "But to tell the truth, I didn't feel they were mine for about six months. Now they are just the way I would have wanted my own kids to be. Unpredictable but thoroughly nice kids."[8]

The Adamses, the Roses, and thousands of other foster parents whose names go unsung have proved what wonders love can work—especially when you mix in with it generous dashes of common sense, humor, and courage. It makes you wish that every single unloved child in the world could find someone like them to be his own.

Perhaps someday this will be so. Meanwhile, it is encouraging to see how much stronger in recent years is the feeling not that there is a child for every home, but that somewhere, if only it can be found, there is a home for every child who needs to be adopted. Would-be parents and agencies alike used to be so fussily insistent upon absolute normality that babies with physical, mental, or emotional handicaps even of a minor sort had to go unadopted. Today, our increased scientific knowledge has made doubtful placements less risky, and, what is more to the point, increasing numbers of adoptive parents, realizing that biological parents take chances too, are willing to accept children who are less than "perfect." It is good to know that every year a few more children with handicaps are finding homes with loving parents who will help them to live instead of just exist.

There is, for example, little Rosemary Wilson, who was two years old when she became ready for adoption. A birth injury had left Rosemary with one crippled leg. She was of average intelligence, but her previous care had been so inadequate that it, plus her handicap, had made her thin and unappealing. She so craved affection that she was jealous of every other child and positively dangerous to babies. She was a chronic and deliberate bed-wetter. She had frequent temper tantrums. It was pretty certain she would always have to wear a leg brace and that surgery would be needed when she was older. For over fifteen months every worker in the

8. Katharine T. Kinkead, "Our Son," *The New Yorker,* March 4, 1950.

agency was on the lookout for a home for her. Few people even wanted to consider her—in fact, only three couples in all that time even looked at her. Two of these, it was obvious, were wrung with pity when they saw her, and it was plain that it was only pity which motivated them, that they saw her not as a child but as a "poor little thing." So the staff had to help them to rule themselves out as possible parents, lest all three lives be wrecked. Finally a doctor and his wife applied, a warm couple who seemed neither shocked nor oversentimental when they were told about Rosemary. They took her home with them, they loved her, they gave her expert medical care and much, much patient help. Rosemary—now seven —limps a little but wears no brace, and is sunny and happy as the day is long.

There are many parents like the doctor and his wife who have helped children like Rosemary—many, in fact, who have made new lives for children much worse off than she was. Take Teresa and Don Blake, for instance. They had been accepted by an agency and had been waiting patiently enough for some months for their baby when Teresa, through her volunteer work at a local hospital, saw and fell in love with a handsome blue-eyed baby boy in the children's ward. He was three, but he looked much younger because he was so scrawny and undernourished. The welfare authorities had brought him to the hospital for some minor surgery. He seemed to be so quiet and so good, and he was so beautiful that Teresa fairly yearned over him. It was quite a shock to discover that he was blind. He always had been and always would be. At his mother's death a few weeks earlier (his father had been killed in the war) he had come under welfare supervision and been put in a foster home only until he could be released from the hospital and institutional care could be arranged—unless by some miracle adoptive parents could be found for him.

The idea took root in Teresa's mind that she and Don were those parents, and she told her husband about the boy. After the natural initial shock, he was more than willing to go to see him, and when he did, he was as much taken with Bobby as was his wife.

They spent several long evenings talking it over and made a point, too, of discussing it with doctors at the hospital and with the local chapter of an organization for work with the blind, in order to have some idea of what they would be up against if they did take little Bobby. In the end they both felt sure, and so they applied to the authorities, and it was not long before they took the child home with them.

That first year with Bobby took all the courage the Blakes had. They had not quite realized, in spite of all they had been told, how very difficult it is for a blind child to learn anything at all. Poor Bobby had been so underprivileged and underloved that he did not talk, and his little face was so expressionless that it was just about impossible to tell when he understood what you were saying to him. Almost all his learning had to be done through his sense of touch; telling and showing wouldn't do it. And there were so many things he had to learn. He had never brushed his teeth, for example: Teresa had to give him the little toothbrush, make him feel it, tell him what it was for (in case he *might* be understanding what she said), then let him hold her hand so he could feel how she brushed *her* teeth with *her* toothbrush, and finally guide him to trying it. It was days before she dared to put toothpaste on the brush!

Getting him to walk was difficult too. He had no idea how it was done, in the first place, and then he had nowhere to go as far as he knew, and so he was content to sit still on the floor and rock himself to and fro for hours, as most blind children do. They had so many things to teach him—it seemed to take hours for each routine function—and at the same time they had to be sure not to push him too hard, not to make him worried or anxious. For the most important thing of all was to build him up both physically *and* emotionally, to cuddle him and play with him, to love him. And he was impassive for a long time: it was a heartbreaking seven months before he seemed to "wake up." But, as Teresa says, "It was worth every minute of it when after months of silence he laughed out loud and said 'Daddy' and 'Mommy' all in the same day!"

Now Bobby is five, and a year and a half ago Don and Teresa

adopted another little blind boy, now three, who is a wonderful companion for Bobby and just as deeply loved by his parents. Both are legally adopted. It has been easier to bring up Tim: not only did the Blakes have less tension and more know-how when he came along, but also he was younger and had not suffered as had Bobby from lack of love and lack of food. A special school has been found for them to go to when they are ready, and Teresa has herself learned Braille, partly out of real interest, partly to be in a position to help them when they need it. It is too early yet to tell what the boys will make of themselves, but the Blakes are not unduly worried about the future. They feel certain that Bobby and Tim will not let their handicap spoil their lives even though it may restrict them. The Blakes, all four, are a happy family.

I have cited these cases to show that "a home for every child" is not just wistful thinking. If Rosemary and Bobby and Tim found parents, so can other children who have defects of one sort or another but have so much love to give—if only someone can be found who will love back. And it must be remembered that these three are extreme cases. There are many, many children whose handicaps are quite minor who also need homes. Children like Johnny, with a high I.Q., a dazzling personality, and an extra finger on each hand, or like Jenny, whose eyes are badly crossed now, although surgery can probably correct this later on.

The stories of the parents who adopt the imperfect child are moving and inspiring. All the men and women who can with their strength and warmheartedness knock out the walls that imprison the handicapped child to let the sunshine in deserve rows and rows of jeweled crowns. But not every one of us can go and do likewise. This kind of adoption is not for everybody.

Is it for you?

Well, let's see what are the things to be considered most carefully when you are wondering about adopting a handicapped child. As you probably know already, you'll need all the maturity, humor, flexibility, acceptance, warmth that other adoptive parents need to have, plus *more* patience. And I mean lots more. Then, too, depending on the kind and the degree of the handicap, it often helps to have a little extra financial cushion, though lack of this is not necessarily a deterrent, because in many instances free or partially free medical help is available: in many states subsidies can be arranged through public health authorities or adoption agencies. But the most important thing in this kind of adoption is to be as certain as it is possible for human beings to be that you want this child for himself, not just *because* he is deaf or blind or crippled. Be sure that you want to help him not just today and next week, but when he is ten and eighteen and maybe always. You will find that the adoption authorities want to make sure of this too. For sometimes the things that have happened to us in the past make us feel a deep need to take on a burden that may be too heavy for us, make us, though we are quite unaware of it, want to sacrifice ourselves. A home with adoptive parents so motivated would be a very unwholesome thing for any handicapped child who needs to learn through the love and the strength of his parents first to accept his limitations, and then to carry on from there with happy matter-of-factness.

This kind of adoptive parent also needs an extra helping of poise and humor to enable him to handle the attitudes of the community toward the new member of the family, particularly if the handicap is just about the first thing one notices about the child. Friends, neighbors, teachers—in fact almost all the people whom your child sees daily—will have to be very delicately "re-educated" lest they unintentionally defeat your best efforts either by withdrawing or by being oversolicitous. In the beginning the child's playmates must be prevented from making fun of him. Once your child shows that he is learning to handle his disability without being a sissy or a bully, he will have everybody's admiration and respect, and most of all the children's. But while he is still learning how to be your child as well as how to live with his handicap, he needs to be protected from damaging attitudes. And this takes tact —lots of it.

Everything that we have said about bringing up adopted children, and especially older adopted children (for among the handicapped the older ones outnumber the infants), applies to children with defects and disabilities—and even more strongly. For it is understandable that the handicap itself has probably already had some effect on the child's personality, making him more unsure of his worthwhileness than most adopted older children. Your biggest job, after making him feel loved and accepted in the ways we have described, is to show him how to handle that handicap.

To do this, he needs to learn two things: first, to accept his disability; and second, to be independent in spite of it. In order to help him, you will want never to seem to ignore the handicap, to act as if it were non-existent. It *is* there. He knows it, and he is aware that everybody else knows it. Be matter-of-fact about it. You wouldn't try to hush up bright red hair if he had it. So there's no reason either to avert your eyes when you see him trying to get his brace through his trouser leg or to rush over and say pityingly, "Oh, it's too hard! Mommy will do that for you." Just say matter-of-factly, "The brace catches, doesn't it? Here, I'll help you." Show him how to keep it from catching, and help him until he can do it alone. Let him do everything that he can and wants to do unless it is downright dangerous. At the same time you will want to help him accept the fact that there will always be some things he can't do without so much effort that it really isn't worthwhile to try. He must learn to do necessary things, even if it's painful and tedious. But try to stop him from feeling that just *because* of his handicap he must learn to do everything his un-handicapped friends do and do it better. You want to help him live in peace with the concrete fact that he can't, that in many instances he must find something altogether different in the line of special accomplishment. Perhaps if, as so often happens, he has a compensating talent, you can help him find it. It will do wonders for him to become known as "the boy who does the magic tricks" instead of "that lame kid."

If you have other children, it takes quite a bit of wisdom and planning to make sure that the added care and attention the handicapped one needs do not shut out his brothers and sisters. They may not need help in dressing or eating as he does, they may not need to be made to feel important as often as he. But you don't want to forget that no matter how self-reliant they appear to be and no matter how much they love and look out for the newcomer, they need to be sure that there is enough love for them too, that they mean just as much to you as he does.

None of this is easy. No kind of parenthood is easy, biological or adoptive, and bringing up an adopted older child, especially one with a handicap, is a good-sized challenge. Not everyone can do it, but there are some who, though they may not know it, are just the right kind of parents for children like these. Perhaps you and your husband are among them, perhaps not. But by all means think it over. Maybe somewhere there is a child who has been waiting for three whole years for you to come along!

8 When There Are Problems

There never was a parent who wasn't faced time and again with what, for lack of a better word, we call a "problem." For children cannot get their growing and learning done without passing through stage after stage of what is frequently irritating or upsetting behavior. Almost every mother of a happy, outgoing baby has been dismayed to see him around his eighth month burst into tears at the sight of a neighbor whom he knows well, or to surprise on his little face an expression of worried unhappiness. The father of an ordinarily independent two-year-old is astonished and often angry to see his big boy suddenly take to clinging to his mother and hiding his face in her skirt. Over and over, parents have been appalled at the sudden "spells" of lying, swearing, using "dirty words," disobedience, rudeness, and so on which seem to show up without rhyme or reason. Often parents blame themselves: they feel they must have failed somehow. Have they overdisciplined their child, have they indulged him too much, have they somehow caused him to feel insecure?

If biological parents react this way, how much more so the adoptive ones, who very humanly want to prove themselves just about the most faultless parents ever to have a child. They love their child and they want him to love them. They want to do everything for him and they want to do it in the right way. And the thing they are most afraid of is that in spite of all this he may somehow feel unwanted. Therefore, let adoptive parents be forewarned that not only are they quicker to panic than biological parents, and quicker to blame themselves, but also more likely to focus their entire attention on the insecurity angle whenever troublesome behavior takes place. Their very natural special anxiety in this area makes them likely to misinterpret what they see, and may also intensify whatever difficulties the child may be having.

So adoptive parents even more than other parents need a compass in this maze of roads. They need to know when they are simply dealing with a trying stage of development and when their child has a real "problem" and may get off the trail. The compass is knowledge. Parents ought to learn all they can about the pattern of a child's physical and emotional growth, and prepare themselves to understand and accept the varying kinds of behavior as they come along. A few parents have an instinctive appreciation of the cycles of growth; most of us must learn from observing children, from talking with other parents, and from books.

As thousands of parents have discovered, one of the most complete and most helpful books on how to bring up children is Dr. Benjamin Spock's *Baby and Child Care,* widely sold under that title and available both in hardcover and paperbound editions which every parent can afford. Aside from the fact that it is just about all-inclusive and is so warm, so friendly, so reassuring, it is of special help in the very field which we are discussing, because Dr. Spock tells us not only *how* the child acts at this age or that, but *why*.

Another book which you may want to use in deepening your understanding of your child's emotional and physical growth cycles is *Infant and Child in the Culture of Today,* by Drs. Arnold Gesell and Frances L. Ilg. To this you may want later to add their book called *The Child from Five to Ten*. It is most important, however, in using these books to remember that they are only guides to the *average* progression of growth. Children differ. You will be letting yourself in for endless and harmful concern if you expect your child to follow any of these patterns more than approximately. Don't be like the mother who arrived at the guidance clinic with a happy, alert toddler in tow. Opening a well-thumbed Gesell at the section on behavior at four years old, she said, "I've checked all these things off—he doesn't do a single one of them and he was four Monday! I'm worried sick about it!"

A book which parents will find useful for many years and in many situations is *The New Encyclopedia of Child Care and Guidance,* edited by Sidonie M. Gruenberg. In this thousand-page book, Mrs. Gruenberg and an advisory board composed of authorities such as Dr. Spock, Josette Frank, Anna M. Wolfe, and many others, tell parents why their children act as they do and what to do about it. The book is especially useful because it deals understandingly and concretely with all sorts of matters which confront parents: allowances, crossing streets, comic books, quarreling, earning money, phonograph records, dating, love, popularity. Parents of adolescents in particular will find much help and illumination in the pages of this book.

Many other excellent books are available about practically every phase of childhood from infancy through adolescence and about family living. A list of some of them will be found at the back of this book. Adoptive parents are rewarded, I think, by reading considerably in the field because they are often in need of reassurance. They find it comforting and strengthening to discover through their reading that they are not the only ones with "problems." And if they give themselves a good grounding in the basic books we have mentioned they are well on the way to understanding what is and what is not a "problem."

All of us use this word "problem" loosely and inaccurately. We use it to indicate not only the trying stages of normal development that exasperate parents and make them anxious, but also the kind of behavior that may indicate that their child is in serious trouble and is asking for help. Parents are likely to say, "We're having such a problem with Donny—he tells these whoppers all the time," when Donny is really not being a problem but is going through a trying but to-be-expected stage of his development. Often parents actually understand this perfectly well and are speaking in the same offhand way in which they might say, "It's such a problem to know what to have for dinner." All they really mean is that it's a puzzle to know what to do. But sometimes, through ignorance or because of a tendency to expect too much of their child, they may think that the behavior points to a real difficulty. Oddly enough, it is often the same parents who start blaming themselves and looking for trouble where none exists who at other times just don't notice the symptoms of what may be a serious disturbance, behavior that actually does point to a "problem."

There really ought to be another word for "problem" when we mean behavior indicating serious disturbance as distinct from the troublesome but natural behavior at certain levels in the child's development. Since there isn't, let us for convenience's sake call the latter a "stage"—a misnomer, of course, for each age and stage brings with it its typical joys as well as its typical difficulties, and we are planning in this chapter to use the word "stage" to stand only for the kind of behavior which, although developmental, may make parents worry. Ages and stages go roughly together, and if you have learned from your reading and from observation and discussion what to expect, you will be far less tense as your child grows and learns. And he will be, too, with the result that his behavior is likely to be less trying.

Unfortunately, none of us can take refuge in the notion that just because our child is going through a "stage" we have only to sit back and let it pass. When our confident three-year-old is suddenly afraid of the dark, when our four-year-old starts wetting the bed after the arrival of his baby sister, when our two-and-a-half-year-old is so bossy we can hardly stand it, we are all prone to think our duty is done when we say, "Well, that's natural! They all do it!" and return in relief to our stocking sorting. It is part of our job to *help* our children do their growing up. There are, of course, many times when it is best to seem not to notice, to leave the child alone. But there are more times when we must give him a boost in the direction in which he needs it. We can try to understand the reasons behind the behavior and show that we do. We can relax our demands on the bossy one, let our timid one have a night light without reproaches, give our bed-wetter more love and attention to allay his jealousy.

In other words, parents must guard a little against the temptation to sit back and say, "This too will pass." If it is a "stage," pass it probably will, with or without our help. But we must be watchful to see that it does, that this particular behavior is a rung of the ladder of growth that is no more important than any other, a rung that is grasped and then let go of when the next is reached, not a place where the child gets stuck. Afraid of the dark at two or three is one thing; a boy of eight who won't sleep without the lights on is quite another. A little girl may suck her thumb off and on from babyhood until she is three or four; if at six she suddenly starts in again, something, big or little, is bothering her.

Nail-biting, thumb-sucking, telling tall stories and lying, bed-wetting, bullying, picky eating are all forms of behavior which most children can and do demonstrate at different ages according to their temperaments and surroundings. Fears also enter into growth patterns in many different disguises: fear of the dark, fear of people, of animals, of thunderstorms. Some of these are innate, like the tiny baby's fear of a loud noise; some are natural concomitants of the child's growing awareness of the complexity of the world around him; some are unconsciously encouraged by parents who have, for varying reasons, never gotten over their own childhood fears. But if one or more of these typical behaviors is carried on well beyond the age when most children have turned to something else, or if even at the age when it is appropriate it is much more marked than with other children, then the parents should be watchful. It is not enough to conclude that the child will outgrow it, for if it indicates, as it may, that for some reason he is not at home in his world, he will either fail to outgrow it or he will simply exchange that habit for another. Meanwhile, whatever it is that is bothering him may go on bothering him, becoming harder to find and harder to dig out with each year that passes. It is generally agreed that adolescent and preadolescent children who have problems and who turn into problems have almost always shown some signs of disturbance before the age of six or so. When these signals are overlooked or dismissed, it becomes much harder later on to help these children find their way back into the happy childhood that ought by right to be theirs.

At the same time, parents need to be careful to keep a sense of perspective, not to overdo the watchfulness. Especially, of course, adoptive parents, and adoptive parents of only children. Continued anxiety, constant supervision, fretting and worrying over the child's behavior may well be to a large extent the cause of whatever symptoms he is showing. And then, if he isn't showing any, he soon will.

Three-year-old Tommy Davis came in from play with a toy fire engine that belonged to his neighbor Jon. He wanted it, so he took it. He certainly never thought of it as "stealing." But Mrs. Davis brought him to a clinic next day, her eyes still red from a night of stormy weeping. That a child of hers should *steal!* The guidance worker tried to straighten her out on a three-year-old's "thinking," and comforted poor, miserable Tommy who knew only that he had apparently done something so awful his mother couldn't love him any more. She helped Tommy to understand that the engine belonged to Jon, that Jon might need it, and that was why it was right to take it back to him. But one wonders, with a mother so perfectionist and overanxious as Mrs. Davis, what "problem" Tommy will develop next—and how soon.

When you are on the prowl for problems, you will be sure to find them. Don't stalk them, then, but try to recognize one that is before your eyes, and do something about it. It is surprising how blind parents can be sometimes. Most psychiatrists and psychologists will tell you that many of the children with whom they work are brought by parents reluctant or positively refusing to take this step until forced to by school or community pressure.

Kickers, biters, pinchers, vandals, terrors of the block and play-ground, many of them, but the parents have closed their eyes until it was nearly too late. And yet the behavior of the destructive child, the cruel child, the bully and troublemaker puts out sirens and flashing red lights that shout for attention. It is much easier to understand how parents sometimes miss the cry for help of the "good" child, the lonely television watcher who is living in a daydream, a cry so muffled that it often goes unheard. And of the two, the child who would rather walk through the looking glass than stay on this side and fight it out is most in need of help.

So remembering always not to be overanxious, try to be aware. If your child has taken his first years in his stride, doesn't stutter, suck his thumb, or twist the tails of cats and dogs, so much the better. But this does not necessarily mean that all is clear sailing from now on except for the "stages" that still remain to be traversed. Sometimes the pressures of school or adolescence re-awaken conflicts that stayed submerged in the earlier years, or stimulate new ones. And with each year that passes your child acquires, even as you and I, another layer of protective shell. The steely sheen of manners, conventions, rules of the group, and the wish to conform, hide more and more of the real "him." That "him" is very likely just about what you would want and expect it to be: a maturing personality which, though it may be having its trials, is sound and strong. But with an adopted child, especially, you want to be as sure as you can that he *is* growing straight and sound and strong, that he is not being warped by self-doubt or hos-tility or fear.

But how do you know? How can you tell? Should you pry? Should you ask him if everything is all right? No—because if every-thing *is* all right, if he is as comfortable as can be expected both in his world and the world of the family, the question will only worry him. And if everything is not all right, you won't find out that way. He will only say, "Yes!" and jerk away from you. Here again, awareness is the key—not the eagle eye, not the spying ear, but a sort of sixth sense that tells you when danger is there. In most parents, that sense exists. You can learn to cultivate it and to listen to it.

What are some of the less obvious ways in which a secretly unhappy child of eight or ten or twelve may be sending up distress signals? What are some of the signs which may activate ever so slightly that sixth sense of an aware parent? I should say that one of the most significant of these may take place in the parents themselves. Does their child make them feel baffled, frustrated, incapable of understanding his motivation for certain repeated behavior? Do they worry and wonder, and then berate themselves for worrying because everybody else thinks their child is so nice, so polite?

For instance, let's take a close look at Margot and her parents. Margot was nine, pretty, and so well mannered that other parents were always enviously exclaiming about it. And she seemed to be fairly popular with children in the neighborhood. In school she had not been doing too well recently, bright though she undoubtedly was, but her teachers had no specific complaint beyond the fact that she was occasionally uncooperative, did not put forth her best efforts, and often procrastinated. This, surely, was not too serious; lots of Margot's friends in the fourth grade got the same sort of report. What baffled her parents was her home behavior at nine—and ten. Without being downright disobedient, she was increasingly hard to handle. Where had their sunny, helpful, companionable little girl got to?

"I always thought," said Margot's mother, "that children had a very strong sense of what was fair, what was just. But Margot doesn't. She *won't* be in the wrong ever. She expects us to do everything for her and she won't do anything for us. She asks me for bacon for breakfast; I cook it and she won't eat it, says it's no good. I just don't understand the child." The parents grew more and more uneasy—but what to do in the face of what they thought was "no symptoms"? The child was growing and gaining, in perfect health. Over and over friends said, "Aren't you proud of her? Such a charming child!" And so the parents stuffed their uneasiness into the corners of their minds and tried to forget it. Margot would surely outgrow this—she *was* growing fast, and no doubt that was a strain on her. One thing they could do was make her go to bed earlier, get more rest. Or maybe vitamin pills would help.

But Margot didn't outgrow it. As the months went on the parents grew more unhappy, more puzzled. They tried to re-examine their own attitudes. Perhaps they had been too strict—on the other hand, it sometimes seemed to them that even Margot thought they were not strict enough. Meanwhile, the side Margot presented to the world, except now and then at school, continued apparently happy and outgoing. But at home it was another story. There she seemed to want conflict, and she got it. Father and Mother tried this and then that: loving, patient acceptance one week, a confident "no-nonsense-from-you" attitude the next. Nothing seemed to work.

Then there came a day when Margot couldn't go to school. It made her sick, physically sick. Two doctors and many tests said there was nothing organically wrong with Margot. And so at length the parents sought professional help for her—and, as it usually turns out, for themselves too, for all three of them had got themselves into quite a tangle.

Margot was an only child. And she was an only adopted child. It ought to be said that, as often happens, there were in her middle years several circumstances quite outside the parents' control which worsened her predicament and which precipitated her inability to play out the role she had chosen for herself. But a very great part of her trouble was that she had been too closely supervised, too closely watched, too suffocatingly loved. Quite without realizing it, her parents expected too much of her and expected it all the time. And when her behavior continued to be so baffling, her helpless parents had unwittingly deepened the gulf that may lie between the only child and his family: the feeling that "they have each other, but I have nobody."

The fact that Margot was adopted was not the *cause* of any of the difficulties, Margot's or her parents'. But it is easy to see how Margot, once she began to feel the weight of her parents' concern, the impact of several upsetting events, and her own inability to cope with the situation, brooded about the adoption as she brooded about many other things. And wondered. Wondered whether she could ever be what her parents expected, wondered if she were really, after all, not much good as a person. Wondered where her first parents were and who they were, and if maybe they had let her go just because she wasn't much good to anybody.

In being unreasonable, selfish, unfair at home, Margot was fighting her troubles in the only way she could. Though her parents tried with all their hearts, they didn't understand. And she could not tell them. She had nobody who could understand—until she found the counselor who listened, and kept listening, until every frightening thing was looked at in the daylight and recognized for what it was, so that it no longer had the ability to terrorize. After a while—though it was a long while—the counselor and Margot and her parents, working together, got them all on the right road again.

The important thing to understand about this "for instance" is that Margot's adoptive parents are not the villains of the piece. Neither is adoption. The fact that she was adopted simply added a plus value to the emotional reactions of both parents and child to a situation that could have come about in any biological family. For it just happened that she ran into a set of circumstances nobody could have foreseen or prevented which were sufficiently upsetting, especially taken all together, to shake any child's equilibrium. It just happened that Margot's temperament needed more support than her parents realized. She had been such a good, bright, and co-operative child when she was little that her parents assumed they knew Margot through and through, that with her they would have no problems. It had probably cost her something to be that way, and as time went on and life got more complex, it took more strength than Margot had to keep that outer shell intact for the outside world and for her parents, too.

We repeat that such a situation can and does come about with children of biological families as well. Handicaps of personality make-up plus handicaps of upbringing plus sheer bad luck may combine to make the child break down—or they may not. Many biological and many adopted children have worked their way successfully through problems such as these without anybody's being the wiser, though people may say, "Jack is a wonderful boy now, isn't he? Will you ever forget what a little horror he was the first two summers at the lake?" But if you have a child, biological or adopted, who can't work his way out of the box without help, there is no need to feel guilty—unless you should deny him that help.

Like all parents, Margot's made many mistakes along the line. But the only one they can logically blame themselves for is not listening sooner to that inner voice that told them something was wrong. It would have been so much easier to help Margot at eight than it was at ten.

It is natural for any parents, and especially perhaps for adoptive parents, to reproach themselves the moment anything goes wrong. Then, besides this almost instinctive tendency, parents of today have heard so often that wounding sentence—"We have no problem children, only problem parents"—that they are afraid to confess even to themselves that things are not going along the way they should. "Problem parents" exist, unfortunately—some of them are the Margots of the world who didn't get help when they needed it —and they do often raise problem children. But that sentence as a whole is unfair and even cruel. Parents make mistakes, of course— some which they can help and some which they can't. But before shouldering a load of blame, fathers and mothers ought to remember that, particularly in the complex and tension-ridden civilization in which we live, parents can't be all-powerful and all-knowing. Children grow up faster than they used to. They know much more. They come into contact with the complexities of life sooner and oftener. Once upon a time, parents were able to share in a natural way many more phases of their child's life than is possible today.

Don't forget that of your child's twenty-four hours as many as six-teen or eighteen may be spent in school and in sleep, not to mention those spent in other activities outside your direct influence. The influence of the home and the strength of the parent-child relationship are tremendously important, of course, but parents can't do everything and be everywhere, even if it were desirable that they should.

So, again, don't look for trouble and don't make mountains out of molehills, but don't smother that sixth sense of yours. Be aware. And should you get that feeling that your child is different from what he used to be, that something's wrong, watch and listen and think for a while before you decide it is just a "stage."

Often, as was the case with Margot, continued difficulties in school can alert the parents when everything else seems to go along smoothly. Teachers vary, and children are the first to know it. But if each successive teacher finds David a troublemaker in class, or consistently failing to do his best work, perpetually quarreling, showing marked disinterest in all the work rather than in a subject or two, there's a danger signal. It is unlikely, after all, that *all* the teachers are cross, overworked though they may be, that *all* the subjects are too hard, that *all* the children pick on him.

There are other weapons that children use which very often indicate secret unhappiness and unexpressed hostility. I say "weapons" because in every case in which a child is struggling against heavy odds he needs a weapon against the giants, the grownups. He is obliged to pick one that he can handle. With some children it's provoking disorder in the classroom, at scout meetings, on the playground, or anywhere else where adults are supposed to ultimately have the upper hand. With some it's arguing about each and every little thing, and slyly shifting ground until the opponent is helpless and exasperated. A mother of one arguer told me, "He makes me feel just like a mouse with gloves on, boxed into the corner of the ring!" Manipulating first Mother and then Father, and vice versa, so as to divide their authority is another weapon that the unhappy, hostile child often learns to use very skillfully. Stealing may be another. So may deliberate lying—the look-you-straight-in-the-eye kind. And so may a pronounced appetite for violence, sadism, and the supernatural in movies, in comics, or on television. So may excessive masturbation, or a secretive cruelty to younger children or to animals, or a persistent passion for lighting matches. So may consistent bullying.

Many of these forms of behavior appear in almost every child at certain ages. Most toddlers and lots of six-year-olds are fascinated by matches. The tendency to masturbate may appear and reappear at certain phases of the child's development. Many, many perfectly well-adjusted children seem to have to be bullies at eleven and twelve. There are few boys who don't welcome a smashing fist fight on television, and a certain enjoyment of the supernatural seems to go hand in hand with adolescence. So the parents who catch Tommy giving his friend of yesterday a really rough Dutch rub, or surprise his sister reading a lurid sex romance, don't have to wring their hands and cry that all is lost. Instead, they ask themselves, is this a habit or is it an episode? Is the child too old for this sort of thing? Does he persist not only in this type of behavior but in related types which make you uneasy? Before you panic, look at your child as a whole. And look at yourselves, too, your way of living, your ways of discipline, the interrelationships of each member of the family. Perhaps your child's problem is something a little insight and some common sense may solve. Or perhaps you and he need some professional help.

The types of behavior which we have been talking about mark the unhappy and hostile child who is also aggressive. He isn't going to take it lying down. Through his behavior he is trying to say something to his parents, trying to tell them that things are all wrong with him, that he wants to be helped. Maybe he needs to feel more accepted and acceptable, maybe he feels he can handle more freedom than he's getting, maybe he doesn't like his own picture of himself. Maybe all these things, or maybe others. But he knows something is wrong, and even if he doesn't know what it is or what to do about it, he is fighting. And if he gets help, the very strength that made him pick up the weapons at hand and flail about with them will enable him the better to find himself. The wish to fight back, once directed into constructive channels, becomes an asset.

The hurt child whose hostility is uppermost among his tangled feelings, the child who fights back, sends out distress signals far more conspicuous than the call for help of the child who retreats from the field, the one who gives up. Such a child, finding no place that is comfortable, no place where he fits in the world he can see around him, little by little builds up in his daydreams a world that is just for himself. In that world he can be strong and superior; he can more than hold his own. Why fight? On television and in books and magazines, as well as in his own fantasies, he can escape for hours into regions where he is as free as the air, with no demands upon him. This is not to say that he deceives himself entirely, that he is actually happy or even thinks he is. Deep down he knows he isn't. But he can pretend better alone. He soon learns the trick of retiring into his secret world even when he is outwardly carrying on a conversation or eating his dinner at the family table. In the beginning he may greet Mrs. Brown at the front door very politely, although in his thoughts he is a million miles away. But when he has become deeply attached to his awayness he will make it a practice to vanish before Mrs. Brown sees him.

This child may have no friends except one or two very close ones, and seem not to miss having them. In fact, he may even quietly avoid children of his own age and spend his outdoor time aimlessly walking down the street, eyes on the ground, kicking a stone along. At home, he is likely to spend most of his time in his room or glued to the television set hour after hour. He is dutiful about his homework, minds when he is spoken to, is often neater and tidier than most children of his age. Often helpful, too, though he may seldom take the initiative.

In other words, such a child may do almost nothing to worry his parents—if that sixth sense of theirs is sleeping. "He's always so good—he's never given us a bit of trouble," they may say fondly, never stopping to think that if he were leading the kind of life he should be leading, he would have to give them *some* trouble. And so, parents should be careful not to be lulled into a sense of false security by behavior which on the outside is exemplary but which actually is disguising a very real difficulty.

This doesn't mean that parents ought to heckle their children into going out, talking with company that comes, staying with the family more. In the first place, everybody needs some time to be alone. We all know the person who has no resources within himself, who is totally at a loss without somebody to talk to. And there are stages in a child's development, especially adolescents, when he must be alone to daydream, to telephone, to work on his stamps, or just to *be*. In the second place, we must remember that children are individuals just as grownups are. Two children in the same family, biological ones as well as adopted, can be conspicuously different in temperament. It would be a great mistake to expect Alice, with her love of the piano and poetry, her introspective turn of mind, to be as outgoing as her sister Jane, who swims, dives, plays a hard game of tennis, and is always the center of a crowd. There have always been and always will be people who are shy, whose special charm shines best in small gatherings. If the parents of Alice, for example, time after time should force her into social situations, make her "speak up," play her piano piece for company, and if they talk about her in front of her, they may well turn her into a "problem."

So, again, look at your child as a whole. Add up his actions, his facial expressions, his "emotional tone" over the course of a week or so. Reflect on the subjects and tenor of his conversation, his relationships with other children and with the family, the trend of his interests in the newspaper, on television, in books and magazines. Think about the kind of person he is, and whether the way he is acting is in general right for him, or whether it may mean that he is backing away, trying not to show that there is something he's afraid he isn't strong enough to handle.

It goes without saying that one has to use a little extra insight with both the overaggressive and the withdrawn child to determine whether the behavior may be largely owing to some isolated circumstance. A serious illness in the family, a flare-up of trouble at school which may not have reached the parents' ears, the loss of a pet with a resultant sense of guilt (deserved or undeserved)—any of these things can throw any child temporarily off the track. At such times he needs respect and support—not cross-examination, not nagging, not apprehension. You will have to decide for yourself whether your child most needs to be left alone to work it out on his own or whether he can and needs to talk about his fears or his guilt. Much depends on his age. The support may, especially if he is adolescent, have to be silent, indirect. But it can still be warm and loving.

It is well to bear in mind that adolescence more than any other stage in the child's development may carry with it many of the kinds of behavior which ordinarily might indicate the possibility of serious disturbance. Arguing, lying, withdrawal, sudden and violent changes of mood, anger, sullenness, failure in school, refusal to cooperate at home—any or all of these earmarks of the emotionally ill child are likely to show up in our adolescent, and yet his development may well be proceeding perfectly normally. Practically all parents, biological and adoptive alike, are so baffled by the erratic behavior of their teenager, his nervousness, his hostility, that they are almost certain the child is seriously disturbed. "Disturbed" he is—there's no doubt about that—often seriously. And of course it is always possible that professional help may be indicated. But all of this turmoil is so consistently a part of the growth pattern of the teenager that this is a time when the parents need to bend over backward to avoid being alarmists.

By many of the criteria we have been discussing, her parents might have reason to be concerned about fourteen-year-old

Carolyn. Carolyn is blond, very pretty, popular, well dressed, and lacks for little either in material things or in family affection. But her school marks have been skidding straight downhill. Her fair skin is beginning to break out, and she is constantly preoccupied about this. She has recently developed all sorts of nervous mannerisms and tensions. For her, at present, there seems to be no middle ground between giggling and weeping. Though she complains bitterly that her mother expects too much of her, that she has no right to "nag" at her about keeping her room in order, doing her share of the housework, and so on, she is on the whole defensive of her maternal parent. She feels Mother *does* understand, in a way. But her father! He doesn't understand *anything*. And both of them are much too strict with her. They seem to think she has no judgment at all, no maturity, no sense of responsibility.

Carolyn is madly and deeply in love with Roger, a wealthy boy from a family of some prominence in the community. One may smile, but this love is very real to her. He is the main reason she can't keep her mind on her schoolwork and is driven frantic by the tiny blotches on her face. Then, too, Roger is rather sophisticated and is allowed a good deal of freedom: here again, she feels, her parents fail to understand and limit her dates and her curfew hours with him. At the same time, she is constantly begging her parents to "do something" about her older brother, Bob. It is embarrassing enough that he is getting a divorce, but at least they could make him see how bad it looks for him to be taking this girl, Peggy, around when the divorce won't even be final for another month!

Carolyn is driving her normally even-tempered parents fairly wild. And with her lightning-fast mood swings, from broodiness and tears to effervescent laughter, her constant tension, her spoken and acted-out hostility, she *does* act like someone who needs therapy. But Carolyn isn't sick.

She's adolescent. Typically, she hasn't yet really learned that the privileges of maturity have to be counterbalanced by its responsibilities. She needs to shine in Roger's eyes, to be worthy of his love by being able to show not only a flawless complexion but also a conventional and irreproachable family background. In her eyes it's all right for *her* to be a little fast, but her brother Bob ought to be made to conform. At her present stage of development she is not able to go beyond herself. Her wants, her moods, her feelings, are the only important ones. *She* is the one who is never understood—not Bob, not Mother, and, of course, never Father. Her parents actually are not unsympathetic or overstrict—in fact, it is the consensus of community opinion that they are not so strict as they might be. Her mother is no jailer or slave driver—she is rightly setting certain limits for Carolyn, and Carolyn, again typically, feels she has to fight them. She truly does not realize that she is insisting on responsibility on everyone else's part and refusing to take any herself. Most of all, she is seriously concerned about the depth and the strength of her feelings for Roger and his for her. She doesn't know whether she can handle these strange new emotions. She is afraid.

Adolescence today is a period of seething turbulence. It always has been, of course. But while the disturbing bodily and glandular changes are what they always were, our swing from rural to urban and suburban life, our changing economic conditions and customs, the ubiquitous automobile, the availability of alcohol and drugs, the stress on sex in books and movies, the threat of riots, war, or nuclear holocaust combine to make it much harder for our teenagers to get their maturing done. Nowadays, adolescence has to be acted out on a bigger stage, in a play with more actors, more and brighter footlights and spots, more properties, more hectic music. And there are more parts than there used to be for these teenagers to play: very demanding ones, too. So all their roles must be rehearsed in the home, with the family as audience. All the personalities which they must try on and strut about in while they are finding their own real ones must be tested first against the family background.

It makes it just a little harder on the audience that these personality costumes are seldom if ever without anachronisms. The hair that has been brushed until it shines may swing against a definitely dingy neck. The new Christmas sweater may be worn above a pair of faded, frayed dungarees a tramp wouldn't envy. And these anachronisms may be of many kinds: it never occurs, for instance, to the competent woman of the world to hang up her clothes, or to the sophisticated ladies' man to gather up the dozen dirty socks from under the bed. And anyone who suggests that it would be a good idea to do so "just doesn't understand." It's no wonder that parents do sometimes feel like throwing in the sponge. It would be so much easier just to wait out the rest of it lying on the ropes. They are baffled, and often they feel guilty, certain that somewhere along the line they must have failed.

Adoptive parents feel this way too, only—understandably enough—more so. Even though they think they have succeeded in working it through, up pops that old failure feeling again, the feeling that they are lesser parents because they were not biological ones. And now, seemingly, they have made a mess of the other kind of parenthood as well! Of course neither premise is true, and it will help both of you a great deal to take out those old feelings and look at them again. Face them for what they are, acknowledge them, accept them—and go on from there. They may not vanish overnight, but at least you will see that you are up against a very natural emotion which you will recognize when it shows up in your reactions to your adolescent's behavior.

Then it is well to remind yourselves that just now he, too, has a very real extra problem which is concerned with the fact of his adoption. For every adolescent is likely to spend a large part of his daydreaming time—which is considerable—in going back over the past. Whether the things he recalls happened the way he thinks they did is unimportant: what he believes or imagines about them *is* important. If you once punished him too severely for stealing, say, he doesn't understand that you did it out of lack of knowledge rather than lack of love. He doesn't realize that your later attitudes prove this; he remembers only that once he *earned* your disapproval. If while you were still learning how to be a parent you were much too strict about his toilet training, he remembers only that he *felt* unloved at that time. Adolescents want and need most of all to feel acceptable, worthy of the love and respect not only of their parents but of their contemporaries. But since parents are only people, with feelings of their own, there can hardly be an adolescent on the globe who has felt accepted every minute, every hour, every day of his life. So most of them, when they hark back, consciously or subconsciously, hit on at least one thing that makes them doubt their worth-whileness, their values as a lovable individual, and about this they brood.

It is easy to see how the adopted child can feel he *really* has something on which to focus his self-distrust. And this is true no matter how good a parent you have been or how well you have handled with him the story of his adoption. It is a fact that his own mother and father did not keep him. He has accepted this without too much hurt and he will again—but until he is finished with the turmoil of adolescence and has learned to stand on his own two feet this will bother him off and on. It may well make him seem even more hostile and unreasonable than his contemporaries.

What, then, can parents do, and especially adoptive parents, to help themselves and their child through this stormy period? First of all, they can try to be honest with him and with themselves. They can recognize their failure feelings and the ways in which these may affect their reactions to him and his behavior. They can recognize the fact that, in common with all parents, they want to hold on to their child and his love; they can see the time is coming when he must be on his own and deep down they want to postpone it, to put it off just a little while longer. They can try to get their child to talk about his feelings and to accept them if he does so. And above all they will want to set limits for him and stick to them— provided that they are reasonable ones in line with what others of his age are allowed to do, and provided that he knows they are open to revision as he grows more mature. The adolescent actually is fearful of his independence even while he is insistent on getting it: he *wants* you to set those limits. He may gripe, he may beat his chest, he may insult you to your face, but it happens, oh, so often, that he is later overheard to tell a friend, "My parents wouldn't *think* of letting me do that!"

But how do you tell what is normal adolescent behavior and what may be something of a more serious nature? What if you feel it just *must* be the latter? Is it a rule never to get professional help for an adolescent? By no means, for if there should be any serious disturbance the child may be totally unable to cope with it *and* the strain of adolescence without help. On the other hand, you can see how threatening it would be to a teenager, already full of doubts about himself, to be carted off to a therapist just on suspicion, even though if all is well a good therapist would be able to give him the reassurance he needs. So it behooves the parents of an adolescent not to jump to conclusions.

If you *do* suspect trouble, it is often a good idea to talk first to some of the people who see a lot of adolescents in action: teachers, scout leaders, ministers, leaders of youth recreation in your community. Their guess will be pretty good as to whether your child is no more erratic than the rest or whether he does seem to have some special difficulty. Then, the school systems, which have psychologists and guidance leaders, offer a helping hand which is extended both to your child and to you. If the psychologist is an able person and one who is trusted by the children, and most of them are, your child may consult her in school hours on his own and be reassured about himself as a result of one or two brief talks. He will learn that he is not the only one who is full of doubts and fears and feelings of inadequacy. Often this is all he needs. But whether or not you think he may have taken this course, it is always your privilege to consult her on *your* own. The chances are that she will be able to clear up most of your worries and to give you some concrete assistance about ways to handle your child.

This is what happened in the case of fifteen-year-old Lars, who came for help because he was so desperately unhappy he had determined to run away from home. Lars was the middle child of three, quite small for his age, of average intelligence, intense but controlled, musically gifted. His grades had dropped rapidly and it didn't matter to him that they had. His mother appeared to be gentle and over-protective, his father remote, old-fashioned, and very, very strict. For two years now Lars had been earning between eighteen and twenty dollars a week on a newspaper route and at a bowling alley where, because of his slight build, he could get to the machines and adjust them when a ball got stuck.

Of this money he willingly turned over more than half to his mother. At home he was an amenable, respectful boy. He helped with the dishes every night. The main trouble, he felt, was that his father would not let him go out of the house after dark—not to a friend's house to practice on the drums nor down to the hamburger stand for a malt, not even if he promised to be home by half-past eight or nine. Lars was no potential delinquent—he didn't want to hang around street corners or shopping centers, to shoplift or look for trouble. "Girls? I got no use for them," he said. "They don't like me anyway and I don't care if they don't." He thrust his hands, thumbs crossed and fingers twisting, between his knees. "Everybody's against me," he said. "But they're so good to me, what can I do? I just got to leave home, that's all. I can't stand it any more!"

With some difficulty the psychologist got Lars' parents to come in for a talk. She tactfully led them to see how Lars could not help feeling that no matter how hard he tried or what he did his father didn't think he amounted to much. And she showed them, too, that Lars further suffered from being undersized—*of course* he cared that the girls passed him by. He cared desperately. After a while the father was able to acknowledge that perhaps he had been mistaken in allowing Lars so very little freedom, and the mother saw that she, too, had wanted to keep him a little boy, to tie him to the home too long, in the old-fashioned way. Together the three of them compromised on a plan for giving Lars a few evenings out without worrying the parents too much, and the parents promised to do what they could about making Lars feel more appreciated, less taken for granted. This, of course, produced no miracles: Lars still must learn to accept the fact that he is short and likely to stay so, nor are his father and mother, at their age, likely to alter their natures completely. But home is a happier place, and now that some of the pressure has been taken off Lars, he has a better chance of developing into the fine boy he really is.

And so with your adolescent, as with your "acting-up" child at any age, take a long look at the problem first. Don't rush off for therapy at the first jolting sign of trouble. Be aware: take a new look at your own attitudes and the emotional climate of the house you live in. Reconsider the limits you have already set, and when you have determined what these fairly ought to be and stated them, stick to them—very gently but very firmly. Accept your child's expression of his feelings all that you can, even though you must prevent him from time to time from acting on them. And if you feel, in spite of all this, that he *must* have some sort of emotional disorder, and that it is truly risky not to determine whether this is so, go about it very slowly and very cautiously.

Suppose, then, that after a period of unobtrusive observation and considerable thought you feel that there is a good chance your child may be disturbed, may be trying to handle a problem that is too big for him and for you as well. What do you do next? I think it helps first to talk to someone who is experienced and sympathetic with children and is acquainted with your child. In rare instances this may be a neighbor—there are neighbors who are gifted with children, who are able to be frank, and who have sufficient detachment to give you real help. Someone like this can often set you straight if it is a case of your having lost your perspective. It is wise, however, to always remember that friends and neighbors have problems too, and it is only human to interpret other people's problems in terms of our own. To lean entirely on the advice of a friend or two is to run the risk of wasting time trying this recommendation and that, from tonics to day camps, precious time which it may turn out could have been spent to better advantage either in therapy or in not worrying had more expert advice been sought first.

Your child's teacher is usually a good person to talk to. She knows your child, she knows children in general, she will have some idea whether you need professional guidance and, if so, whether you can get it within the school system. All this is providing, of course, that when you talk to her you find her wanting to help and willing to listen. There is the occasional teacher who for one reason or another has little use for parents and uses such interviews solely to lecture the unfortunate mother on her short-comings and Junior's misdeeds. In that case you are no better off for having talked to her—except, of course, to have, perhaps, more fellow feeling for Junior than you have recently been experiencing! In most instances, however, a mother will gain a good deal from an interview with the teacher. She may find that the teacher, too, feels that something is bothering Junior. Perhaps she doesn't know what it is, perhaps she has found clues in his classroom behavior or in his dealings with the other children. Or perhaps she can honestly reassure you, can make you feel that not only does she think that your child is as well adjusted as any, but also that she probably knows what she is talking about. In that case, you can go home feeling heartily relieved, and determined just to "leave Junior grow" for a while—without, however, burying that sixth sense ten feet deep.

If, however, the warm and intelligent teacher with whom you talk seems herself to be puzzled and disturbed by your child's behavior, indicates that she has more "trouble" with him than with the others, or that he doesn't get along with the other children or both, it is more than time to prick up your ears. By all means take advantage of her perhaps hesitant suggestion that he have a talk with the school psychologist if there is one. And if not, ask her what recommendations she may have as to professional guidance and where you can find out about it.

Either way, whether there is or is not a school psychologist with whom you can work, you will want to take your child for a thorough physical checkup. You want to make sure, first of all, that there is nothing organically wrong to account for his troubles. In case the doctor finds nothing of this sort and is inclined to agree with you that some kind of psychological help may be indicated, your physician is an excellent person, knowing your personalities and your pocketbook, to ask how and where you may best find that help.

You will be most unusual if you get even this far without considerable stress and strain on your emotions. The parents are rare whose hearts do not beat a little faster when they are faced with seeking this kind of help for their child. Much of this emotional stage fright is natural, like the apprehension you have for your child before even a minor operation. You wish you could have the operation for him; you wish you could better explain to him what it is all about. In the case of asking for psychological help, or even in ascertaining whether it is needed, the apprehension is stronger because it is complicated by feelings of self-blame, of shame, and of sheer dread of the unknown. The first two of these are often felt even more strongly by adoptive parents.

To guide yourself toward the relaxed acceptance which can be your greatest safeguard, try your best to get rid of that feeling of guilt. You are not obligated to have it; this turn of events is not a punishment. You might feel dismayed and sorry, but not guilty, if in spite of your conscientious helpings of vitamins, milk, and sunshine your child developed a tendency to rickets or to bad teeth. There would be no reason to blame yourself. But all parents—and, as we have said, adoptive parents particularly—are inclined to feel branded as failures when their child is found to need help with his emotions. They are ashamed; they feel the whole thing *must* be their fault. They go over and over the past trying to puzzle out what they "did wrong"—probably a futile and certainly a tormenting task. It is perhaps impossible for parents to be wholly objective in this regard, but it is of tremendous help to try. Look at it this way: somewhere along the road you missed a turning. Perhaps you have gone off the course only a little way, perhaps you have wandered afield a good distance. It is not your fault that there are so many ways to go astray, that storms came up, that you floundered into a couple of bogs you could have gone around if you had known they were there. Think only that there *is* a road back, and you and your child will find it.

As for that feeling of shame, there is no reason at all to feel stigmatized or set apart just because your child needs help for an illness of the spirit, of the personality, any more than if you were having to seek medical advice for weak arches or sinus trouble. Children are bound to share the subtle but powerful tensions under which we all must function in the world of today. Parents, teachers, and doctors who understand this are taking advantage of the widely increased knowledge of how we can lessen these tensions in our children—so much so that the services of guidance clinics, psychologists, and psychiatrists are in tremendous demand everywhere and there is need for many, many more. So there is nothing to feel ashamed or embarrassed about. You would be surprised if you knew under how many roofs in your very neighborhood parents and children are in a like predicament and are extricating themselves in a like way.

It is wise, though, not to talk too much about your problem and the ways in which it is being remedied while treatment is under way—not because such treatment is a skeleton in the family closet, but because you want to protect your child's privacy. Some grownups are careless of others' feelings; they don't stop to think that their own children may be listening to and misinterpreting their comments about John's visits to the clinic—with the result that John may be made the subject of their not always silent curiosity. Other grownups are capable of being tactless directly to John himself. And so while the fact that he is going for treatment need not be a deep, dark secret, for your child's sake it ought not to be broadcast—particularly if he is adolescent. His progress will be greatly impeded if he has reason to believe that his innermost feelings are the subject of even the kindliest conversations over the coffee cups.

If you can rid yourselves of the feelings of guilt and of shame about needing this kind of help for your child you have taken a big step. But what about that feeling of fear, the panic that overtakes you when you realize that you don't know what you may be letting yourselves in for? At the last moment, and perhaps even after, you want to draw back. Maybe things aren't so bad, after all. Maybe it would be better to see if he outgrows the trouble. After all, you know so little about it—what will the counselor or therapist do exactly, and how long will it go on? And will it really help?

The answers to these things your professional advisor can give you. Don't be afraid to ask. He or she may not be able to be positive about how long it will take, for he can't tell until he has worked with your child enough to gauge the depth of the disturbance, but he can reassure you, clear up some of your worries, and give you an idea of what to expect.

A word of caution here: if in the first or second interview with him you feel antagonistic toward him, feel, perhaps, that he is cold, or remote, or that he doesn't get what you are driving at and seems disinclined to, don't go further unless you are sure you can't find someone else equally reputable whom you can warm up to and trust and believe in. Don't be afraid, if you have any choices— and usually you do—to search for the expert who inspires confidence in you. This does not imply in the least that your second choice is a more skilled person than the first; it simply means that he happens to be a person you can, all three, work with better. For work all together you must, and if your personalities don't jibe, you will find that it becomes harder and harder for you to help him help your child. And if you wait until well into treatment to decide that you simply don't "click," this is most unfair not only to him but to your child, who will have overcome with considerable difficulty many of his own fears and shynesses in order just to talk to this counselor, only to have it all to do over again with a new one.

Everybody knows that many an excellent physician inspires confidence and liking and friendliness in one person and not in another. Mary gets along beautifully with Dr. White and thinks he is the most sympathetic doctor in town, while you have always felt him to be brusque and hurried. The relationship between doctor and patient is always important, but nowhere more so than between the therapist, the child he is treating, and the family. For such treatment may continue over a long period of time, and, long or short, will deeply involve the emotions of the father and mother as well as those of the child. Especially if your child is older and the roots of his disturbance a bit deeper, the going from time to time will be very hard on you as well as on him. In every situation of this kind the parents are bound to have doubts occasionally of the wisdom of their course. For in any fairly extensive treatment there must be peaks and valleys and plateaus. There will be, there must be, intervals when the parents, no matter how much they basically like and trust the therapist, wonder if they wouldn't have done better to leave "well enough alone." Especially if the cause of the disturbance is deep-seated, there will be many times when it seems as if all of them were losing ground instead of gaining it. The child is harder to handle than ever before; the pressures he is undergoing make him veer like a weather vane from one kind of behavior to another. His parents feel like a pair of zeros; all the authority, it seems, must come from the therapist, and the parents are likely to imagine for a time that all the child's affection is directed toward him, too. They feel futile, shut out, even disliked. All this is not easy, and it may have to go on for a long time.

While it is happening, it helps a little to remember that it is by no means easy for the child, either. On the contrary, to be in therapy is very painful. It's no fun to turn yourself inside out, as it were, to be led to look at yourself just as you are. But this must be done before the healing can begin. All the hostility the child feels must first come to the top and overflow. Meanwhile, most of it, rightly or wrongly, must be directed against Father and Mother.

Their child must get worse before he can get better. And so the parents, with the sympathetic guidance of the therapist, must just ride out the storm, knowing that when they are all on an even keel once more, when the healing is completed, their child more than ever before will be truly theirs and truly himself.

9 Breaks in the Family Circle

When you first bring your baby home, however much you love him and wanted him, it takes a few days to get used to the idea that now there are three of you instead of two. This adjustment, however, is one we all make very quickly, and in no time at all it seems as though your family has always been three—and always will be. What's more, you unconsciously think and feel as if this close circle of father, mother, and child were as fixed a relationship as that of the stars in a constellation. You tend to think this way even though you are aware of the fact that school and high school, clubs and activities will take your Tony—or your Susan—more and more away as the years go by, that you will run into difficulties and anxieties along the way as all parents do. You know, too, that there are fields in which you as adoptive parents will have to take special care, and you plan to take that care. Just the same, during your baby's first few years all that seems remote. You have the comfortable feeling that adolescence will be your first major hurdle, that until then you can count on the familiar, cozy *status quo*. Today and tomorrow are pretty much routine, rewarding and happy routine, to be sure, but still the predictable circle in the square— the three of you snug inside your four strong walls.

This is a natural feeling for beginning fathers and mothers to have, and having it doesn't mean that you're vegetables. On the contrary—for quite aside from the turmoil of contemporary living, life with a child is anything but vegetative. Each day has its drama, its moment of decision, its anger and its joy. But all of us are inclined to take our way of life for granted, to assume that next year will be about the same as this year. Particularly do we feel this when we are conscious of the need to insure the emotional security of our adopted child. And so we are inclined to act as though things will continue to go along much as they are going, that except for happy surprises tomorrow will be pretty much like today. We feel as though our circle will never be broken into.

Of course we know that this isn't really so. Things are bound to happen. Things happen inside of us and our children as we grow and change—and things happen *to* us as well. Some of these are natural and to-be-expected concomitants of our children's growing up; others are quite beyond our control, and, good or bad, may deeply affect all the members of the family. The pattern of family life constantly alters in small ways and large for the parents as well as for the child. We can't and don't expect growth without change, but often the little breaks and strains—and sometimes the big ones—come before we are quite ready for them. Going to school, for example, often opens up the circle before parents quite realize all that it may mean to their child. A new baby in the family is an even bigger break, and this, too, the parents must be ready to help the child accept. And moving into a new house and neighborhood, often a fairly stiff adjustment even for adults, can be thoroughly unsettling to a child. As time goes on, other really disturbing alterations may take place, like the death of a grandmother or a dearly loved uncle. And there may even be the cataclysmic break of parents' separation or divorce.

Every family has to learn to handle some of these situations. It is hoped that you will not have to meet many of them. Particularly is it to be hoped that you will not have to undergo the splitting asunder of your family group by death or divorce. But though most of these crises are, we pray, remote and unlikely, it will help enormously, should they ever come to pass, to know and understand a little of what even the small alterations in family living can mean to a child so you can help yourselves and him gain strength from the little ones with which to meet the big ones.

For even the most normal alterations in the family routine tend to shake the children's security just a bit. Adoptive parents will want, without being overanxious and tense about the effect of such changes on their child, to understand his real feelings at these times in order not only to bolster up his security whenever a break occurs, but also to nurture his ability to meet them on his own in later life.

In many families the first event that seriously alters the home and family as the small child knows it is the arrival of a new baby. This can be a very trying time for the older child in biological families, as many of your friends can testify. To the adoptive parents and their child it will be just as trying and, under certain conditions, even more so. For to a child, biological or adopted, the arrival on the scene of a little brother or sister really seems for a while to break up the family. The child's hurt and resentment may be obvious or it may be covered up, depending on the child's age and temperament, but whether it shows or not, it is there, and he needs help to learn to handle it.

Just what does a child—in any family—feel when it really begins to penetrate his pretty solid little ego that this baby about whom he has heard so much and in whom he is somewhat interested —but only somewhat—is a permanent fixture, a fourth member of the family? That he's not here just for today and tomorrow (or that infinite space of time, a week) but for always, and apparently owns just as much of Mommy and Daddy as he does—or maybe more? No matter how well the older child may have been prepared for it all, even though he may have been warned that he may not love the baby *all* the time, he has no way of anticipating how sudden and strong—and frequent—his angry feelings will be. He doesn't know they're natural feelings. All he knows is that he would like to do something to this *baby* that they're always talking about, always feeding, always hugging and cooing at. It helps if Mommy and Daddy see to it that he still has his special times alone with them, that he is listened to and hugged and rocked and loved. It helps a great deal. But it doesn't alter the fact that somebody else is the baby now, somebody else needs more of Mommy's time than he does. "That baby" gets cuddled and held at feeding time—which is often—while he is supposed to be a big boy now and eat with a spoon and drink out of a cup. And no matter how much he enjoyed the grownup style of doing things before the baby came, he just doesn't *feel* like a big boy now. He knows he can no longer be the first-loved, the best-loved. He would like to go back to being the baby again.

The older child's resentment of the newcomer is not constant and not necessarily intense. He can and does feel real affection for and interest in the baby, but every now and then the other feelings will probably have to come up to the top. A child will act out this resentment, either directly or indirectly—sometimes both—because he is incapable of putting it into words. He may revert to wetting his pants and his bed, he may refuse to drink his milk, he may go in for defiance and tantrums, he may suck his thumb. In all these ways he is showing that he wants to be a baby once more —wants to be the *only* baby. Many children take out their anger on the baby and his belongings, either shyly or openly. They may shake the carriage hard, or turn a cooling pet into a teeny pinch, or give the legs of the bathinette a kick.

These things, of course, cannot be permitted. It is more than all right for you to show your child that he must not do them, as long as you show him also that you understand and do not yourself resent the feelings that make him want to. Tell him, "I know how you feel. You want to hit the baby. You think you wouldn't care if you hit him hard. You feel angry. That's all right. But I can't let you hit the baby or his carriage or his crib. Tell me about it instead. The baby makes you feel mad inside, isn't that right?" The words, of course, will depend on the age and understanding of the child. The important thing is to show him that you can accept the way he feels about the baby and that though there are certain things he may not do, it is not a wicked and shameful way to *feel*.

Remember that much as he thinks he would like to do something to the baby, he wants even more to be stopped from doing it. It is up to you to stop him, and to manage the daily doings so that opportunities for hurtful and destructive aggression—hurtful and destructive most of all to himself—are few. Also, you will want to let him know that you don't think he is bad for wanting to hurt and destroy. If in addition you can lead him to talk a little about how he feels, much of the antagonism and jealousy will drain away.

Sometimes older children, and especially girls, will be so "good" with the baby that parents are deceived into thinking that the child feels no jealousy or resentment whatever. It is far more likely that he does and that he feels so guilty about it that he must play-act "love the baby" all the time, stuffing his anger way down, trying to pretend it isn't there. This isn't good for him. For the sake of his emotional well-being those stuffed-down feelings ought to be ventilated. Of course with a child who is trying so hard to be and do what he thinks is expected of him it is not easy to help him to his own release. If the child is old enough to understand, sometimes talking will do it. But it shouldn't be forced. Don't insist, don't ask questions that seem to accuse, but instead introduce the subject casually, assuming, as it were, that your child, like everybody else, good though he is with the baby, can get pretty tired of him sometimes. "I remember how I felt a lot of the time about your Uncle Jim when he was my baby brother," is often a starter—if you *do* remember! Or some mothers have said, "Oh, my, I'm glad the baby's asleep! I do love him, but he takes a lot of time away from us, doesn't he?" Some of these openings or others may lead your child to express himself. If he can, he will feel better for it, and will have room inside really to love the baby as part of him wants to do.

If the child is not old enough to be talked with in this way, there is not too much you can do except to give him all of the single-minded love and attention you can manage. And as time goes on be sure you don't expect too much from him in the way of helping with the baby just because he is so willing. It is very easy for all of us, without realizing it, to take advantage of our conformist children just because they are so reliable, so eager to please.

What about the adopted child when a new baby comes in the family? Are his feelings different? Have they a "plus value"? How could they have if he is so small he barely knows what "adopted" means except that it's good? Or even if he is old enough thoroughly to understand the story of how he came to you? How, you say, could his reactions to the new baby be complicated by the adoptive factor?

The answer is that they often are—perhaps not consciously so at the time, but in a deep-down way that may leave small or large scars on his emotions. This may happen for two reasons. One is that the adoptive child may have subconscious memories of rejection which the biological child has never experienced. These constitute a very real force which can intensify his natural resentment at being displaced by the new baby. The other reason is that special tension of non-biological parents around the area of adoption which *may,* even though they seem to have worked it through successfully, make it more difficult for them to keep their attitudes toward the older child natural and relaxed.

It may be a little easier for the child who is at home with the story of his adoption to accept the newcomer than it is for the one who is too young to understand, provided that the baby is adopted as he was. Even a fairly young child, however, may suffer from a double resentment if the baby is a biological one, and if he does not consciously feel this at the time, it is quite likely to flare up now and then when he fancies himself less loved than the "own" child. Especially when he is adolescent is this feeling likely to reassert itself and be brooded upon.

What can adoptive parents do to help their child adjust himself to the new member of the family with the least hurt to his ego? First, as with biological children, comes proper preparation. This ought to be just a shade more on the casual side than the enthusiastic, and the child should not be given so much advance notice that he has time to worry about it. If the new baby is to be adopted, time enough to tell him about it when you have seen the baby and are sure that in a few days you will bring him home. (It would not be wise to tell him in advance that you are going to "find" or "choose" his baby brother and then in case you and the baby just don't take to each other or something in his history disturbs you, be faced with the explanation of why you're not going to bring him home after all! Much wiser to make sure, first, that the placement will go through, and then ask the agency for an extra few days in which to prepare your child for the baby's arrival.)

If the new baby is to be a biological one, it is well to explain to the older child several times over a period of about three weeks or a month (sooner, of course, if the child should be curious about his mother's increasing bulk and you feel that this provides a good opportunity for sex instruction) what is going to happen. If you are not too insistent and too prying about his reaction to the news, he will accept it quite easily. You might also prepare yourself to be on guard against the many well-meaning but thoughtless friends who make a great to-do over the idea of your producing your "own" baby after having adopted. It is probably impossible to stop this kind of gushing, but if you know it is coming, you can be properly casual about it and indirectly convey to your child by look, gesture, and affection that while outsiders can carry on about it in this way, you and he know that he's still your baby and always will be.

When the new arrival, biological or adopted, comes home, try from the first so to organize his care that you have plenty of time alone with the older child. Make allowances for him during this period when he would like so much to be the baby again: cuddle him a lot, lovingly tuck him in at night, try to accept temper tantrums, bed-wetting and the like, as casually as you can. And do what you can to help him talk out his feelings about the baby.

In other words, in this situation, just as in so many others, adoptive parents only need to be *aware*—aware of their child's hidden feelings and of their own. Just as intelligent and sensitive biological parents do, they will take a few extra pains to avoid giving their oldest child left-out feelings, feelings of bewildered hurt which then or later may bruise a child's ego and which are often more keenly felt and more surely remembered by the child who did not come into his family by birth. On the other hand, adoptive parents particularly want to avoid going too far along this line by making too much fuss over the older child and "playing down" the baby. For if they attempt to hide or stifle their perfectly natural love of and delight in the baby, the older brother or sister will wonder himself either then or later, "They don't seem to think so much of him! Sometimes they act as if they don't even want him! I wonder if *I* was wanted. . . ."

Perhaps your adopted child will be an only child so that you will not have this particular opportunity to lay the foundation for his acceptance of the changes which will come along one by one. But there are many other occasions of the child's moving into life when it is just as important to be sure that as we help him through the doors we do not give him the feeling either that we are pushing him through or that he must be shielded from whatever is on the other side. Many of these situations we have discussed in Chapter 5—introducing your child to babysitters, first trips to dentist and barber, getting acquainted with school, going to the hospital. Having someone stay with him while Mother and Father go out is of course one of the earliest and commonest experiences of this kind. Making visits with Mother is another good way of extending your child's horizon beyond that of the home and the family. For the very young child these ought to be brief and may have to be omitted temporarily when the toddler reaches the stage of grabbing everything in sight—unless your hostess is used to children or perhaps has a youngster his age with whom he can play. Bringing one or two toys along is always good strategy, but better short visits or none at all than a constant battle between him and you for possession of the hostess's valuable bric-a-brac.

When your child is two and three it is especially important to encourage sociability rather than to keep him too much by himself or with you. For short periods he can play well with another child and will even accept his mother's leaving him briefly if he has been used to this and is not suddenly introduced to it just now. It is worth a good deal of effort to keep him moving among people at this age as much as you can without forcing or pushing him to the point where he begins to get tired and cranky. "Short but often" is a good rule of thumb for these visits and playtimes.

As your child gets older you will want him very occasionally to sleep away from home. Spending the night at a relative's house is a good way to start, because familiarity with the house and the people doesn't put too much of a strain on the child. An excellent first visit is often made with a family of slightly older children when, as often happens, they initiate the idea and are really enthusiastic about having him. This kind of stay always has the aspect of an adventure and usually the visiting child handles himself very well. There are two important things not to forget about visiting. First, if the child has an old doll or towel or something of the sort which he is accustomed to take with him to bed, be sure it's packed with his nighties and toothbrush and that his hostess understands his word for whatever it is. And second, be explicit about what time you are picking him up in the morning and be true to your word.

The child who has been used to seeing people both in his own house and in theirs and who has enjoyed the companionship of other children as a fairly regular thing, can usually accept nursery school or kindergarten and first grade without too much difficulty. Children do vary, however, in their readiness for this to them quite complex experience, and we repeat, be sure to move very slowly and gradually if your child seems fearful or worried about it. Better to take more time to fit him into nursery school, should he seem unready, than to force him to go and have trouble later on.

How about camp? Many parents, both biological and adoptive, ask this, particularly if they are city dwellers and can't help wondering if the being away from home at a comparatively tender age wouldn't be balanced by the advantages of country air and camp activities. The answer with any child depends on him and on the camp. By and large, adoptive parents will want to be surer than biological parents need to be that the child is ready for the experience and wants it, and that the camp is right for him. In some communities summer day schools can be found at moderate prices, where the child has the advantage of group play outdoors with trained supervision and still has the comfort of knowing he can come home in the late afternoon to his own family and his own bed. A season or two of day camp is a good springboard for regular camp if the child has enjoyed the experience. Even if this is the case, however, don't send your adopted child away from home too young. Unless he is quite outgoing and carefree, ten or eleven is likely to be much safer than eight or nine for any child.

In selecting a camp it is a good idea, after checking on such basic things as location, cost, sanitation, variety of activities, rest periods, availability of doctor, quality of food, number of children assigned each counselor, and so on, to visit, if you can, the camp or camps which seem to you to rank high by these standards. Sometimes it can be arranged to meet and talk with the director and some of the counselors in a nearby city before the season opens. If this is not possible where you live, perhaps you can judge from talking to parents whose children have gone there what sort of camp it is and whether it is likely to suit *your* child. It is well to remember that the personality as well as the training of the adults who run the place are more important than the plant, especially for a first camp experience. Better a simple layout and counselors who truly like and understand children, than four new aluminum canoes and overstrict regimentation or a camp policy that puts more stress on competition than on learning to enjoy and find oneself in camp activities.

As the camp people will tell you, acute homesickness for the first week is much more common than not. They will advise you to take leave of your child cheerfully and casually, and strongly urge that you plan to visit him only when he has been in camp for four or five weeks and is at home there. Many camps limit the visits to one during the season and then to a single weekend known as "parents' weekend," when the children are descended on by all the parents at once and all activities are arranged with this in mind. Frequent visits only upset the child by reawakening the homesickness with which he began his stay. If, as rarely happens, the child does not get over his misery as soon as the others do, the skilled camp staff will be able to determine whether a few more days will help or whether the child is still not ready for the experience and should be taken home perhaps to try again next year.

The tone of the letters he gets from home is an important factor in helping the child to adjust to camp. If they are unconsciously woebegone, full of plaints about how much he is missed, how lonesome Daddy and Mommy are without him, how his dog keeps looking for him, the child is forced to continue the struggle he had on arrival. Pulled in two directions, he can't possibly enjoy camp. So make your letters casual and happy, brief but frequent. Mention in passing that all are well at home. Make some of the letters funny if you can. One mother cheered and amused her child with letters purporting to be from his dog Butch, who, it appeared, was also away for the summer experiencing his first year at "Dog Camp." Johnny and his cabin mates got a great deal of fun out of Butch's struggles with bed-making and canoeing (he always *was* a clumsy dog), and with his account of the evening campfire where Counselors Shepherd and Pinscher led the group in the camp song, "Bark Among the Birches."

One shift in the family home circle which often comes both unexpectedly and inopportunely is moving. Whether the move is simply one to a new house a few blocks away or whether it involves a more drastic change, leaving a familiar home is likely to be an upsetting experience to any child. The younger he is, the more easily he can take it, but no matter what his age one needs to be prepared for tremors in his security. If the parents have no choice about where or when the move is to be made, all that they can do is to be aware of what it means from the child's point of view and to alleviate any anxiety he may have by discussion and casual reassurance. Letting him have a suitcase which he can pack with his favorite toys and some of his play clothes often helps, though it is well to make it clear that not everything will fit in this, and you will see to it that the rest of the things get there safely. Try to prepare him for just what will happen: how the moving men will take out all the furniture, how it will travel in that big truck, how you will go to the other house in the car or by train or plane, how all of you will decide where the furniture goes in his new room, and so on. Give him as much time as you can manage in all the rush, and make an adventure, if you can, out of the last hasty breakfast, closing all the bags, the picnic lunch, and so on. It is a good idea to let him carry a favorite toy with him on the trip.

If the move is one of your own choice, the opportunities are of course greater for you to make your child's adjustment as easy for him as possible and to make sure that the new home and community will offer at least as many opportunities as the old. Looking for a roof over our heads these days is such an involved affair and it is so hard to find the home we want at the price we can afford, that sometimes we neglect to check on those intangibles that as the years go on may be much more important than a fireplace in the living room. We need to look not just at fireplaces and plumbing, school transportation and shopping centers, but also at the community as a whole. We need to see whether it is one into which we can fit happily as parents and whether it provides companions of appropriate ages for our children, space for them to play, church or temple, Scout and Brownie groups.

We want, if possible, to live in a place where his friends are accessible to our child, where he can pop out of the front door and be within hailing distance of other children, rather than have to be carted hither and thither in the family car for playtimes. If it is possible for us to set the time for moving, we want especially, if our child is under school age, to make the change in the season of the year when children play outdoors, so that our child can meet and make new friends more casually and frequently than when everybody is snowbound. We like to find, if we can, a house with a feature that especially attracts our child and makes up to him in a way for having lost the old familiar home and playmates—such as a bedroom that has more space for his hobbies, or a tree big enough for a swing, or a basement rumpus room where the gang can come after school. Sometimes the new home is an ideal one for pets whereas the old one was not. Any obvious advantage that relates particularly to the child and his interests will make him more pleased and excited about the move and also give him the important assurance that *his* feelings have been considered, too.

Preparation for the move, especially with some discussion of the child's feelings and his likes and dislikes, is important. Sometimes this is not possible, of course, but where there is time to talk about the move and some element of choice as to the new location, it makes a child feel more secure to be consulted about at least some of the things the family is looking for and considering, even though he knows that the final decision must be his parents'. Then, too, it is important for all parents, and especially for adoptive ones, not to blind themselves subconsciously to a child's immediate needs because of the long-range possibilities of a situation. In another two years, parents say, he'll be in junior high— the place will be more built up then and his friends will live nearer, and besides the outdoor barbeque will be wonderful for teen-age parties. True enough—but that can't make up for the fact that *now* is when he needs to put his roots down in the new community, now is the time when he should make the friends he will be inviting to those parties.

There is no question but that the most difficult time for children to pull up stakes is at adolescence. Especially in the first year or two of high school it is truly painful for them to break out of the circle of their "crowd." If it must be, it must, but if it happens, parents should be prepared to be extra understanding, extra patient and watchful, while their child is trying to make his way into the new circle, which is probably just as tightly closed to newcomers as his old one was. It may take quite a while for him to become accepted in the new group, especially if he is rather shy, and there is not too much that the parents can do in a concrete way to help him except to move themselves actively but not pushingly in *their* new groups, so that he can at least feel that there *is* movement between the family and the community. There are times when the parents can foster entertainment of his new acquaintances at the house, but as a rule this is delicate ground. It is far better at first to let the social aspect grow gradually and spontaneously with after-school droppings in and so on. Prepare to keep soft drinks on hand, be ready for occasional sudden dinner guests, be warm but not insistently glad-handed with the new boys and girls—and then sit back and hope for the best.

Adoptive mothers whose husbands are in the armed services are often concerned about what all the moving around will do to their child or their children. Many aspects of this kind of life—the frequency of the moves, the broken schooling, the friends made and lost and made and lost again—*are* hard on children, and there is no question that parents of adopted children must take pains to emphasize security of other kinds. A spirit of adventure and a sense of the opportunities travel offers will help a great deal. And some sense of "home" ought to be always present whether the family has alighted in a hotel room or the massively furnished wing of a granite mansion in Germany. It may not be possible to shift the family furniture wherever you go, but even if you are traveling light it is always feasible to carry a few personal things that stand for home to you and the children. A couple of family photographs, a bright scarf and a cushion or two, a pottery jar and a lacquer box are not much in themselves, but when they go where you go and always pop out of the suitcase as soon as you have your hat off, so to speak, they help create home and a sense of continuity.

Don't forget that while these many moves may be hard on your child in some ways and may demand extra wisdom from you in order for him to maintain his sense of security, if you are successful they can develop in him many personality strengths that otherwise might never have had a chance for exercise. Perhaps he *did* miss decimals when you went from Washington to Texas in the middle of the fifth grade, but decimals can always be made up, and think what he has seen meanwhile of our country and the people who live in it, perhaps of other countries and their people. And think, too, of the wonderful opportunity you are giving him to learn to enjoy meeting new situations and new faces.

The family unit which must consist of the mother left with the child or children while the father is away in military service, or earning the livelihood in some profession that requires his long and frequent absences, labors under a more serious handicap. It is almost impossible for either parent to be father and mother both. There are, however, some constructive things that the parents can do in situations like these.

The father ought to write often directly to the child, even when the letter will have to be read to him, and he can well afford to put real and concentrated effort into making these letters specific and personal. He can describe the things he is seeing on his journeys that would interest the child—pets, trains, children, bridges, bull-dozers—and even draw a sketch or two now and then, never mind how crude. And he can make use of the information the mother will be giving him in her very detailed letters about the child's current interests and the hobbies father and child have shared to-gether. He can tell him that he wants to hear the new piano piece as soon as he comes home, that he has an idea for a special kind of tower they can make together with the new erector set, that he will bring some new slides for the viewers, or new stamps for their collection. Such letters, interspersed with interesting post cards and a very occasional inexpensive gift, will do much to keep alive the contact so that Daddy doesn't seem a stranger when he does come home.

When that fine day arrives, most mothers will need to watch lest they project themselves too much into the renewal of the ac-quaintanceship between the child and his father. Let the "briefing" about health, school progress, the current stage or undesirable new habit be brief and of course conducted out of the child's hearing

—then let them go ahead and enjoy each other, with Mother joining in when she's wanted, but not hovering to make sure Daddy handles things just right.

It ought to be said that very young children—from a year and a half to three, for example—often resent the father's reappearance and won't have anything to do with him when he comes. This can, in fact, happen even when Father is home all the time: it is an age when sometimes it seems impossible for the child to be at ease with him. About all the father can do in such a case is to try to be relaxed about it, and above all not to push or force his way into the child's affections. Time, patience, and matter-of-factness will eventually turn the trick.

When fathers are away for a long time it is a good idea, especially with little boys, to try to provide some substitute for Daddy's companionship. Perhaps an uncle or a neighbor or a man teacher—somebody about Daddy's age whom they know well and like—can be counted on to come around every once in a while and play catch or fly kites or take the child to movies and ball games. Or just to visit—it doesn't matter so much what they do so long as the child enjoys and benefits from the comparative novelty of male strength and companionship and occasional male discipline. Groups that function largely or wholly under male supervision, such as swimming classes, camps, Scouts and Cub Scouts, are very valuable for the boy in this situation.

There is another kind of awayness with which we must deal sometime. It is the problem of all parents sooner or later to help their child accept the idea of death. Just how they do this depends very much not only on the child's age but also, of course, on the closeness of the relationship with the one who has died. It is to be expected that the death of the household pet will hit him harder and frighten him more than being told of the passing away of a relative whom he has seen only occasionally. But the death of a person whom he knows well and sees often may shock an older child deeply. When children are quite small—under four, say—the idea of death doesn't mean very much to them, even though they may ask questions about it and may seem to accept the answers. As they grow older, periods of real concern and anxiety about it, including the realization that it may happen to their parents and even to them someday, alternate with spells of such matter-of-factness that their attitudes may seem shockingly callous. Children of seven and eight, and often at other ages, too, are full of what may appear to grown-ups a morbid interest in what happens after a person is "put in the box." They are wont, for example, to have elaborate funerals for dead birds and other animals, and it is not uncommon for curiosity to lead to digging them up again some days later. It is hard for parents not to be shocked about things like this, but unless the morbidity persists and seems to have an overtone of real anxiety, parents should try to accept it as a natural step in learning about death. Remember that it takes a long, long time for children to really understand and accept the fact that death puts a positive stop to action, that when a person or animal is dead, it isn't just "asleep" but can no longer walk or eat or even breathe. But as a rule by the time the child is ten or eleven he is able to grasp the idea of death and accept it more or less philosophically.

It is kindest and wisest, however, not to just sit back and wait for this understanding to grow of itself, but to prepare your child gradually in occasional talks about death. Here, as with sex instruction, if questions do not come voluntarily—and they may well not—you can perhaps pick them up in his play and his play talk and judge from them what his questions might be if he did put them into words. You will want to move very slowly and not tell him more than he is ready for. He needs plenty of time to digest each bit of information. Usually it is enough at first just to answer honestly his one or two questions and show him you are ready to answer others any time he wants to talk about it. Sometimes it is best to make just one observation in line with his interest—"Yes, the goldfish was dead. He couldn't swim around any more, could he?"—and let him pick up from there either then or later.

Above all, be honest with him. It is kinder to tell him when he asks why his baby sitter doesn't come any more, to say, "Mrs. Bender died, dear, like the little kitten did, so we won't see her any more," than to tell him that she went on a trip or moved away. For if he is very young, the fact will probably not disturb him greatly, and if he is older, the straightforward telling will not only help to prepare him for a time when death may come closer but also will show him that he can depend on you to tell him the truth. For with death, as with other crises that come to a family, his natural anxiety will be lessened if he knows what is going on. For this reason it is best when a death is expected to prepare a child for it as gently as you can rather than to let it come as a shocking surprise. It may seem hard to do this, but if you can manage it you will find that it makes things easier for him, and also for you. Naturally you will not want to harp on it, but a couple of discussions and very occasional references to it will dilute and reduce the intensity of his fear and grief—and also of your own.

Perhaps the most important single thing to remember in helping children—and especially adopted children—find a wholesome acceptance of the death of someone near and dear is to make sure that they do not retain any belief that that death was in some way caused by them. To feel guilty when someone close to us dies is a deep and natural reaction. All of us willy-nilly add to our load of real grief a good-sized heap of remorse. How we wish we had been warmer, more sympathetic, less engrossed in our own affairs! How we wish we hadn't been so snappish about Grandma's way of canning tomatoes, that we had been less impatient with Grandfather and his hypochondria! As a rule this is needless: probably we have done pretty well. Family life has to have its up and downs, generations must disagree about ways of doing things, and no doubt Grandma and Grandfather, too, reproached themselves for many things every time death deprived them of someone. Eventually, we are able to accept this and to go on as we must go on. But a child's understanding is limited; he is bound to misinterpret much of what he sees and hears. And he is accustomed not only to feeling but to expressing his natural and frequent bursts of anger and frustration. "I hate you!" he often says to the grownup he loves the very best. Sometimes he cries, "I wish you were dead, you old *thing,* you!" And so for years he may blame himself because he remembers yesterday's rudeness to Grandma not just remorsefully, which would be painful enough, but in panic because he thinks maybe that was what made her die. He was told so often to be good for Grandma, and he knows he was bad. He was so angry he wished for a minute something would happen to her. And then something did. So it must be his fault.

Sometimes comments made at the time can be wholly misinterpreted even by an older child. My friend Jenny carried such a burden for years. She and her little brother had been roughhousing amiably with Uncle Joe just before supper, and the next morning they were told that during the night Uncle Joe had died of a heart attack. The news hit Jenny like a blow: perhaps the roughhousing had done it. He started it, and she hadn't known he had a heart condition—all the same, she couldn't help blaming herself. As a matter of fact, Uncle Joe had known for many years that he had a bad heart. He had been warned to take it easy, not to work. But Jenny didn't know this. And so she interpreted as applying to the roughhousing the many remarks of sympathetic callers to the effect that, "He should have known it would be too much for him." It never occurred to Jenny's parents that she was taking these comments so personally. It was not until Jenny was in her late teens that she was able to talk to the doctor who attended Uncle Joe and learn that the mild romping probably had had nothing to do with the attack that carried him off. He was even able to lead her to see that even if it had, it was not a ten-year-old child's responsibility, and that Uncle Joe not only wanted but probably benefited by the laughing relaxation with the children he loved. If only Jenny's parents had guessed her feelings at the time and had reassured her, she would have been saved years of self-reproach.

So when death comes to your family, if your child is beyond babyhood and especially if he is adopted, lead him to talk about it with you and make as sure as you can, without overinsistence, that he is not harking back to some piece of naughtiness or freshness and reproaching himself with it. Naturally, you won't want to put any ideas into his head that aren't there, but if at such a time he shows in word or act that he is feeling guilty, or ashamed, it is safest to make it crystal clear that nothing he said or did had anything to do with the dying. Tell him that whenever a person dies everybody wishes that they had been nicer—but that everybody's angry feelings come out now and again. So there *never* is anybody anywhere in any family who can truthfully say, "Well, I'm certainly glad I was always good and always nice and never got mad at him."

This clearing away of possible self-blame is especially important, of course, if it is a parent whom death takes away. Fathers and mothers, in the very nature of things, have to represent so many frustrations to their children that it's almost a reflex action for a child to accuse himself instantly of having caused that death by his tantrum of yesterday or his shouting defiance of last week. It is essential for the parent who is left to make sure such feelings of guilt are not allowed to fester.

Again, although it is an easy thing to overlook at such a time, a child must be allowed to share in the mourning to a certain degree, depending on his age. By this we do not mean that he must be subjected to all the sorrow in its every grim detail nor that he should be expected to be silent and subdued all the time, but simply that he not be ignored or brushed aside, made to feel that the house is full of secrets. If he is old enough to go to the funeral and if he wants to, let him, explaining to him first about the proceedings so that he won't feel totally at sea by not knowing what is expected of him. If he is too young to go or if he does not want to go, it is well to take a little time to reassure him that his not going is all right, is an accepted thing, and no one will think it strange. Above all, try not to let him have the feeling that all this is not his business, that he is expected to just wait quietly until it's all over. Don't subject him to scene after emotional scene, but don't feel you must keep a stonily cheerful face always before him, either. This, after all, is the family's grief, and he is an important part of the family; he must be allowed to share the grieving in a healthy way. This is particularly important for the adopted child who, even though he is quite small, may feel doubly deserted and doubly guilty if at such a time he feels pushed outside of the family and denied the right to mourn.

When an adopted child loses a parent, it is even more important for him than it is for the biological child to be allowed and encouraged to keep the memory of that parent alive—not in a maudlin or sentimental fashion, but in a wholesome way. The parent who is left will want casually and without insistence to keep the other one a loving and remembered person. A father may smilingly tell his daughter that she has her mother's laugh, or her mother's way with flowers; a mother may say to her boy that he has his father's knack of making visitors feel at home. It is well, of course, never to say things like these unless you really mean them, and not to overdo it. It is too easy that way to slip into the habit of implying—or even saying—that the child is taking the dead parent's place, is being a "little mother," or being "the man of the family now." This is a convention it is best to stay away from, for a child feels every bit of the weight of such a responsibility, much more than you mean him to feel, and it makes him more anxious and more afraid. He is not a husband and father, she is not a wife and mother: they are children still, and it isn't fair or wise to make them carry a burden so far beyond their years.

What about adopted children and divorce? Remembering how our adopted child has been deserted once before, and remembering on top of that our fond reassurances to him that we wanted *him,* wanted to be his real Mommy and Daddy, it frightens us to think what the revelation that he isn't to have a whole family any more may do to him. And rightly so. For there isn't a doubt in the world that adopted children suffer more when their parents are separated or divorced than do biological children.

Does this, then, mean that their suffering can't be alleviated?

Does it mean that at all costs we must keep the family together or destroy the child? No, because it is just as true of adoptive as of biological children that a loveless home, a home full of anger and hate either given free rein to in loud quarreling or suppressed behind masks of cold politeness, is every bit as bad for them as a broken home—and often worse. If the parents must separate and if the child is told why, this is at least a reality, something he can get hold of and learn to live with.

For the tendency of any child—and it is far more powerful in the case of the adopted child—is to blame himself for his parents' not getting on. Indeed, it often happens that there is perfectly good logic behind this, as in the many situations where his behavior and upbringing have served as the handiest bone of contention for his unhappy parents to lay hold of. In addition, the parents, distracted by their emotional problems and often by their inability to come to a decision, are likely to be giving vent to irritation far more readily than they used to and making him feel that they don't like him any more. Sometimes crossness and impatience are alternated with bursts of wild and tearful affection—which only serves to confuse him utterly. The child always knows far sooner than the parents guess he does that something is seriously wrong. He needs to know just what is going on.

When parents first begin to realize that they are in such straits that separation and possibly divorce are to be seriously considered, they will want, for the child's sake if not for their own, to make sure before they discuss it with him that there is no other way out. They will want to give themselves time—time to see if, after all, they cannot settle their own difficulties, time to see if experienced outside counsel can help them to do this. If they have honestly tried to mend the situation and the breakup of the home still seems the only way out, then it is time to tell the child the truth. He needs to hear his parents put into simple, honest words the fact that they are not getting along any more, that they are too often angry with each other. If the parents are planning on a trial separation, they will want to tell the child that they are going to try living apart for a while in the hope that they can straighten things out. If, on the other hand, a divorce is definitely afoot, he must not be led to believe that this is a temporary living apart, that things will some-day be as they were. Don't, don't deceive him—your stake is great in this. If plans are still unsettled as to where you will live, whether he is to stay with Father or Mother, this, too, the parents must tell him, emphasizing always that they are trying to make the best arrangements for *all* of them, and that this is not easy to do. Along with giving him the facts, or such of them as they know, the parents must take pains to reassure the child, probably many times, that this state of affairs is not caused by him or anything he did, and that both Daddy and Mommy still love him. If it has been one of those situations where the child *has* been the focus of many disagreements and knows it (as he practically always does), the parents will want to go a step further and say to him that al-though they did fight a lot about him, it was because they were angry anyway: if they hadn't fought about him, they would have fought about something else.

If you as adoptive parents find yourselves in this turmoil of impending divorce or separation, you should be prepared for some of your emotions *as* adoptive parents to complicate further the con-fusing emotional currents to which all divorcing parents are sub-ject. Every husband and every wife in this situation feels resent-ment, and hurt, and above all, wherever children are concerned, guilt—acknowledged and unacknowledged. In your case there is extra guilt, a double helping, first because of that deep-down but now reawakened feeling that you first "failed" in your marriage when you were unable to become parents in the way in which most people do, and second because of the knowledge that although you cannot help it you are contributing to the second abandonment, as it were, of the child you then adopted. But you can help your-selves a great deal if you acknowledge that these feelings are there, and that they make it harder for you to see things as they are, to deal as wisely and lovingly with your child's emotions as you wish you could. But try to remember that in putting forth a consistent and constructive effort to plan a "good" divorce for the child, to make as healthy a breakup as possible since breakup there must be, you will be helping yourselves, too. You will find that in seeking sound ways to allay his anxiety, his resentment, you do much to allay your own.

A final caution: be ready for quite a lot of hostility on the part of your child, especially if he is young or in his middle years. His very first reaction may be a complete refusal to accept the situation. This is understandable—he wants both parents, and he will not hear of any other arrangement. You will probably have to tell him a good many times that this is the way things must be, that you are trying to work things out in the way that is best for everybody—for Daddy and Mommy and for him. Of course this is a time when in all your discussions with him you will want to be kind and gentle rather than punitive, but it is important to remember that it is a time when you must also be firm. You are sorry things must be this way, you understand how he feels, and you are prepared to accept some of his anger; but for his own sake you must set limits to this. Don't ask for the role of scapegoat, don't let him say things he later will be truly sorry for or feel guilty about.

In these situations the adoptive parents and their child are undoubtedly subject to disturbing special stress. When these are added to the deep emotional turmoil that must accompany any divorce, the accumulation can seem overwhelming. For this reason it is often wisest to seek special counsel even though there is no question but that separation or divorce must go through. A good marriage counselor or psychologist or psychiatrist can help you keep the situation on an even keel, can be a safety valve for those bewildering resentments and frustrations, can help ease those extra emotional storms which the adoptive factor sets in motion. And he can guide you to the best way to prepare your child for the break and keep him strong in spite of it.

Above all, try not to feel guilty yourselves because this unhappy situation has come about. It is not the end of the world for you and your child. You can and you will handle matters in such a way that he may come out of this experience far healthier and stronger emotionally than if you endeavored to keep intact for him a set of parents who are enemies or, worse still, polite strangers. This is the real abandonment, the real rejection. If your honesty and your courage now can make him feel that he is still truly loved by a father and mother who simply made a mistake, he can feel accepted and worthwhile. He still has a real mother and a real father, even though it happens that the four walls of home don't hold them together any more.

10 A Talisman for Adoptive Parents

When does adoption begin? When do adoptive parents really start to build their families? In one sense, of course, the beginning is the day of the legal adoption, when society and the law put their seal of approval on this special relationship. That important and moving ceremony puts into the parents' hands once and for all the final authority and the final responsibility.

But most parents feel that the real beginning is the day they bring their baby home. And they are right, for it is then that the child really joins the family. It is then that the family starts being built.

All families build, as the children and parents mature, as personalities take shape, relationships form and re-form, but an adoptive family builds in a very special sense and in a special way. Its cornerstone is the father's and mother's acceptance of the fact of adoption; their knowledge that the emotional overtones inherent in that very situation will be continuously significant, is the cement that holds all the other stones together.

This child is now yours, for better or worse, for richer or poorer, in sickness or in health—in most ways just as much yours as if he had been born to you. You are proud of him, you feel humble and lucky and grateful to have been given him. Chubby or lanky, placid or bouncy, quick or slow, he's just like other children—except that he has a certain plus value.

He was adopted. He has another father and another mother. He was not born from inside of you, his real mother. You know all this now; he will know it later. Day by day and bit by bit you *become* his real parents and he your real child, so much so that you will often forget that he came to you in any way but by birth. But he did. And if you gratify the very human tendency to deny this, if you pretend too hard, you are endangering the family's stability just as much as if you *never* lost sight of it, never let yourselves forget it.

Adoption is an artificial situation and it creates families in an artificial way. This does not mean that the family you are making is less good than your mother's or your friend's or Mrs. Baker's biological family—or any better. It's just different. It's best not to sidle away from that, for it's a fact. Look at it. Try to accept it, assimilate it, examine it from all angles until you can feel relaxed about it, just as you tried to do when you were screening yourselves for adoption.

For the deeper and calmer this basic acceptance is, the more secure and confident you will be as parents. Make up your minds that as adoptive parents your job will be different and probably harder than the job all other parents hand themselves. You are handicapping yourselves if you pretend, even secretly, that you are biological parents. Any doubts deep inside, feelings of unworthiness because you may happen to be unable to be biological parents, can make you so insecure in the situation that you look for trouble where none is (and consequently create it), or go so far in denying the reality that you may make your child feel unwanted even as you conscientiously tell him about his adoption in the accepted words at the recommended age. But with honesty, common sense, and the wish to succeed you can do it.

All parents feel from time to time in the bringing up of their children that over some undefined abyss they are teetering on a narrow plank between the "right way" and the "wrong way." Adoptive parents sometimes feel as if the plank were a tightrope! And it *is* like tightrope walking in a way, this job of bringing up an adopted child. It's a real challenge. The chasm below is as deep, the scenery much the same, the journey about as long. But the footing is just a little more precarious, the balance just a bit harder to maintain.

There is a talisman for parents highheartedly setting out on this adventure. Those wise and experienced in the rewards and trials of adoption counsel: "Always remember he's your own—and never forget he's adopted."[9]

"Always remember he's your own . . ." He *is,* now. And you are his. Just as much as if he'd been born to you, you will both rejoice in his health and his growing, worry when he's ill, repeat his funny sayings and show off his snapshots, be humanly exasperated when he misbehaves. Almost at once, or in a very few days, you will beam like any other new parent at the visiting relatives and friends. The idea of *not* having him will be quite unthinkable.

As witness a woman who brought home her adopted baby on the day her husband lost his job—at a time when jobs were not easy to get. A friend said, "Why, I *know* if you called the agency they'd take her back! Just explain what happened!" "Take her back!" the woman exclaimed. "Why, we wouldn't dream of such a thing! Suppose I'd had her in the hospital, and John lost his job the day we brought her home—would I want to send her back? It'll be hard sledding for a while, but we'll just have to take the rough with the smooth together!"

And so you do—you all take the bad breaks when and if they come just as everybody has to. You *may* have some bad ones. So do biological families. I can think of a delightful family with three happy, healthy children. The youngest, just walking, has been found to be congenitally deaf. He will have to start special training right away.

I think of twin boys, as strong and well and attractive as their older sister, but blind from early infancy. They are going to a special school, and are happy and well adjusted, but the worry and

9. For this thought the author is indebted to Dorothy Hutchinson (who at the time the book was first published, was Professor of Social Work, New York School of Social Work) who said, "In all successful adoptions the adoptive parents make the child their own and at the same time can acknowledge that he is adopted."

financial burden have been and will continue to be a strain on
the parents. I think, too, of a mentally defective child, the second
oldest and the only boy in an otherwise normal family of four normal children, who has been in a special home since he was five. All
of these situations have meant difficult adjustments on the part of
the parents, who in each case have worked out the best solution
possible.

These tragedies can and do occur with "own" children as well
as adopted. But when a similar misfortune turns up in an adoptive
family, people are likely to lose sight of that fact, and to focus
all their attention on the fact of the adoption itself.

If, as very seldom happens, an extremely serious condition develops in your adopted baby, one that calls for institutionalization
and years of expensive care, judges and agencies agree that adoptive
parents should not be penalized emotionally and financially by
assuming the entire burden of the care of this child with whom
they have hardly had time to get acquainted. The cost will usually
be met in part or in whole by the state, and the agency will place
a healthy baby with the parents as quickly as they can. Nor is
there any reason for the parents to feel guilty about having re-
linquished the first baby.

In such a case, of course, you would take time to make as sure
as you can that this is the right decision for you and for him. I
know of one pretty little adopted girl who seemed so slow in walking and talking, so behind-hand in everything, though happy and
sweet-natured, that her worried parents had her undergo an ex-
haustive series of tests, both physical and mental. Physically she was
fine, but mentally, they were told on the best authority, she would
never advance beyond the age of three or so. She appeared to be
a mental defective, and their wisest course would be, they were
told, to return her to the agency. Heartbroken, they did, and
almost immediately they bitterly regretted it. The distraught parents
felt they could not give her up, no matter what happened; they
would rather have her the way she was, and take on the unremitting
care that would be necessary, than not have her at all. So they

took her back, and loved her and cherished her even more tenderly than before. And how did it all turn out? Well, she is now a happy, helpful, affectionate girl of eleven; no one would know to look at her and talk to her that she is several grades behind her age. Schoolwork is not easy for her; she needs a great deal of help with it, and high school, if she gets there, may prove to be too much for her. But the parents don't care; they are as proud of her as if she were a gold-star scholar, and so is their old family doctor, who said all along that she would turn out all right, "just needed to take her time and drink up lots of loving."

So, again, always remember your adopted child is your own— just the way he is. You can help him in many ways to be his best self, but you can't make him over into something he isn't—and you don't want to. Just as your biological daughter might turn out to have a bit more of her grandfather's stubbornness than you might have put in if you were doing the mixing, your adopted daughter may turn out to be a little more aggressive than your ideal. Or maybe a bit too much on the dreamier side, not enough of a doer. Maybe she will coordinate poorly, when you'd hoped for a third sports enthusiast in the family. Well, let her be the way she is. Respect her abilities whatever they may be, guide her whenever you can, understand her, and help *her* make the best of what *she* has to work with.

And remember *you* are not capable of being perfect, either. All mothers and all fathers are people, with flaws and blind spots and petty vanities. Nobody can be right and unruffled all the time. Flashes of insight will alternate with baffled bewilderment, confidence of handling with black misgivings. Most parents today have become a little on the defensive from the recent bombardment of blame showered on them from schools, from churches, from psychologists, from law-enforcement officials, from just about everybody. It is perhaps only natural that adoptive parents feel even more on the defensive; for emotionally, if illogically, these parents feel as if they must continually *prove* themselves fit to bring up the child they have been given, that they can afford to make no mistakes. They are also likely to be unusually sensitive to criticism. Now and then, sometimes in imagination, sometimes in reality, they encounter the implication that a "real" mother is an instinctive mother—that adoptive parents are automatically less skilled. So to parents who may feel a little dubious of their capabilities for this job—just remember he's *your* child, and no mother or father ever lived who did not make mistakes along the line. You two are certainly not going to be the exceptions.

And he *is* your own. What's yours is his now: the medal Daddy's grandfather won in the Indian wars, your collection of glass animals, Grandmother's recipe for baked beans, the Bible Daddy was awarded in Sunday School. Family jokes and sayings, your special ways at Christmastime, the living grandparents and aunts and uncles, the yellowed snapshots of Mommy and Daddy as children—all these are part of his family tradition now, and will become more so each year you live together. In the long run it will not matter that you know and he knows he had had other parents and grandparents; he's more than willing to take yours on as if they had been his, if you will, without insistence but naturally and lovingly, help him feel that this new nest is a strong one, and a warm and cozy one as well.

It is amazing, too, how quickly and how easily you will feel your child always *has* been yours, how natural it is to exclaim to your husband, for example, "Now if that isn't your father all over again! Isn't it, Harry!" without stopping to think that whoever it is all over again, it isn't Harry's father. With our own adopted boy I found myself thinking more than once, "Well, maybe he is going to be left-handed. After all, I am. . . ." Amazingly strong family resemblances often come about too, partly because the baby probably came from very similar racial strains, partly for the same reason that married people grow to look like each other—love and close association. Just about as often the adopted child bears little resemblance to either new parent—and this can happen in bio-logical families, too. Anna Perott Rose tells with delight in *Room For One More,* her heartwarming account of the raising of her three own and three foster children, about the stranger who approached her on the beach after several days of speculating on which child was which. She knew the little blond girl couldn't be theirs because Mrs. Rose and her husband were dark and she wasn't a bit like them, and of course she knew the little dark one was theirs because he was the very image of his father. She couldn't decide about the others—would Mrs. Rose please set her straight? Actually the little blond girl was their very own oldest daughter, and the little dark one was their "ready-made" boy, a miserably underprivileged little fellow (until he landed with them!) who came from a very bad background indeed!

"And never forget he's adopted." This is the other end of your balancing pole, or, to use a simpler metaphor, the second side of the adoptive parents' talisman. And it's just as important as the other half. "Always remember he's your own."

Let us first understand that when we say "Never forget" we hardly mean it in the literal sense. Nothing could be less conducive to a relaxed and loving relationship than steeling yourselves to remember every day and every minute that he's not your biological offspring. If you are continually anxious and concerned about this, and about how he may sooner or later regard it, you cannot help infecting him with your anxieties and fears. He will be bound to come to the conclusion that there must be something quite peculiar and uncomfortable about being adopted. The same thing is likely to happen if you go around reminding others that he is adopted. Not many people do this, but some do. Occasionally an adoptive parent (mothers particularly are inclined to do this) cannot resist exclaiming in delight each time the child's strong resemblance to his father is commented on, "And he's adopted, you know!" More often, people, just from a sense of honesty, volunteer the information at every turn—to the barber, to the policeman who helps the children across the street, to the piano teacher. Even though it may be done in a proud and happy way, it isn't wise. It's overemphasis. Remember that the entire community will take its attitude from your own. Your friends and neighbors will, of course, know that your child is adopted, and they will be interested and pleased. After the first excitement is over, and your baby is taken for granted just as are the other new babies on the block, you want your relatives, your friends, your child's friends, the tradesmen, the milkman, the policeman, to be as casual and relaxed and matter of course as you are about this relationship. And they will be, if you don't go around stressing it.

In spite of the fact that many parents seem to have done it successfully (or is it only "seem"?), I think that an annual "adoption day" with cake and candles like a birthday is unwise. It sets the child apart from his contemporaries. It makes him different. *Birthday* parties are what everyone else has, and what your child will want to have, too. Far better, I'd say, to celebrate the birthday with pomp and circumstance, as families ordinarily do, than to remind him annually, in a very separate way, that he did not come into your family by birth. Another disadvantage of an "adoption day" that people don't stop to consider in babyhood days is: when do you stop? Even though it may by then have become strictly a family celebration, many adolescents, no matter how well adjusted, would take a pretty dim view of an "adoption-day cake"; they would prefer to skip it. And yet, such is the prickly nature of the teenager, if you, his parents, seemed to decide it was an outworn family tradition, he might perversely wonder if that meant you were bored with him!

So what do we mean when we say, "Never forget he's adopted?" Two things, really: to make sure that he knows it and is comfortable with it, and to be aware yourselves that this fact of adoption may *sometimes* color your, and his, reactions to otherwise ordinary situations. The problems which adoptive parents face are no different from those which others have to contend with: thumb-sucking, bed-wetting, tantrums, defiance, running away. But in an adoptive family these problems have, or may have, a different connotation to both parent and child, and as a rule need a different kind of handling.

A very good "for instance" is the experience of friends with their adopted boy and the puppy that all three picked out at the animal shelter on the boy's eighth birthday. A year or more later they were nearly distracted with the problems that the dog, Skipper, presented. They'd gambled on a smallish dog—he grew to boxer size. They had hoped he'd be on the quiet, gentle side—he was tremendously powerful, very stubborn, and quite high-strung. (He'd turned out to have mange when they got him, and the vet insisted the poor dog was neurotic.) Affectionate and devoted he was, and the family was very much attached to him. But the boy, though he tried to hide it, was afraid of him, as were the many small children on the street, so the dog had to be always on a leash, which made him thoroughly unhappy and which left all the dog-walking to the grownups, as he was too strong for any child to control. The boy was no fun for the dog and vice-versa; besides, everybody (except the dog) had agreed that the boy was old enough to assume most of the animal's care.

Problems these, but no insurmountable ones, for they all loved Skipper and he loved them. But as time went on it seemed obvious that he was too much dog for the little house. He would pop out of it like a jack-in-the-box at every opportunity, bowling over the arriving guests and knocking down toddlers like ninepins. It seemed that Skipper would be happier in a place where he could run, and a big farm was found where he would be loved and be as free as he needed to be. The parents discussed this very gently and carefully with their boy, not once but several times. He obviously felt that Skipper *would* be happier on the farm. He seemed somewhat reluctant, but no more, they thought, than was natural; though downcast at the thought of losing Skipper, he appeared quite mature in his reactions. But one day, while arrangements were being made, the parents faced the reality they hadn't really faced before, and found they just couldn't let Skipper go, however logical the solution. They loved him too much—he was part of the family. He'd just have to stay with them and make the best of it. When they told their child of this change of mind, his relief was literally hysterical. It was perfectly obvious that way down underneath he had felt that what was going to happen to the dog they had all "picked out" to come and live with them might, happen to him!

What those few weeks took out of the boy is only to be guessed at—and it all could have been prevented if the parents had been *aware,* if they hadn't "forgotten" their boy was adopted! "Own" children might have been disturbed at the loss of their dog, more or less deeply according to their temperaments, but there would be no reason for any parallel to strike them.

Adoptive parents have to learn that often, but not always, their emotions and those of their child may be interpreted in terms of the adoption. Situations continually arise in which they must be aware of the possibility of undercurrents, as in the instance just given. And it is just as important to know that they will have to guard against looking for whirlpools when the stream is actually flowing a placid course.

Maintaining this balanced awareness would be a great deal easier, as would many relationships in this world, if we could momentarily change places with our child, just to keep in touch. We can't really remember what it is like to be a child. Some of the times we felt afraid or threatened we may recall, but most of them we have succeeded in burying deep. But if it were possible to be part of the children's world again, how quickly we should feel the difference! And feeling differently, how differently we should act and speak! But since turning ourselves into children again is impossible, we must just do the best we can, especially in adoptive parenthood, to observe, to listen, and to weigh, remembering that on this occasion there may be real fear or resentment centering around the adoption, on that occasion there may be nothing more than a perfectly normal reaction.

Don't forget that not only your child's feelings but your own are bound to be affected by the knowledge that yours is an adoptive situation. Sometimes it is to a small degree, just a faint flick across your consciousness, a split second of doubt of uncertainty. Sometimes it's a temporary loss of perspective, wherein you complicate an ordinary behavior problem common to dozens of children, own and adopted, with the questions, "What have we done wrong? Did we cause this?"

A mother who has one biological and one adopted child, and so is in an excellent position to compare both kinds of motherhood, told me about an episode which illuminated for her quite suddenly and brilliantly the typical "reflex," we may call it, of the adoptive parent.

It happened one rainy day when five-year-old Ronnie, the biological child, and Benjie, the adopted one, who was almost two, had a spat. Tempers sparked suddenly, and Ronnie ran to his mother and shouted, "He's no good! Why don't you take him back?"

For a split second the mother was heartsick. Was this the companionship she had thought so solid? Had Ronnie all along, perhaps, in his own mind put the baby on probation? Take him back! Was it for this they had talked so warmly of adoption, bent over backward to leave Ronnie no reason for jealousy, and been so delighted at his warmhearted acceptance of the child?

Luckily, her common sense came quickly to her aid. She realized that in families up and down the land this scene takes place. The novelty of the baby has worn off, and the fact that the older child can no longer always have his way keeps looming large. Everything was much nicer before the baby came. Therefore, take him back. The phrase bore no relation in the child's mind to adoption. Like older brothers and sisters everywhere, at that moment he only wished the baby to be subtracted from the household, and it was the *mother's* awareness that the baby was adopted that made her read too much into words that *any* child would have used.

A period when children's hostility is likely to be misinterpreted by parents and child alike is adolescence. Many "own" parents can honestly confess to deep hurt when their children have arrived at this tumultuous stage with its seeming contempt for all the family stands for, its selfishness and withdrawal, its broodiness and irritability. When biological parents feel rejected and pushed aside at this stage of the game, how much more so the adoptive parents, who can't help wondering whether their child treats them this way because he feels unwanted, because in some way they have not measured up as "real" parents may have done. Bobby next door may be just as offensive at this stage of his growing-up as your Tom, and Janet across the street may be every bit as openly scornful of her mother's ideas as Ann is of yours. But at least Bobby's and Janet's parents, however concerned and temporarily discouraged they may be, just don't wonder whether things might be going more smoothly had they conceived and given birth to their difficult offspring!

As a matter of fact, it is more than possible that all four of these children, own and adopted, may have fantasies about their "real" parents. It is a very common thing (think back—very likely it happened to *you!*) for an adolescent to fancy that he is actually the child of distinguished, handsome parents who, for some unknown but surely romantic and dramatic reason, were obliged to turn him over to another family for raising. Someday they will come to claim him, in a long, glistening car, amid gratifying publicity. It makes no difference whether or not he was actually born to the parents he has now and knows it beyond a doubt. He feels that they are of far less sensitive clay. They don't understand him, don't appreciate his sensibilities. They are continually outraging his deepest feelings, on the one hand doubting his ability to manage his own affairs, and on the other expecting of him the judgment of a Solomon. They have no idea, apparently, of what goes on in his head and in his heart. How *could* they be his real parents?

Of course, all this is usually in the realm of day-dreaming, a sort of narcotic fantasy, and is outgrown quite quickly. You can imagine, however, how much more validity this little dream of glory assumes when the adolescent *is* adopted, when he ponders that somewhere in the world, maybe in the next town or even on the next street, his real mother may be going about her business, unconscious of his nearness and his need for somebody who *really* understands him. Unlike the biological child, he has just enough basis for this daydream to make it more real and more disturbing to him, and to lend to his natural temporary rejection of his parents a knife edge—with which they are very likely to wound themselves needlessly, solely on account of the adoptive situation.

Again, the whole area of discipline—the *how* of being authoritative—is affected to a greater or lesser degree by the child's adoptive status, and by his and his parents' consciousness of it. Most parents try to steer a middle course between being too harsh and too soft. They know that overstrictness on their part may breed feelings of resentment and inadequacy in their children, just as they know that, on the other hand, too much leniency not only leaves the child without the guidance he both needs and wants, but also will create in him the very same destructive feelings. This balancing of discipline, which is hard enough for any parent, is doubly difficult for the adoptive family. Lack of sureness, unconscious pity, a fear that a mistake or two may be disastrous, and above all a strong if unacknowledged wish so to arrange matters that the child may never want to lay any unhappiness at the door of his adopted mother and father make a consistent and strong approach to discipline just a bit harder for the adoptive parents.

I am inclined to believe that most such parents, when they err, err on the side of permissiveness. This is especially so when the youngster outgrows childhood and his world expands beyond the family and its do's and don'ts. His parents see him taking his place among his contemporaries, like them an adult in the rough, a baffling mixture of articulate and secretive, callous and loving, rambunctious and fearful. They watch him with pride and with anxiety, too. Subconsciously they may feel that there is one thing his contemporaries have that they can never give him, and they may try to put their consciences at ease by letting him have more freedom than he is ready for, or by giving him more "things" than are good for him. Or they may be fearful lest *he* feel this distinction between himself and his friends, and so overindulge him in a subconscious wish to prove to him that he is no less well off for all that he was "chosen" instead of being born into their family.

As we have said, the problems of all parents are much the same, but it is very easy for adoptive parents to be so conscious of their difference from biological families that they can distort a normal situation quite out of focus. For example, many an "own" child has been known to rush off to a neighbor after a scolding and announce that he hates his mother and is going to find another one. Nobody thinks anything of it. It is the adoptive mother who in this situation may find it easy to lose her perspective. She is likely to feel unduly mortified and embarrassed, and the unfortunate part of it is that her child will be on the receiving end of her reactions, whether these are highly punitive out of wounded vanity or whether they are overprotective and sentimental because of an unwarranted sense of guilt.

Often the method of handling an ordinary problem is affected—or ought to be—by the fact that the child is adopted. For instance, running away is a common problem, and one that is often dealt with—not always successfully—in a permissive way. Here is Davey, an only child of seven, very secure in his parents' love, healthy and happy since babyhood. Neither he nor his parents need worry about adoption as a factor in his or their behavior, for he is, as it happens, their biological child. Right now, however, his world is all out of kilter. His parents' standards are perhaps a little rigid, and when he comes home from school cross and cranky from the still-difficult job of adjusting to the ways of the group and the teacher, he needs a little approval, a boost to his confidence. It is hard when he finds his mother engrossed in the dress she is cutting out. It is harder still to find that she *does* have time to step on him for slamming the door and throwing his jacket on the stairs. Later he is rebuked for not coming home from play on time. At supper his table manners are criticized. Daddy and Mommy haven't the slightest intention of badgering him; their comments are routine. They just have forgotten how hard it is to be seven, and how much teasing he has already taken today from Pete and Janie and Mike. So on this particular Thursday they are aghast when, red-faced and in tears, Davey slaps his spoon into his custard and

says, "I hate you! I hate you both! I'm going far away from here!
I don't want to live with you any more!" Immediate efforts to quiet
the storm meet with failure and Davey tears upstairs still shouting. Bangs and door-slammings accompany the angry monologue.

Daddy and Mommy belatedly realize that they have torn their
child down when he needed building up, that what he is really saying to them is, "You don't love *me* any more! You don't *want* me
here!" Upstairs they go, and while he sobbingly gathers up pajamas
and toothbrush and paper bag, they do their best to make the
peace, to assure him that they do love him and do want him. They
love him all they can without mussing up his dignity. Still he is un-
convinced; he seems incapable of unwinding. They offer to help him
pack. Daddy finds his slippers under the bed and Mommy gets her
little overnight bag. All the while they make it clear, over and
over, that they *do* want him, they always will want him. If he
wants to leave, they won't make him stay, but they do so hope he
will change his mind and come back, no matter how late it is. And—
it is to be hoped—within an hour of his departure in peeps a tear-
streaked Davey, already tired of his fling, and only too glad to see
the lights of home and to be put lovingly to bed.

This is not to recommend such a procedure. It has been used,
and it may work, depending on the age of the child and his temperament (notably, the amount of stubbornness in his make-up), the
neighborhood, the hour and season, and lots of other things. But
especially with an adopted child, such a method of dealing with
hostility is distinctly danger-ridden. For his greatest fear, conscious
or otherwise, is that he may really *not* be wanted. He knows that
he and his first mother were somehow removed from each other,
and to a varying degree, according to his age, deep inside he may
feel hurt about this. If you help him to run away, therefore, no
amount of telling him how much you love him can alter the fact
that you are apparently willing to see him go. And to put him in
the position of having to decide whether to go or stay is asking entirely too much of him.

It ought to be, and I should like to think it is, unnecessary to point out how cruel it is to punish an adopted child by a threat to "send him back." Believe it or not, people have been known to say this, people you would not think capable of it, out of rage or temper or frustration. The damage this might do to an insecure, sensitive child is obvious and appalling; even a quite well adjusted little extrovert might feel his world sway beneath him if such a possibility took shape in words.

Far better in all these eventualities—with adopted children as well as with biological—to help your child to talk about how he feels, and show him that you accept those feelings, just as he is learning to accept yours when you are tired and nervous. Let him understand that you know everybody has angry feelings, fathers and mothers as well as children, and that nobody is angry with him just for having them, but only wants to help him straighten out what is wrong. What you want most is to have him feel that he is a part of the family, and that you accept him with all his good and bad feelings—just as he accepts you two with yours. That's what you must manage with any child, in order to help him achieve his best self. The only difference here is that it may be harder for your adopted child to be sure of his acceptance than a "born" one—and so it never does any harm to stress that in *all* families everybody gets out of sorts at one time or another, and that it is part of being a family.

But we say again, never forgetting that he's adopted does not mean to fret and worry and wonder as if he and you were struggling under the handicap of the ages. It simply means that while you yourself must be on guard against remembering it too often and too quickly, you must also protect your child in many situations where a biological child might not be disturbed, and make as sure as you can, every step of the way, that he feels secure and wanted, and that he knows you like him not just because you "chose" him, but because he's a likable person.

Now that we have seen some of the ways in which each applies to the function of child raising in the adoptive family, let us put the two halves of our talisman together: "Always remember he's your own, and never forget he's adopted."

If you can steer your course by this saying *as a whole,* you will be well on the way to a rewarding and successful adoptive parenthood. You may find, however, that you need to guide your feeling and thinking a little more toward one side in order to compensate for a natural inclination to stress the other. For instance, you may find that you tend to push the adoption into the forgotten area—or you may find that you are too often concerned and fearful about it. Either slant may be caused by your personal make-up, by your own experiences as a child, by your own security or lack of it, by the depth of your hurt at not having a child of your blood. Whatever the tendency and whatever its cause, teach yourselves to understand that reflex—"he is adopted"—so that you can make it work for you and not against you.

Parents who let it work against them become over-solicitous, fearing that their child may in the future suffer from being adopted, may feel less worthy, may feel unwanted. They probe for "hidden" conflicts. They reassure. Over and over they tell him how special he is, how happy they are that they chose him, even how much dearer to them he is just for having been adopted. Such constant concern will sooner or later awaken in the child conflicts he might never otherwise have had—not to mention the needless emotional wear and tear the parents force themselves to undergo. Parents like these remind me of an aunt who wanted to make sure I would not suffer any blow to my self-esteem from the glasses I was obliged to wear at an early age. "Never you mind about those glasses, dear," she would say almost daily. "Everybody who loves you knows there's the same sweet little girl behind them, and you won't have to wear them always." The glasses had opened up a wonderful new world to a very near-sighted little girl, who would have worn them happily and unselfconsciously had it not been for the repeated implication that they were a deplorable disfigurement.

Another danger in this insistent attitude toward adoption is that problems, when they arise, may be blamed on the adoption and dismissed, or mistakenly dealt with on that basis alone, when actually they may be caused by something entirely different: by a chilly emotional climate in the home, by financial troubles of which the parents assume the child to be unaware, by a time of temporary stress in the couple's adjustment to each other, or even by a purely physical factor like anemia. It is never wise for anyone to automatically assume that adoption is at the bottom of an adopted child's difficulties. If his problems are serious ones, there is no doubt of the fact that the adoption makes them more serious —perhaps *much* more. In all probability, however, the adoption of itself is not the sole cause of the trouble.

Among those parents who find it all too easy *never* to forget their child is adopted are the fathers whose sights become focused on material success for the family, and for the child the best schools, the best marks, track and football stardom, the lead in the class play. These are the mothers who spoil and overprotect, who postpone the first haircut, who are upset when their girl goes through the tomboy stage, who are everlastingly "afraid" of bikes and football and wet feet. Of course many biological mothers and fathers also have these drives and these fears, for varying reasons. Their children will also suffer from the pressures, and may or may not be able to meet them successfully, but at least none of these children is laboring under the extra handicap of wondering if "real" parents wouldn't have accepted him the way he is instead of trying to make him over.

The same sense of failure which motivates some parents to be overconscientious in their attitude toward the adoption may make others try to forget their child is adopted. Among these are the parents who would like to live out the three lives as if the child had been born to them. They may even pull up stakes and move home and business far away in an attempt to preserve the fiction. Or if they bow to the advice that the child should be told, they find the telling unnatural and even painful, and cannot help handing out the information in such a way that the child, no matter how well chosen the words which are used, absorbs the feeling that there must be something "not quite nice" about being adopted—a very damaging feeling to have about oneself!

Such parents are not *building* a family—they are making a tower of playing cards, trusting to luck that it won't topple. The ones who have kept the adoption a secret must live in fear lest by some accident they be found out. The ones who have informed with reluctance and a "now that's done" feeling must always remain insecure within the whole area of adoption; conversation of adults or children about it, articles or books that find their way into the house, make them feel uneasy, at a loss for the "right thing to say" should the child put questions to them.

So we come back again to the foundation stone—an acceptance of the fact of adoption, as nearly whole-hearted and relaxed as within the limitations of our personalities we can make it. Without this we cannot create a safe and enduring structure. With it, we can build a house that is happy and lit with sunshine, and strong enough to take the hurricane.

State Departments
of Public Welfare

A wise first move for would-be adoptive parents is to write to the State Department of Public Welfare at the state capital for the most complete and up-to-date information about the agencies within the district.

ALABAMA

State of Alabama
Department of Pensions and Security
Administrative Building
64 North Union Street
Montgomery, Alabama 36104

ALASKA

Department of Health and Social Services
Division of Family and Children Services
Pouch H
Juneau, Alaska 99801

ARIZONA

Arizona State Department of Public Welfare
1624 West Adams Street
Phoenix, Arizona 85007

ARKANSAS

Arkansas Social Services
P.O. Box 1437
Little Rock, Arkansas 72203

CALIFORNIA

State of California
Department of Social Welfare
714 P Street
Sacramento, California 95814

COLORADO

State of Colorado
Department of Social Services
Division of Public Welfare
1575 Sherman Street
Denver, Colorado 80203

CONNECTICUT

State of Connecticut
State Welfare Department
1000 Asylum Avenue
Hartford, Connecticut 06105

DELAWARE

Division of Social Services
P.O. Box 309
Wilmington, Delaware 19899

DISTRICT OF COLUMBIA

Government of the District of Columbia
Department of Human Resources
Social Services Administration
Child Welfare Division
122 C Street, N.W.
Washington, D.C. 20001

FLORIDA

Department of Health and Rehabilitative Services
Division of Family Services
P.O. Box 2050
Jacksonville, Florida 32203

GEORGIA

Georgia Department of Human Resources
47 Trinity Avenue
Atlanta, Georgia 30334

HAWAII

State of Hawaii
Department of Social Services and Housing
P.O. Box 339
Honolulu, Hawaii 96809

IDAHO

State of Idaho
Department of Public Assistance
P.O. Box 1189
Boise, Idaho 83701

ILLINOIS

State of Illinois
Department of Children and Family Services
524 South Second Street
Springfield, Illinois 62706

INDIANA

State of Indiana
Department of Public Welfare
Room 701
100 North Senate Avenue
Indianapolis, Indiana 46204

IOWA

Department of Social Services
Lucas State Office Building
Des Moines, Iowa 50319

KANSAS

The State Department of Social Welfare of Kansas
State Office Building
Topeka, Kansas 66612

KENTUCKY

Commonwealth of Kentucky
Department of Child Welfare
403 Wapping Street
Frankfort, Kentucky 40601

LOUISIANA

Department of Public Welfare
P.O. Box 44065
Baton Rouge, Louisiana 70804

MAINE

State of Maine
Department of Health and Welfare
State House
Augusta, Maine 04330

MARYLAND

Department of Employment and Social Services
Social Service Administration
1315 St. Paul Street
Baltimore, Maryland 21202

MASSACHUSETTS

Commonwealth of Massachusetts
Department of Public Welfare
600 Washington Street
Boston, Massachusetts 02111

MICHIGAN

State of Michigan
Department of Social Services
300 South Capitol Avenue
Lansing, Michigan 48926

MINNESOTA

State of Minnesota
Department of Public Welfare
Centennial Office Building
St. Paul, Minnesota 55155

MISSISSIPPI

State Department of Public Welfare
Fondren Station
P.O. Box 4321
Jackson, Mississippi 39216

MISSOURI

State Department of Public Health and Welfare
Division of Welfare
Broadway State Office Building
Jefferson City, Missouri 65101

MONTANA

State of Montana
Social and Rehabilitation Services
P.O. Box 1723
Helena, Montana 59601

NEBRASKA

State of Nebraska
Department of Public Welfare
1526 K Street, Fourth Floor
Lincoln, Nebraska 68508

NEVADA

State Welfare Division
201 South Fall Street
Carson City, Nevada 89701

NEW HAMPSHIRE

Department of Health and Welfare
Division of Welfare
1 Pillsbury Street
Concord, New Hampshire 03301

NEW JERSEY

State of New Jersey
Bureau of Children's Services
163 West Hanover Street
Trenton, New Jersey 08625

NEW MEXICO

State of New Mexico
Health and Social Services Department
Social Services Division
P.O. Box 2348
Santa Fe, New Mexico 87501

NEW YORK

State of New York
Department of Social Services
1450 Western Avenue
Albany, New York 12203

NORTH CAROLINA

State of North Carolina
Department of Public Welfare
P.O. Box 2599
Raleigh, North Carolina 27602

NORTH DAKOTA

North Dakota Department of Social Services
Capitol Building
Bismarck, North Dakota 58501

OHIO

State of Ohio
Department of Public Welfare
Division of Social Services
Oak Street at Ninth
Columbus, Ohio 43215

OKLAHOMA

Department of Institutions, Social and Rehabilitative Services
State of Oklahoma
Sequoyah Memorial Office Building
Oklahoma City, Oklahoma 73125

OREGON

Children's Services Division
Department of Human Resources
Public Service Building
Salem, Oregon 97310

PENNSYLVANIA

Commonwealth of Pennsylvania
Department of Public Welfare
P.O. Box 2675
Harrisburg, Pennsylvania 17120

PUERTO RICO

Commonwealth of Puerto Rico
Department of Social Services
Box 11697
Santurce, Puerto Rico 00910

RHODE ISLAND

Division of Community Services
Family and Children's Services
The Aime J. Forand Building
600 New London Avenue
Cranston, Rhode Island 02920

SOUTH CAROLINA

State Department of Public Welfare
P.O. Box 1520
Columbia, South Carolina 29202

SOUTH DAKOTA

Department of Public Welfare
State Office Building #1
Pierre, South Dakota 57501

TENNESSEE

State of Tennessee
Department of Public Welfare
State Office Building
Nashville, Tennessee 37219

TEXAS

State Department of Public Welfare
John H. Reagan Building
Austin, Texas 78701

UTAH

State of Utah
Division of Family Services
231 East 4th South
Salt Lake City, Utah 84111

VERMONT

Vermont Department of Social Welfare
State Office Building
Montpelier, Vermont 05602

VIRGINIA

Commonwealth of Virginia
Department of Welfare and Institutions
429 S. Belvidere St.
Richmond, Virginia 23220

WASHINGTON

Department of Social and Health Services
Social Services Division
P.O. Box 1788
Olympia, Washington 98504

WEST VIRGINIA

West Virginia Department of Welfare
State Office Building No. 3
Charleston, West Virginia 25305

WISCONSIN

State of Wisconsin
Department of Health and Social Services
Division of Family Services
1 West Wilson Street
Madison, Wisconsin 53702

WYOMING

Wyoming Department of Health and Social Services
Division of Public Assistance and Social Services
State Office Building
Cheyenne, Wyoming 82001

Some Books
for
Further Reading

Ames, L. *Child Care and Development*. Philadelphia: Lippincott, 1970.

Anderson, David C. *Children of Special Value; Interracial Adoption in America*. New York: St. Martin's Press, 1971.

Bettelheim, Bruno. *Dialogues with Mothers*. Glencoe, Illinois: Free Press, 1962.

Bricklin, Barry and Patricia M. *Strong Family Strong Child*. New York: Delacorte Press, 1970.

Chinnock, Frank W. *Kim—A Gift From Vietnam*. New York: Paperback Library, 1971.

Dywasuk, Colette Taube. *Adoption—Is It For You?* New York: Harper & Row, 1973.

Farnham, Marynia F., M. D. *The Adolescent*. New York: Collier Macmillan, 1962.

Fremon, Suzanne Strait. *Children and Their Parents: Toward Maturity*. New York: Harper & Row, 1968.

Gardner, G. E. *The Emerging Personality; Infancy Through Adolescence*. New York: Delacorte Press, 1970.

Gesell, Arnold, M.D., and Ilg, Frances L., M.D. *Infant and Child in the Culture of Today* Revised. New York: Harper & Row, 1974.

———. *The Child From Five to Ten*. New York: Harper & Row, 1946.

———. *Youth: The Years From Ten to Sixteen*. New York: Harper & Row, 1956.

Ginott, Haim G. *Between Parent and Child*. New York: Macmillan, 1965.

————. *Between Parent and Teenager*. New York: Macmillan, 1969.

Gruenberg, Sidonie M. *The Wonderful Story of How You Were Born*. Revised. New York: Doubleday, 1970.

————, Editor. *The New Encyclopedia of Child Car and Guidance*. New York: Doubleday, 1968.

Hartog, Jan de. *The Children: A Personal Record for the Use of Adoptive Parents*. New York: Pantheon Books, Inc., 1969.

Ilg, Frances L., M.D., and Ames, Louise Bates, Ph.D. *Child Behavior*. New York: Harper & Row, 1955.

Meredith, Judith C. *And Now We Are a Family*. Boston: Beacon Press, 1971.

Neisser, Edith. *Mothers and Daughters: A Lifelong Relationship*. Revised. New York: Harper & Row, 1973.

Newton, Niles. *Family Book of Child Care*. New York: Harper & Row, 1957.

Rondell, Florence, and Michaels, Ruth. *The Adopted Family* (2 vols.: *You and Your Child* and *The Family That Grew*). Revised. New York: Crown, 1965.

Rose, Anna Perott. *Room For One More*. Boston: Houghton Mifflin, 1950.

————. *The Gentle House*. Boston: Houghton Mifflin, 1954.

Scheinfeld, Amram. *Heredity in Humans*. Philadelphia: Lippincott, 1972.

Schweinitz, Karl de. *Growing Up*. New York: Macmillan, 1968.

Spock, Benjamin, M.D. *Baby and Child Care*. New York: Hawthorn, 1968.

Strain, Frances B. *Being Born*. Revised and enlarged. New York: Hawthorn, 1970.

Wasson, Valentina P. *The Chosen Baby*. Philadelphia: Lippincott, 1950.

Wolf, Anna. *The Parent's Manual; A Guide to the Emotional Development of Young Children*. New York: Ungar, 1961.

Index

Abortion, 6, 28
Adolescents, 16, 24, 108, 123, 124, 169, 172, 173, 181, 182–189, 201, 208, 228, 231–233, 237; *see also* Teenagers
"Adopted Adult Discusses Adoption as a Life Experience, The" (Hagen), 94
Adopted children, follow-up study of, 45
Adopted Family, The (Rondell and Michaels), 81
Adoption, 3, 4, 222; announcement of, 65; of "bad" children, 158–159; at beginning, *see* Beginning of adoptive parenthood; of blind children, 161–163; changes in, 4–5; of handicapped children, 9, 38, 39, 161–166; interracial, 47–48; laws on, 5, 9, 67; legalization ceremony of, 70; of older child, 137–166; overseas, 48; private, 40–43, 44, 49; by single person, 9, 22–23, 137; subsidies in, 7; telling children about, 71–96; of toddler, 138–139, 140–147; of twins, *see* Twins; *see also* Adoption agency; Babies; Beginning of adoptive parenthood; Children; Family
Adoption—Is It For You? (Dywasuk), 48
Adoption agency, 4–11 *passim,* 19, 20, 21, 25, 31, 137; and age of adopters, 7; child's interest protected by, 6–7, 25, 37, 68; church-rated, 9; fee charged by private, 46; flexibility of, about

age of adopters, 7; private, 46; and "probation" of adoptive parents, 68–70; and public funds, 46; religious requirements relaxed by, 9; residence requirements by, 9; screening by, 10, 21, 22, 24–25, 31, 68; waiting to hear from, 55, 59–60, 64
Advisor, professional, 193
Agency, adoption, *see* Adoption agency
Amatruda, Catherine, 43, 44, 46
And Now We Are a Family (Meredith), 82
Anderson, David C., 48
Anesthesia, child informed about, 114–115
Announcement, adoption, 65

Babies: age of, at adoption, 38–39; black market in, 40, 41, 42, 50; and crying after homecoming, reasons for, 63–64; developmental tests of, 35–36, 37; gray market in, 40, 42; homecoming arrangements for, 62, 63; memory in, 111, 112, 113; toilet training of, 60, 100, 101, 186; weaning of, 60, 101; *see also* Adoption agency; Beginning of adoptive parenthood; Children; Family; New baby
Baby and Child Care (Spock), 168
"Baby book," 66
Barber, child's first visit to, 116
Bassinet, 59
Bathinette, 59